RECIPES

YOUR MOTHER KNEW

BY HEART

RECIPES

YOUR MOTHER KNEW

BY HEART

Delicious Connections volume 2

Marina E. Michaels

Athena Star
PRESS

Disclaimer. The recipes in this book have been carefully tested. To the best of our knowledge, they are safe and nutritious for ordinary use and users. For those people with food or other allergies, or who have special food requirements or health issues, please read the suggested contents of each recipe carefully and determine whether they may create a problem for you. All recipes are used at the risk of the consumer. We cannot be responsible for any hazards, loss, or damage that may occur as a result of any recipe use. For those with special needs, allergies, requirements, or health problems, if in any doubt, please contact your medical advisor before using any recipe. If you are uncomfortable with this, please return the book to the seller.

The author and publisher have no affiliation with any of the brands or companies mentioned in this book. All brand names are trademarks of the respective companies. Anything the author recommends is from her experiences with purchasing and using the product.

A note from the author. Understanding the hard work that goes into making any kind of book, and especially a cookbook, and knowing the possibilities for error on the path to publication even despite extensive recipe testing and editing, I can appreciate how errors creep in. I fervently hope I haven't introduced any. If I have, it would be a great favor to me if you were to let me know. You can contact me by writing me care of the publisher, or emailing me at marina@sonic.net. Thank you!

Athena Star   Press
2467 Westvale Court
Santa Rosa, California 95403
athenastarpress.com
publisher@athenastarpress.com

Library of Congress Control Number: 2020947787

Paperback ISBN 978-1-60038-022-8

eBook ISBN 978-1-60038-023-5

Printed in the United States of America with chlorine-free ink and on acid-free interior paper stock supplied by a Forest Stewardship Council-certified provider.

First Edition June 2021

Credits: Body text and ingredients are in Museo and Museo Slab, fonts designed by Jos Buivenga. Cover titles are in Fontin, also by Jos Buivenga. Headings, chapter titles, and recipe titles are in Gabriela, designed by Antonio Mejía Lechuga and published by Latinotype México. Drop caps and bold are in Hyun-Seung Lee, Dae-Hoon Hahm, and Dong-Kwan Kim's Core Sans CR, published by S-Core. Poppy graphic copyright CanStockPhoto.com, artist: blackmoon979

Always and forever, to my beloved daughter, Elisabeth

without whom life would be so much poorer

Contents

Contents

Breads. 85

Breakfasts 115

Desserts................... 129

Meat, Fish, & Cheese Dishes......... 167

Contents

Pickles, Ferments, and Preserves 237

Salads & Salad Dressings 255

Savory Sauces & Spices 279

Appendix A: Recipe Guidelines 317

Appendix B: Weights and Measures . . 321

Index 329

Preface

Caretakers have always been busy, and cooking is just one of their many jobs. Although cookbooks are incredibly helpful and have been around for millennia, many times a cook doesn't have time to look up something in order to bake or cook it. Instead, we memorize our favorite recipes.

Cooking has been this way for thousands of years.

Unfortunately, sometimes those memorized recipes are lost. The person whose special recipe it was didn't realize how precious their recipes were, and so the recipe died with them. Sometimes the only way to preserve a recipe was for someone else to sit patiently with the cook as they made their special recipes, writing down the ingredients and instructions, as I did with my mother.

And that's how this cookbook got its name.

Although this book's title uses the word "mother," that's mostly in recognition that historically, mothers were the cooks. It's not to be taken as a slight to those many fathers, grandparents, and other caregivers who are also actively involved in cooking. If you are one such, or had one such in your life, know that I recognize the contributions made by you and yours. Some of my favorite recipes come from fathers who love to cook for their families.

About This Series, Delicious Connections

This book is volume 2 in my *Delicious Connections* series of cookbooks. As a friend's grandfather used to say, "Eat dessert first. You never know what's going to happen." So volume 1 in this series is *Delectable Desserts*. That book has the majority of my favorite dessert recipes, but not all. This book has close to three dozen more favorite dessert recipes. (You can never have too many.)

Why did I name the series *Delicious Connections*? My cookbooks have a lot of rare, old, original, and international recipes. Unfamiliar food is a safe, easy way to open doors, to connect us with our fellow human beings, to safely try that "little bit of this and that."

And that's why I call this series *Delicious Connections*: because food is one of the many ways in which we humans connect with each other, share our stories, our cultures, our ideas. It's easy to like food, right?

Food has connected humans with each other since the beginning of time. Anthropological evidence shows that our early human ancestors took care of each other even when a member of the group was unable to care for themselves. It's my belief that we humans care for each other from the heart, and the only thing that separates us is fear—fear of the unknown, fear of the unusual, fear of the unfamiliar.

Call me an idealist, call me an optimist, and you will be 100% correct. I believe in my fellow human beings. I believe in you. I believe we all have the capacity to learn and grow, even if just a little bit (and a little bit is okay), and I believe that food is one excellent—and delicious—way to do so.

How This Cookbook Series Was Born

My mother was an excellent from-scratch cook. Breads, cakes, frostings, cookies, muffins, biscuits, soups—everything that people were more likely to make from a box or can, my mother made from scratch. Because of this, I took an early interest in cooking. In my teens, I began collecting recipes from my mother, other family members, friends, neighbors, and coworkers—over the back fence, at picnics, pot lucks, small parties, chatting on the telephone, when attending small local plays, and so on.

All the recipes in this book are from the tip of the iceberg of my collection. Some recipes have been in my family since my mother, or her mother, or her mother's mother, was a child. Others are long-time favorites of other families. Some I've picked up along the way, loving them, enjoying them, and modifying them until they better suited me. Still others are original inventions from family, friends, and yours truly.

In true seat-of-the-pants cooking style, whenever I add a recipe to my collection, I put my own stamp on every recipe. Although I follow a recipe to the letter the first time I make it, the next time I make it, I change proportions, ingredients, instructions, and cooking times to suit my ideas of what works best.

Every time I make any recipe, my own or anyone else's, I jot down notes on how to further improve the ingredients, quantities, or instructions, incrementally improving every recipe. I streamline instructions, eliminate unnecessary steps and ingredients, and simplify the entire process.

Initially, many of these recipes were in the form of hastily handwritten instructions on the back of an envelope, or in an ancestor's shaky elderly handwriting on recipe cards, or the occasional typed recipe (using a typewriter), or notes scrawled on a handy piece of paper when I was inventing, all of which I kept rather untidily in a binder.

When I got my first personal computer in the early 1980s, I started typing up my recipe collection, which continued to grow. As the internet became part of everyday life, people started sharing their recipes online, and some of my more recent favorites came from there as well.

After collecting recipes for decades, I realized that I had a unique collection; a collection of recipes that are true Americana, presenting a mix of cultural heritages and regional specialities, spanning at least three centuries, and presenting an almost anthropological view of cooking in America.

My focus with a recipe is substance and flavor, not presentation. So although my meals look appetizing, works of art they are not. However, I use the best quality ingredients I can, and the ingredients and the love I put into cooking and baking create delicious food. Cooks who care about retaining taste while gaining as much time as possible; who understand that good ingredients create flavorful meals, and that looks aren't everything when it comes to food, will understand what I mean. If it comes to a choice between presentation and flavor, I'll go for flavor every time.

I hope you enjoy these recipes as much as my family, friends, and I have over the years, and that you use them to connect with your fellow human beings.

What You Might Love About This Book

First, this cookbook is for cooks. Like many, many cooks who are in their kitchens every day, creating yet another mouth-watering meal or delectable dessert for their loved ones, we don't have the time or money to waste on untested recipes. As a conscientious cook, I've **tested every recipe** in this cookbook, all of which are favorites, multiple times. In many cases, I've made a recipe so often I've lost count.

A large number of these recipes are originals—my own and those of family members and friends—often invented on the spot in the kitchen, then carefully recorded so we could make them again. The remainder I learned from someone else through cookbooks, magazines, blog posts, coworkers, strangers, and just about anyone and any place where people were willing to share their recipes—then heavily adapted to make it my own.

Although technically, because I so heavily changed them, I could claim almost every recipe in this cookbook as my own, I don't. I respect the original sharers and am intensely grateful for their recipes. They've brought so much pleasure to my kitchen. So I give credit for all recipes whose origin I remember. I do claim my originals as my own, as is right and proper.

This cookbook is **readable by design**. The main font (the one you're reading) is dyslexia-friendly and large enough to read. Each recipe gets its own page, so you can focus on the one recipe. (Some recipes require more pages.) The index is careful and thorough; if you want to look up recipes that use egg whites, you'll find them listed under *egg whites* in the index.

I made it easy to find a recipe in several ways:

- The recipe names are in the table of contents and in the index.
- The chapters and the recipes in each chapter are in alphabetical order.
- I simplified most recipe names so they are logical and straightforward. In some cases, the name was charming enough or well-known enough that I kept it.

Each recipe includes an item of information called *Total time*. This time represents how much time you can expect to spend preparing a recipe, from initial preparation to when the food is ready to eat. It includes the amount of time it takes to perform all preparation tasks (grating, chopping, measuring, and so on), as well as all mixing, cooking, cooling, and setting-up times. If a recipe calls for 1 cup diced celery, I include the dicing time in the total time.

Using these times, you can plan your meals without having to read the entire recipe and figure out how much time it will take. No surprises. (Though I encourage you to always read a recipe through anyway.) It also gives you the flexibility to choose another recipe that takes less time.

The total times are as accurate as I can make them based on my own experiences. However, take them as approximations. Many things can make a difference in the amount of preparation and cooking time required for anything. For example, your oven may run hotter or cooler than mine. You might be using a convection oven instead of a standard one. You might buy some prepared ingredients (diced onion, celery, and carrots, for example), or maybe you chop faster than I do. Take all these factors, and your own experience and cook's intuition, into account when planning to make a recipe.

Acknowledgments

I have so many people to thank. First, the many cooks who have shared their recipes and wisdom from their cultures, not just with me but with whomever asked. And not just now, but throughout time. Without their generosity, this world's tables would be sadder and poorer places. Food bloggers, that includes you. I think only another cookbook author would understand just how much work a good cookbook is. I've written hundreds of software manuals and many thousands of pages on highly technical topics, topics I needed to make clear and easy to understand, but not one of those manuals was ever as much work as putting together a cookbook. I've loved every minute because of the connections I feel with other cooks throughout time and space.

My thanks to friends and family who have supported me, encouraged me, and accepted my long absences while I worked on this cookbook series:

- Elisabeth Michaels, my daughter, who has been with me every step of the way and who has encouraged me and cheered me up. My life would be infinitely poorer without you. This cookbook series is your family legacy.

- Floyd and Ruth Norskog, my long-lost dad and new mom, recently come back into my life. Floyd, having you back in my life healed a long-broken part in my heart. Ruth, someday soon I hope we can meet in person.
- Dawn Keiser, a force of nature and my associate publisher. Thanks for your help with the Library of Congress. You're an all-around awesome person. There never has been, nor will there ever be, another person like you, and I'm so glad you're my friend.
- Bryan Munoz, Jordon Rader, Heidi O'Claire, and Linda DeRose-Droubay. You mean so much to me and have never questioned whether I could write these books. You've given me feedback and perspective on life in general, and only the best kind of friend does that.
- Lynne, Gil, and Morgan Harrington. You've been accepting and patient, and have given up most of our virtual social nights as I've put the final touches on this book.
- Louise Nicholson, my friend since we met at Santa Clara University, oh so long ago. It touched my heart when I found out you not only have kept a home-printed early version of this cookbook all these years, but use my mother's tasty and foolproof pizza dough recipe regularly.
- AJ McInnis, friend, former husband, and excellent cook in your own right, thank you for all your original recipes, the many cooking-related gifts, your support and encouragement, and your appreciation of my cooking.
- Jon Rioux. I often say that authors shouldn't cheer lead their readers, but that doesn't mean we can't cheer lead our friends. Your cheer leading has meant much to me. And thanks again for the keyboard!
- Kulwant Singh, you may have forgotten me, but I've never forgotten your kindness in teaching me how to make a simple masala chai in the late 1970s. When you and your friends in the Sikh community welcomed me to a day-long celebration, with warm hearts and without question or criticism, I was feeling separate and alone. The welcome I received opened my eyes to possibilities. I'm sure my love of Indian cookery is based in part on the warm community I experienced, however briefly, that day.
- Ruth Hashimoto, when I was 10, you welcomed me into your home as your daughter's best friend and treated me like family. Over the next several years, I experienced many new foods in your kitchen, and with those experiences, I acquired a lifelong love of Japanese culture and cookery.
- Jos Buivenga, thank you again for your awesome fonts (Museo, Museo Slab, and Fontin) that I've used in this cookbook series, and for your help solving my fraction problems when I was working on *Delectable Desserts*.
- Thank you, those who purchased *Delectable Desserts*, the first cookbook in this series, and told me how much you've enjoyed the recipes. Your praise and five-star reviews have warmed my heart and encouraged me.

Appetizers, Party Foods, and Snacks

When entertaining, many people purchase pre-made appetizers and party foods to just heat and serve. And why not? After all, the main point of a get-together is to enjoy one another's company, and if you are too busy fixing food you lose out on quality visiting time.

Still, it's nice to offer a few homemade treats to your guests. Many of the tasty recipes in this chapter are both fast and easy, and you can make several ahead of time. You could also put together a variety of the recipes in this chapter and make a meal of snacks.

Charcuterie

Total time: 1 hour   Yields as much as you want

By the strictest definition, charcuterie (pronounced *shahr-ku-TREE*, with a slightly rolled "r" on the last syllable, or sometimes *shahr-ku-tuh-ree*) is cooked or cured pork products, such as pâté, sausages, salami, and sliced ham. If you serve those items on a board, that's called a charcuterie board.

Less strictly speaking, charcuterie includes other meats as well as pork, along with cheeses, fruits, nuts, crackers, and more.

A charcuterie board involves no cooking. You just buy the ingredients and lay them out artistically on a serving board or platter.

The quantities and variety will depend on how many people you're serving. You can be as simple or as elaborate as you wish.

For a small gathering (six to ten people) , I like to have

- two types of salami
- one other type of sliced meat
- three types of cheese that contrast in texture, color, and flavor
- one type of bread and one to three types of cracker
- two or three kinds of fruit
- two or three types of jam
- one to three types of pickles
- nuts
- one or two vegetables

Here are details on each of those items.

Start with the meats: sliced deli meats, such as peppered salami, soppressata, Genoa, and prosciutto (all preferably uncured, to avoid sodium nitrate or nitrite), plus roast beef or ham and some good-quality smoked salmon.

Some people recommend just a few slices of meat per guest, but I come from the "never leave guests wanting" school of hosting, and I serve at least eight ounces per person. Besides, the leftovers from a charcuterie board make great sandwiches later.

Select good-quality cheeses that include a range of textures (from soft to hard) and flavors (from sweet to what I call "manly goat"). A favorite cheese is the double-crème Fromager d'Affinois. It's like a triple-crème brie made in heaven. (Though brie-like, d'Affinois is a not a brie.) For cheeses, lay out ¼ to ½ pound cheese per person.

Slice a sourdough or French baguette and include crackers that complement the cheeses. If you can find them, Boudin's twice-baked sourdough crackers are perfect with just about everything. I prefer serving one kind each of bread and crackers, but sometimes I find some interesting crackers and serve those along with ones I know are suitable and tasty. For example, try Cheddar Cheese Wafers (page 4).

Choose a variety of fruits—sweet, juicy grapes; crisp slices of slightly tart apples; sweet dried apricots; organic strawberries. (I prefer organic fruit, but I'm not strict about it—except when it comes to strawberries, which are consistently in the Environmental Working Group's dirty dozen list of fruits and vegetables with too many pesticides.) When available, I include blackberries, raspberries, and some cubes of fresh pineapple.

Consider jams and fruit spreads as well. We've found that Dalmatia brand's fig or sour cherry spreads are a perfect complement to d'Affinois or cream cheese.

Add some **marinated and pickled items**: cornichons (tiny, tart, crunchy pickles; the English call them gherkins); pickled onions; marinated artichoke hearts, sun-dried tomatoes; and a variety of olives, including kalamata (my favorite).

Add nuts, such as toasted almonds, walnuts, pine nuts, or other nuts. Serve in small, attractive containers. I have a set of blue Pyrex ramekins I use all the time in kitchen (for separating eggs, for example); they're also good for holding nuts, pickles, and what not in a charcuterie board.

For a nod to vegetables, add a simple, tasty dip (several of which you'll find in this chapter); sliced celery; and cherry tomatoes (which, yes, technically are a fruit).

Arrange everything on platters or wooden cutting boards on a cloth-covered table. Be sure to have everything sliced, rolled, or otherwise ready for eating. You don't want your guests holding up other guests as they wrestle with the food. Include whatever tools and utensils people might need, such as small utensils to dip out the fruit spread or spread the soft cheeses. And of course small plates for your guests to pile high.

A vase of flowers dresses up the table.

Depending on how many guests you have, this array can be quite inexpensive, and could even be your entire extended meal for an afternoon or evening of company. (With beverages, of course!)

Et voilà! You have a buffet meal full of variety and interest that's far less trouble than it sounds.

Cheddar Cheese Wafers

Total time: 2 hours 45 minutes   Yields several dozen small crackers

This recipe, which makes a type of cracker, takes time, but most of it is "sitting" time. Also, it produces prodigious quantities of wafers that taste like the real cheese you use in making them. You can make the recipe a few days ahead of time and refrigerate the dough until you are ready to cook and serve the wafers. Best served hot and fresh out of the oven, but they'll keep if you want to bake them ahead. You can also freeze the dough for a few months. The recipe calls for cheddar cheese; experiment with your favorite cheeses.

⅓ cup cheddar cheese, grated   ½ cup all-purpose flour
¼ cup unsalted butter,   ¼ teaspoon dry mustard
   softened

1 Mix cheese and butter together until a creamy paste.
2 Cut in flour and mustard.
3 Form into a long roll about 1½ inches thick.
4 Wrap in waxed paper and chill for at least 2 hours. You can chill up to 2 days.
5 Just before serving, cut into thin slices and bake at 375° for 15 minutes or until a golden brown.

Clam Dip

Total time: 1 hour   Yields 4 cups

Clam dip is traditionally made with sour cream and cream cheese. This unusual variation uses sour cream and cottage cheese. You can use the dip immediately, rather than letting it sit overnight in the refrigerator, though the flavors marry better with after sitting. For a vegetarian version, omit the clams and add some spices; for example, try garlic powder or minced fresh garlic and some fresh minced parsley. Some people might add a tablespoon of Worcestershire sauce. Serve with celery sticks, crackers, potato chips, or whatever sparks your imagination.

2 cups cottage cheese
2 cups sour cream
2 teaspoons lemon juice

1 (8-ounce) can whole baby clams (or more, to taste)

1 Combine cottage cheese, sour cream, lemon juice, and clams. Mix well.
2 Chill in refrigerator for about 1 hour.

French Onion Dip

Total time: 1 hour 15 minutes   Yields 2½ cups

Also known as California dip, French Onion dip has been around since 1954, when it was invented in Los Angeles, California. This dip is always popular at parties. To reduce the calories while retaining the deliciousness, use fat-free or low-fat mayonnaise and sour cream. For a vegetarian or vegan version, use vegetarian/vegan sour cream and mayonnaise. Serve with any dippers you like: potato chips, tortilla chips, small wedges of pita bread, or whatever seems right and good.

2 cups sour cream
½ cup mayonnaise

1 (1.9-ounce) package dry
    onion soup mix

1   Stir together sour cream, mayonnaise, and onion soup mix until well mixed, then cover.
2   Chill for 1 hour.

Delicious Dill Dip

Total time: 2 hours 10 minutes   Yields about 1½ cups

Dill is a hearty, lovely, fragrant, and ever-useful herb. Named the 2010 herb of the year by the International Herb Association, the culinary version of dill grows wild, along with wild mustard and wild radish, throughout Sonoma County in Northern California. Local lore says dill was brought here by the early Italian settlers, and that those early dill plants readily self-sowed. The leaves are called dill weed, and the seeds are called dill seed. (As with coriander seed, dill seeds are the fruits of the dill plant, not seeds.) Both dill weed and dill seed are great in a wide range of recipes. I don't remember the long-ago co-worker who shared this simple and unusual dip. I enjoy the refreshing sharpness of the dill combined with the green onions, celery seeds, and garlic. Give it a whirl! For a vegetarian or vegan version, use vegetarian/vegan sour cream and mayonnaise. Use it as you would any dip—with potato or tortilla chips, or spread on small slices of sourdough baguette.

⅔ cup sour cream
⅔ cup mayonnaise
1 tablespoon minced green onions
1 tablespoon fresh parsley, minced

1 teaspoon dill weed (fresh or dried)
½ teaspoon celery seeds
¼ teaspoon garlic powder or minced fresh garlic
⅛ teaspoon salt

1   Combine sour cream, mayonnaise, green onions, parsley, dill weed, celery seeds, garlic powder, and salt.
2   Chill for a few hours or overnight.

Deviled Eggs

Total time: 30 minutes   Yields 24 half eggs

A classic recipe that almost everyone loves and has their own favorite version. Here's mine. Deviled eggs are also known as stuffed eggs, Russian eggs, or dressed eggs. The "deviling" refers to making a dish spicy. The History Channel says a version of deviled eggs dates back to Roman times, "where eggs were boiled, seasoned with spicy sauces, then typically served at the beginning of a meal—as a first course known as *gustatio*—for wealthy patricians." (I recommend reading the entire fascinating article—it's full of ideas for ways to make deviled eggs: history.com/news/the-ancient-history-of-deviled-eggs). So when you make deviled eggs, you're connecting with wealthy ancient Romans. You can double or triple this recipe as needed.

1 dozen large eggs
½ cup mayonnaise or to taste
1 tablespoon dry mustard
¼ cup diced dill pickles
¼ cup sliced green olives or capers

paprika to taste (smoked if you have it)
fresh parsley or cilantro, chopped, for garnish

1 Place eggs in a large, heavy pot. Cover eggs with cold water to a depth of 1 inch above the eggs. (Starting with cold water reduces the number of cracked eggs.)
2 Bring water to a boil, then immediately remove from heat.
3 Cover pot and let sit for 15 minutes.
4 Drain eggs and plunge them into cold water to stop the cooking.
5 When eggs are cool enough to handle, peel them and cut in half lengthwise.
6 Being careful not to tear whites, carefully scoop out yolks and place them in a medium bowl.
7 Mash yolks a bit with a fork, then add mayonnaise, mustard, pickles, and olives to yolks. Mash some more until well mixed.
8 Fill scoops in egg whites with yolk mixture. Heap high. (For a fancy touch, pipe the mix into the egg halves.)
9 Sprinkle generously with paprika and parsley and serve immediately, or refrigerate and serve within a day.

Filled Hot Bread Rolls

Total time: 1 hour   Yields about 12 rolls per filling

T his isn't so much a single recipe as a collection of five fillings for bread rolls. Each roll is a handheld mini meal. To make, you hollow out dinner rolls, fill with one or more of the savory fillings, wrap in foil, and bake. Quantities are hard to predict—it depends on how deeply you hollow the rolls and how big the rolls are—so the number of rolls per filling is approximate. Try this with the fabulous Dinner Rolls on page 96.

Preparing and Filling Rolls

1 Prepare 12 dinner rolls by cutting off tops and scooping out as much of the center as you wish.
2 Fill each roll with a tablespoon or two of filling.
3 Wrap each roll in aluminum foil and bake at 325° for 30 to 45 minutes.

Filling 1: Cheddar and Hardboiled Eggs

1 pound shredded cheddar cheese
½ teaspoon chili powder
¼ cup minced onion

1 can (4 ounces) sliced olives, drained
1 tablespoon butter, melted
3 large hardboiled eggs, chopped

1 Combine cheese, chili powder, onion, olives, butter, and eggs.
2 Stuff rolls and bake as described.

Filling 2: Cheddar, Green Onions, and Olives

1 pound shredded cheddar cheese
5 green onions, minced

12 stuffed olives, minced
¼ cup butter, melted
2 tablespoons tomato soup

1 Combine cheese, green onions, olives, butter, and eggs. Thin with tomato soup.
2 Stuff rolls and bake as described.

Filling 3: Crab, Lobster, or Chicken and Cheddar

½ pound cooked crab meat or cooked lobster meat or or cooked chicken
¼ cup minced fresh parsley
1 tablespoon prepared mustard

¼ cup mayonnaise
⅛ teaspoon salt
⅛ teaspoon ground black pepper
½ cup shredded cheddar

1   Combine seafood, parsley, mustard, mayonnaise, salt, and pepper.
2   After stuffing a roll, but before putting the tops on, sprinkle with cheese. Bake as described.

Filling 4: Hardboiled Eggs

5 large hardboiled eggs, coarsely chopped
¼ cup olive oil
¼ cup hot pepper sauce
1 small green pepper, minced

1 small can (4 ounces) sliced green or black olives, drained
½ cup shredded cheddar cheese

1   Combine eggs, olive oil, hot pepper sauce, green pepper, and olives.
2   After stuffing a roll, but before putting the tops on, sprinkle with cheese. Bake as described.

Filling 5: Ham, Hardboiled Eggs, and Cheddar

½ pound ham, minced
½ pound shredded sharp cheddar cheese
3 large hardboiled eggs, coarsely chopped

¼ cup dill pickle relish
1 tablespoon prepared mustard
2 tablespoons mayonnaise
1 tablespoon butter, melted

1   Combine ham, cheese, eggs, relish, and mustard.
2   Thin with mayonnaise and butter. Mix well.
3   Stuff rolls and bake as described.

Garlic Bread

Total time: 1 hour 30 minutes   Yields 1 loaf

This recipe takes a bit of preparation, but is well worth it. Use more or less garlic to your taste. Traditionally in the US, garlic bread is served as part of a spaghetti dinner (along with a crisp salad with tangy vinaigrette dressing), but of course with food there are no rules. Enjoy this whenever and however you like.

1 cup salted butter, softened
3 garlic cloves, minced
1½ teaspoons Italian
   seasonings

1 loaf French or sourdough
   bread

1 Blend butter, garlic, and Italian seasonings. Set aside at room temperature for about an hour to marry the flavors.
2 Slice bread into ½- to ¾-inch thick pieces (or as thickly as you like).
3 Generously slather both sides of each slice with softened butter mixture.
4 Put slices back together to make a loaf again.
5 Place loaf in the middle of a sheet of aluminum foil large enough to wrap the entire loaf. Bring the foil's edges to the top and crimp firmly.
6 Place loaf on a large baking sheet and bake at 350° for about 25 minutes. Serve immediately.

Hot Artichoke Dip

Total time: 45 minutes   Yields 2 cups

Delicious served with baguette slices, small triangles of pita bread, or whatever you like to use with dip. Sturdy dippers are better because this dip is firm and thick. Great as a part of a charcuterie board (page 2). Keeps for about four days in the refrigerator; you can fix in advance, then reheat before serving.

1 (14-ounce) jar marinated artichoke hearts
3 garlic cloves, diced
½ cup mayonnaise
½ cup sour cream
⅓ cup grated Parmesan cheese
¼ teaspoon cayenne

1   Drain and chop artichoke hearts. If you want, reserve liquid to use in another recipe; for example, as a base for salad dressing.
2   Combine artichoke hearts with garlic, mayonnaise, sour cream, Parmesan, and cayenne. Stir until well mixed.
3   Spoon into a small ovenproof dish.
4   Bake at 350° for 30 minutes or until bubbly.
5   Cool 5 to 8 minutes before serving.

Hot Crab Dip

Total time: 45 minutes   Yields 1 cup

This crab dip is delicious with French bread. If you don't have fresh crab meat, you can use a 6-ounce can of crab meat, drained. For a seafood theme, pair this dip with the Clam Dip and the Salmon Cheese Ball (page 18). If you're avoiding gluten, make sure your hot pepper sauce is gluten-free.

3 ounces cream cheese, softened

½ cup mayonnaise

6 ounces fresh crab meat

¼ cup minced white onion

1 tablespoon lemon juice

⅛ teaspoon hot pepper sauce

1 Beat cream cheese until smooth.
2 Stir in mayonnaise, crab meat, onion, lemon juice, and hot pepper sauce.
3 Spoon into a small ovenproof dish.
4 Bake at 350° for 30 minutes or until bubbly.
5 Cool 5 to 8 minutes before serving.

Minty Garlic Dip

Total time: 10 minutes   Yields 1¼ cups

During COVID-19, I subscribed to an organic farm box. The service offered fruits and vegetables, but also many other add-on items: milk, eggs, cheese, meat, rice, and so on. It was a blessing and a relief to reliably get groceries every week. One of the extra items I tried was a minty garlic dip. We loved it so much I decided to learn how to make it myself. Turns out you can find many versions of the recipe online. After some trial and error (not everybody's recipes worked) and a few characteristic flourishes, I came up with this.

¼ teaspoon cumin (whole seeds or ground)
½ cup fresh mint
2 large garlic cloves, minced
1 tablespoon lemon juice

1 cup plain Greek-style yogurt
1 teaspoon salt
⅛ teaspoon red pepper flakes or cayenne

1 If using cumin seeds, lightly toast cumin seeds in a dry skillet over medium-low heat for 1 minute. Remove from skillet and set aside to cool.
2 Remove mint leaves from stems. Discard stems in your compost.
3 Blend the mint leaves for a few seconds, then add the garlic and lemon juice. Blend another minute.
4 Add yogurt and blend well (2 to 3 minutes).
5 Add the cumin, salt, and red pepper flakes. Blend for 30 seconds.

Onigiri (Japanese Rice Balls)

Total time: 2 hours   Yields about 12 onigiri

Onigiri (おにぎり, pronounced oh-nee-gee-ree) is a Japanese snack made from rice compressed in a shape (triangles and balls are popular) around a small dab of filling and wrapped with sheets of nori (dried seaweed). When I visited Japan in 2013, every day I bought a few triangles of onigiri from a grocery store on the ground floor of the hotel where we were staying, then snacked on them throughout the morning. When I returned to California, I purchased the book, おにぎりレシピ 1 0 1 (*Onigiri Recipes 101*, called *Everyday Onigiri* in English), by Reiko Yamada (Pot Publishing, 2014) from Kinokuniya, my favorite source of Japanese language books in San Francisco. Although I give one filling in this recipe, you can make many different kinds, including vegetarian or vegan. An onigiri press makes it easier to compress the rice. The methods of cooking the rice and forming the onigiri are essential. For step 5, I highly recommend using a rice cooker. You must use freshly cooked rice; cold cooked rice won't do. Also, don't use table salt; use a good-quality sea salt, like Celtic salt or Himalayan salt. Serve immediately; onigiri don't keep for more than a few hours.

2 cups white sushi rice
2 cups water (for cooking rice)
¼ cup good-quality salt
4 sheets 12-inch-square nori,
    each cut into strips of 2
    inches by 12 inches

1 cup filling (try a fairly dry
    tuna or chicken salad to
    start with)

1   Wash your hands thoroughly! You'll be forming the rice balls with your hands.
2   Rinse rice repeatedly in fresh cold water (not the cooking water) until rinse water is nearly clear. When rinsing, swish rice around with your hands.
3   Rinse rice three more times. This time, as you rinse, "scrub" rice by gripping it gently with your hands several times.
4   Drain completely, then put into cooking pot with the two cups water. Cover and let sit 30 minutes.
5   Cook rice by bringing water to a boil, then reducing heat and cooking 10 to 12 minutes (still covered). Remove from heat and let sit 10 minutes. The rice should be firm but tender—no hard grains!
6   With a flat wooden paddle, carefully fluff rice, taking care not to smash the grains. Now you're ready to make onigiri.
7   For each person making onigiri, set out a small bowl of plain water and a small bowl of salt with a salt spoon or other tiny spoon in it. Also lay out nori and a plate for finished onigiri.

8   Put rice into a bowl in the middle of the work area.

9   Moisten your hands with water—not too much—then rub a good pinch of salt on your palms. You should see the salt grains on your palms. You don't want the salt to dissolve. As you work with onigiri, you'll develop a sense for how much water and salt to use.

10 Place a few tablespoons rice in one palm and firmly compress it with your other palm.

11 Press a finger into the center of the rice ball. Fill with at most a tablespoon of filling.

12 Fold rice over to cover filling and start compressing and shaping. As you compress, start shaping rice into whatever shape you want. (I like triangles.) Don't compress too much or too often.

13 Once you have the desired shape, wrap onigiri with two strips of nori, one wrapped one direction and the other wrapped the other way. So, for example, if you wrapped the first nori strip from top to bottom and around the back, wrap the second strip from left to right and around the back.

14 Set onigiri on plate and keep making onigiri until you run out of ingredients.

Pimento Cheese Spread

Total time: 20 minutes   Yields about 10 ounces

This yummy pimento cheese spread is my own recipe. I tasted a commercial pimento cheese spread long ago (before the internet) and didn't know there were recipes for it, so I experimented until I came up with something that matched what I'd tasted. You can serve this spread immediately with crackers or slices of baguette, but the flavor improves considerably if you let it sit overnight.

8 ounces aged white extra sharp cheddar cheese, finely grated

2 tablespoons mayonnaise

¼ teaspoon lemon juice

4 teaspoons (half of a 4-ounce jar) pimentos, drained

a dash of cayenne

a dash of freshly ground black pepper

1   Mix cheese with enough mayonnaise to make it wet but so you can still see the shreds of cheese. You want to retain the structure of the cheese shreds, as they add interest to the spread.

2   Stir in the lemon juice, pimento, cayenne, and black pepper.

Salmon Cheese Ball

Total time: 3½ hours   Yields 1 large cheese ball

Very tasty and cheesy, this firm ball goes well with crackers and good cheer. It's great on a charcuterie board. You can use leftover smoked salmon, leftover cooked salmon, or even drained canned salmon.

1 pound cooked salmon
8 ounces cream cheese, softened
1 tablespoon lemon juice
2 teaspoons minced red onion
1 teaspoon prepared horseradish

¼ teaspoon salt
¼ teaspoon liquid smoke
½ cup chopped pecans or walnuts
1 tablespoon minced fresh cilantro

1   Remove skin and bones from salmon. Put salmon in medium bowl.
2   Beat together cream cheese, lemon juice, onion, horseradish, salt, and liquid smoke until smooth.
3   Add salmon and stir until well mixed.
4   Shape into a large ball. Chill 3 hours.
5   Combine nuts and cilantro on waxed paper.
6   Roll ball in nuts and cilantro until covered. Serve immediately or chill for a day.

Stuffed Grape Leaves (Dolmadakia)

Total time: 2½ hours   Yields about 3 dozen

Dolmadakia is the Greek name for "little stuffed grape leaves." Dolma is the Turkish word for one stuffed grape leaf; the Greeks added the diminutive -aki and the plural -a. (You'll also see them called dolmades.) The grape leaves are stuffed with rice or a rice/meat mixture (often lamb), then rolled into small logs, simmered in broth, and served warm or cold with lemon wedges and plain yogurt or drizzled with olive oil. I love these and make them for a meal, though they're also a nice appetizer or accompaniment to a full Middle Eastern feast. This recipe is one approach to making dolmadakia. Instead of presoaking the rice, you can instead cook it until it's softened but not completely cooked.

1 cup short-grained rice (white or brown, doesn't matter)
2 jars (8 ounces each) grape leaves (about 56 leaves)
1 small onion, finely chopped
¼ cup olive oil
3 garlic cloves, minced
1 bunch green onions, finely chopped
8 ounces ground lamb or beef
1 teaspoon ground cinnamon

1 teaspoon ground allspice
1 tablespoon finely chopped fresh mint
¼ cup pine nuts
¼ cup currants, soaked in white or red wine
¼ cup lemon juice
1 quart chicken broth
1 bay leaf
2 sprigs fresh thyme or 1 teaspoon dried thyme

1 Cover rice with water. Set aside to soak for about 50 minutes.
2 While rice soaks, carefully remove grape leaves from jar without tearing them. Carefully separate leaves, rinse, and drain. Snip stems as closely to leaf as possible. Set leaves aside.
3 Sauté onions in 2 tablespoons olive oil until just translucent.
4 Stir in garlic and green onions.
5 Immediately stir in lamb and cook until lamb is brown.
6 Add cinnamon and allspice and cook a few more minutes.
7 Drain rice, then, being careful not to break rice grains, stir into meat/onion mix.
8 Drain currants, then add mint, pine nuts, currants, and 1 tablespoon lemon juice to rice mixture.
9 In a separate pot, combine chicken stock, bay leaf, and thyme. Bring to a boil, then reduce to a simmer.
10 Spread out one grape leaf, vein side up and the tip of the leaf facing away from you. As you work, set aside torn and tiny leaves—you'll need them later. Stuff only the larger leaves.

11 Place a scant tablespoon filling on base of leaf.

12 Fold the leaf end over filling once.

13 Fold each side of leaf inward over the middle, then roll the entire leaf. You want the roll to be tight, but not too tight—you need a little room for the rice to expand. The result should be a small cigar shape about 2 inches long by about ¾ inch thick.

14 Repeat steps 10 through 13 until you've used up the filling. You should have leftover leaves. That's okay—you need those for the next step.

15 Cover bottom of a large pot or deep 12-inch sauté pan with leftover leaves. Bring leaves up the pot's sides a bit. This step protects the stuffed leaves and keeps them stable while they cook.

16 Carefully place the stuffed leaves on the lining leaves, seam side down. Snug together, but not too tightly.

17 When you're done placing all stuffed leaves in pot, sprinkle them with 2 tablespoons olive oil and 2 tablespoons lemon juice.

18 Gently pour the broth you made in step 9 over stuffed leaves. (No need to strain broth.) Cover stuffed leaves completely. If you need to, it's okay to add a bit more boiling water.

19 Place an ovenproof plate on top of stuffed grape leaves (to hold them down while they cook).

20 Bring broth to a boil.

21 You have two choices for the final cooking step.

- Turn heat to low, cover pot, and simmer for about 1 hour, or
- cover and cook in the oven at 350° for about 1 hour.

22 To test for doneness, cut open one stuffed leaf. The rice inside should be tender. If not, cook another 15 minutes.

23 Once stuffed leaves are done cooking, drain off broth and chill stuffed leaves. **Save the cooking broth**! You can use it to cook a fantastically delicious pot of rice, or as a soup stock, or even to make another batch of stuffed grape leaves. Store broth in refrigerator for up to three days.

Stuffed Mushrooms Supreme

Total time: 45 minutes   Yields 16

I don't remember the name of the woman who shared this recipe with me, but I still have the index card in her handwriting and I remember her taking me under her wing in a loving and motherly fashion for a brief while during a rough time in my life. She was empathetic and compassionate. The memory of her unquestioning friendship and quiet company remain with me.

16 large mushrooms
1/3 cup unsalted butter, melted, plus more for buttering baking dish
1 clove garlic, minced
1 large hardboiled egg, chopped
1/2 cup cooked spinach, drained and chopped

1/2 cup fine bread crumbs
1/4 teaspoon ground black pepper
1/2 teaspoon salt
1/8 teaspoon ground nutmeg
1/2 cup evaporated milk
1/2 cup grated Parmesan

1 Prepare a baking dish by buttering it.
2 Wash mushrooms and trim stems down to underside of caps.
3 Chop stems into small pieces.
4 Dip mushroom caps in melted butter, then place skin side down in prepared baking dish.
5 Combine chopped stems with garlic, spinach, bread crumbs, pepper, salt, nutmeg, and evaporated milk, and blend well.
6 Carefully fill mushroom caps with mixture. Heap high.
7 Top with Parmesan and bake at 350° for 30 minutes.

Beans, Soups, and Vegetables

Legumes (beans, lentils, green beans, and so on), and vegetables are versatile foods. You can use them in a large number of ways, and they play a supporting role in recipes throughout this cookbook. In this chapter, they take center stage, starring in a variety of wholesome dishes. They can be warm and hearty curries, soups, and chilis, like my Sweet Potato Tempeh Curry (page 56), the classic New England Clam Chowder (page 48), or Tempeh Chili (page 57). They can be richly complex, like Dal Makhani à la AJ (page 36). They can be super simple and yet still deeply satisfying, like the Greek-Style Lemon Potatoes (page 43).

You can serve most recipes in this chapter as a main dish. Most recipes in this chapter are vegetarian or vegan, or can be made so with a few simple substitutions (such as using olive oil where a recipe calls for butter).

Cooking Beans

Beans are a staple around the world, and no wonder. They are delicious, versatile, highly portable, low-fat, high-fiber, nutrient-packed little marvels, high in protein and in calcium and other minerals, that plump up to two or more times their size when cooked. A pound of beans, an onion, some celery, possibly a can of tomatoes, and some spices and seasonings can create a delicious meal for six, and no one will walk away hungry. Enhance with some Rich Cream Biscuits (page 105) and you're in heaven.

This chapter has several recipes for beans; once you have tried a few, if you aren't already familiar with the ways of beans, you will start to get the idea of how to create your own bean dishes.

Soaking Beans the Quick-Soak Way

You can soak beans had to soak for eight hours or overnight before you cook them. However, research has shown that you can speed up the process considerably by using this shortcut.

1   Rinse and sort the beans.
2   Place the beans in a large stock pot and cover with water.
3   Bring water to a boil.
4   Boil for three minutes.
5   Turn off heat, cover, and let beans sit for one hour.
6   Drain and rinse beans again, add required water, then cook according to the recipe.

Soaking Beans in a Pressure Cooker

You can cook wonderful beans in a pressure cooker. For the best results, follow this process, which I've adapted from the Mealthy website. (I love my Mealthy pressure cooker and Mealthy's fantastic customer service, but everyone's pressure cooker is awesome, no matter the brand.) For any bean recipe in this chapter, you can use this method to cook the beans instead of the soaking/cooking methods in those recipes.

1   Rinse and sort the beans.
2   Place the beans in the inner pot of your pressure cooker and cover with water.
3   Cook on high pressure for 1 minute.
4   Quick-release the pressure.

5 Pour beans into a colander, discarding the cooking liquid. Rinse thoroughly with cold water.

6 Rinse the cooking pot, then pour beans back into it. Add 3 cups water for each cup of beans.

7 Add any other ingredients (from a recipe, for example), then cook at high pressure for 15 minutes. You can also just cook them plain, though I recommend at least adding a bay leaf and some spices; maybe some diced onion and sliced celery and carrots.

8 When the beans are done cooking, release pressure naturally.

Eat More Vegetables

I don't need to tell anyone that vegetables, and lots of them, are great for your health. You've heard it all many times before. It can get confusing, though—what kinds? What colors? Which ones are best? Root crops? Above-ground crops? Eat the rainbow? It's all a lot of work. And then there's the shopping—finding what you want, picking fresh, undamaged veggies. And the food prep—the washing, peeling, chopping, dicing. And so on. Is it worth it?

Yes.

In the research I've done, it seems to boil down to two simple principles (your doctor's advice taking precedence): eat the vegetables you like, in as much variety as you can. Aim for at least two cups a day of vegetables. Another two cups a day of fruit. It's a huge amount, but it's all good, and however much you eat is likely to be more than you were eating before. You may not always meet that goal, but as for me, my health is better when I consistently eat that much.

Black Bean Soup

Total time: 5 hours   Yields 6 servings

I invented this recipe in the late 1980s. Like me, this soup is quite forgiving and allows for many additions, substitutions, or omissions. However, for best flavor, you
should at least use the black beans, tomatoes, spices, olive oil, and ham hock. For a
vegan pot of beans, leave out the ham hock. Serve with a hearty whole wheat bread
or fresh French bread. To make your own Italian seasonings, see page 300.

2 pounds dry black beans
3 quarts water
1 large or 2 small ham hocks
1 can (14 ounces) diced
    tomatoes
2 tablespoons Italian
    seasonings
¼ teaspoon cayenne

2 teaspoons ground cumin
1 clove garlic, coarsely
    chopped
1 can (28 ounces) stewed
    tomatoes or 4 cups coarsely
    chopped fresh tomatoes
½ cup olive oil

1   Wash and sort beans.
2   Place in 1 quart of water in a large ovenproof soup pot or Dutch
    oven.
3   Bring to a boil. Boil 5 minutes. Remove from heat, cover, and let
    sit for an hour. At the end of the soaking, the beans will have
    completely absorbed the water.
4   When beans have absorbed the water, add ham hock, diced
    tomatoes, Italian seasonings, cayenne, cumin, garlic, stewed
    tomatoes, and olive oil. Stir well.
5   Cover and cook in oven at 350° for 3 to 4 hours or until beans are
    tender and have a lovely, thick, delicious liquor.

Carrots with Fresh Basil

Total time: 30 minutes   Yields 6 servings

I don't think I ever would have thought of the flavors of carrots and basil together until I came across this recipe in the early 1980s. It's an amazing combination, and is a nice way to use that abundance of basil you're growing in your garden.

2 quarts water
1½ pounds small carrots
½ cup firmly packed fresh basil, minced

¼ cup olive oil
½ teaspoon salt
3 tablespoons lemon juice

1 Bring water to a boil.
2 Add carrots and cook 10 to 15 minutes or until barely tender.
3 Drain carrots (a colander is handy for this) and rinse under cold water, slipping off skins if desired.
4 Pat carrots dry, trim ends, and cut into quarters.
5 Combine basil, olive oil, and salt in a skillet.
6 Add carrots and cook over moderate heat, stirring, 3 to 5 minutes or until just tender and well coated with the basil and oil.
7 Transfer to a warmed serving dish and sprinkle with lemon juice.

Carrot-Ginger Soup

Total time: 1 hour   Yields 8-10 cups

When I was recovering from cancer surgery in 2018, I bought weekly meals from the Ceres Community Project, a group created to support people in situations like mine. They served many delicious foods, the recipes for which you can find in Cathryn Couch and JoEllen DeNicola's *Nourishing Connections Cookbook*, second edition (Ceres Community Project, 2016). This soup, which my daughter loosely based on a recipe in that cookbook, became one of our favorites.

1 tablespoon olive oil
1½ cups chopped onion
5 cups carrots, scrubbed and sliced into ½ inch slices (no need to peel)
6 cups water

2 tablespoons coarsely chopped fresh ginger (no need to peel)
1½ teaspoons sea salt
3 slices fresh orange peel (optional)

1   Heat oil in a large, deep stock pot.
2   Add onions and sauté lightly.
3   Add carrots. Sauté until onions are translucent but not browning.
4   Add water, ginger, salt, and orange peel. Bring to a boil.
5   Reduce heat to a simmer and cook until carrots are tender (about 40 minutes).
6   Cool soup slightly. Remove orange peel and put it in your compost. Purée soup in batches until smooth. The soup's texture should be velvety. Take care in puréeing; warm soup gets even warmer and expands in a blender. You can also use an immersion blender in the stock pot.

Cheese Mashed Potatoes

Total time: 2 hours   Yields 4 to 6 servings

My friend Louise shared this hearty mashed potato recipe with me decades ago. Using canned soups always feels like cheating. But sometimes the speed and convenience they add to a recipe makes it worth the compromise. If converting to a vegetarian version, use a vegetarian "cream of" soup (cream of celery, for example), or make your own cream of vegetable soup using the basics from the Cream of Broccoli Soup recipe (page 31).

6 medium russet potatoes
¼ cup unsalted butter
¼ cup bread crumbs
1 can (10.75 ounces) condensed cream of chicken soup, undiluted

½ cup chopped green onions
1 pint sour cream
salt and pepper to taste
1½ cups grated medium cheddar cheese

1 Butter a medium casserole dish.
2 Wrap each potato in aluminum foil.
3 Bake potatoes for 45 minutes at 400° (or until just tender).
4 While potatoes are baking, mix butter and bread crumbs together. Set aside.
5 Remove foil from potatoes, then cool. When cool enough to handle, peel potatoes and grate the flesh.
6 Combine potatoes with soup, green onions, sour cream, salt, pepper, and cheese.
7 Put into a medium casserole dish. Top with butter/bread mixture.
8 Bake at 350° for 45 minutes.

Colcannon

Total time: 1 hour 15 minutes   Yields about 4 servings

This traditional Irish recipe was an instant favorite the first time I tried it in March 2021. In Ireland, each cook has their own version; for example, some people add green onions or bacon, or use cabbage instead of kale. (If you make it with green onions *instead* of kale, it's called champ.) I got the original version of this recipe from Farm Fresh to You, a local(ish) farm that delivers fresh organic produce to my door. Farm Fresh was a godsend throughout 2020 because, while my local grocery stores were unable to supply most of my food needs, Farm Fresh always had something. I make this recipe with Yukon Gold potatoes, but you can use any type of potato you like, from starchy russets to waxy reds. It's important to de-stem and chop the kale well; otherwise you'll have large, chewy chunks of kale in the finished dish.

3 pounds potatoes, cut into 2-inch chunks (no need to peel)
2 tablespoons olive oil
2 cups kale, stems removed, leaves chopped into small pieces
¼ cup diced shallots or onions
1 teaspoon salt

½ teaspoon freshly ground black pepper
6 tablespoons butter (salted or unsalted), plus more for topping the finished dish
⅔ cup whole milk, half and half, or cream (depending on how rich you want your potatoes)

1. Add potatoes to a large pot with enough water to just cover. Bring to a boil over high heat. Reduce heat to medium. Cook until tender, 20 to 25 minutes.
2. Drain potatoes and set aside (not in the pot).
3. Add olive oil to pot and heat over medium heat.
4. When oil is hot, stir in shallots. Sauté until slightly softened, 1 to 2 minutes.
5. Add kale and cook 3 to 4 minutes or until wilted and soft.
6. Turn heat to low. Add the 6 tablespoons butter. Stir until melted.
7. Add potatoes to pot. Mash potatoes together with kale and shallots until well mixed.
8. Stir in salt and pepper.
9. Add milk a little at a time until potatoes are creamy but still firm.
10. Serve immediately. When serving, form a small well in the center of each serving and add a generous pat of butter.

Cream of Broccoli Soup

Total time: 30 minutes   Yields about 4 cups of soup

I used to make this recipe with leftover broccoli. That was when my daughter was young and not a broccoli fan. But she loved this soup, especially with cheese. Now that she's older, we hardly ever have leftover broccoli, so I make this soup with fresh broccoli. I adapted this recipe from Jean Anderson and Elaine Hanna's *The New Doubleday Cookbook* (Doubleday, 1975), one of the world's best and most under-appreciated all-purpose cookbooks. You can make any cream of vegetable soup with this recipe. Try asparagus, butternut squash, cabbage, carrots, cauliflower, celery, onion, leek, pumpkin, spinach, or sweet potatoes, or combinations of any of these. You could also use this soup base with carrots, celery, onions, and cooked or canned chicken to make cream of chicken soup.

3 tablespoons butter (no substitute)
3 tablespoons all-purpose flour
2 cups chicken broth or water
¼ cup diced onion

3 cups broccoli florets
1 cup heavy cream
¼ cup cheddar cheese (optional)

1   Melt butter in a large skillet.
2   Stir in flour to make a light roux. (The roux should puff slightly and not get brown.)
3   Stir in broth and heat, continuing to stir, until it boils.
4   Add broccoli.
5   Cover and simmer for 10-15 minutes or until broccoli is soft.
6   Purée the soup, then stir in cream and cheese and heat a few more minutes.

Cumin Potatoes

Total time: 50 minutes   Yields 6 servings

Adapted from Yamuna Devi's *Lord Krishna's Cuisine: The Art of Vegetarian Indian Cooking* (Dutton - Penguin Putnam, 1987), this simple recipe produces delicious potatoes. The slight sharpness of the mustard seed blends well with the mellow sweetness of the coriander seeds and the cumin's warm earthiness. The turmeric's bright deep yellow orange creates an interesting patina on the potatoes. When I make these potatoes, I never have any leftovers. To make this dish vegan, use olive or avocado oil instead of butter. Red or golden potatoes work best; russets are too mealy. You can leave out the cayenne entirely, or vary the amount for more or less heat.

⅓ cup unsalted butter
2 tablespoons cumin seed
2 teaspoons coriander seed
½ teaspoon mustard seed

3 pounds potatoes, cut into ½-inch cubes (no need to peel)
1 teaspoon ground turmeric
1 teaspoon cayenne
4 tablespoons water

1 Melt butter over medium heat in a deep, heavy pot.
2 When butter is hot, add cumin, coriander, and mustard. Fry a few minutes until seeds darken a bit or mustard seeds pop. Watch closely to make sure nothing burns.
3 Add potatoes and coat them as best you can with butter and spices.
4 Fry potatoes, stirring constantly to scrape up sticking bits, until potatoes are slightly browned (about 10 minutes).
5 Reduce heat to low and add turmeric and cayenne, mixing as well as you can. I say "as you can," because the spices and butter make a scant covering. You might think you need more, but you don't. These quantities are perfect.
6 Add water, sprinkling well over potatoes.
7 Cover and cook on low heat, stirring frequently, for 20 to 30 minutes or until potatoes are tender. As you stir, check for signs of sticking on the bottom of the pot. If this happens, scrape up potatoes and add more water, a tablespoon at a time, as needed.

Curried Lentils

Total time: 1 hour   Yields 4 servings

Lentils (*Lens culinaris*) are a great source of protein and trace nutrients. They have a mild, earthy flavor and a tender, mealy texture that makes them quite satisfying to eat. Lentils offer the advantage of cooking quickly and with little fuss. In India, several types of legumes, peas, and beans, including lentils, are collectively called *dal* and are all cooked in an endless variety of curries. This straightforward recipe is made with onions, tomatoes, and several curry-adjacent spices. I vary the ingredients according to what I have on hand. It's delicious served with generous dollops of yogurt or sour cream on top of each bowl of lentils. (I prefer yogurt with this recipe.) Curried lentils are a good side dish for my Lamb Curry (recipe on page 206).

- **2** tablespoons olive oil or butter
- **2** large yellow onions, coarsely chopped
- **3** medium tomatoes, coarsely chopped, or 2 tablespoons canned tomato paste
- **1** cup whole brown lentils, sorted and rinsed
- **3/4** teaspoon salt

- **1** tablespoon curry powder
- **1/2** teaspoon ground cumin
- **1/4** teaspoon ground turmeric
- **1/4** teaspoon ground coriander
- **1/4** teaspoon ground cardamom
- **1** tablespoon diced fresh ginger (no need to peel)
- **1** quart water

1   Heat oil in a medium saucepan.

2   Add onions and sauté until tender (about 8 minutes).

3   Add tomatoes. If using tomato paste, add 2 tablespoons of water with the tomato paste.

4   Continue to cook, stirring, another 2 to 3 minutes.

5   Stir in lentils, salt, curry powder, cumin, turmeric, coriander, cardamom, and water. If needed, add more water to cover lentils.

6   Bring to a boil, then reduce heat to medium low.

7   Cook for about 25 minutes or until lentils are tender. The soup will be thick and the lentils will absorb most or all of the water. If desired, add 1 more cup water to thin the lentils toward the end of cooking.

Curried Potatoes with Peas

Total time: 1 hour   Yields 6 servings

For such a simple recipe, this recipe, one of the first Indian dishes I learned, is incredibly tasty. It's moister than the Cumin Potatoes (page 32), and, of course, has the peas to add extra bites of goodness. For the potatoes, red, russet, or yellow all work well; or try some of the more exotic varieties. The butter is for flavor; substitute olive oil for the butter if you want to make this vegetarian/vegan. My Madras-Style Curry Powder (recipe on page 303) is perfect in this recipe.

3 tablespoons olive oil
2 tablespoons unsalted butter
1 tablespoon curry powder
1 teaspoon cumin seed
1/4 teaspoon cayenne

3 pounds potatoes, cubed (no
    need to peel)
1 1/2 cups water
1 cup peas, fresh or frozen

1   In a medium saucepan, heat oil until hot.
2   Add butter, curry powder, cumin, and cayenne. Stir well and cook a few minutes.
3   Add potatoes and water and bring to a boil.
4   Cover, reduce heat to medium low, and cook for 15 minutes.
5   After 15 minutes, if using fresh peas, add them now, reduce heat to low, cover, and simmer until the potatoes are soft and the peas are tender (about 20 to 30 minutes). If using frozen peas, add them during the last three minutes of cooking. The goal is for the peas to be piping hot.

Curried Vegetables

Total time: 1 hour 15 minutes   Yields 4 servings

People who don't normally like peas or curry love this recipe. (Another one of my "throw everything together" recipes.) You can double or triple this recipe with the following changes: if you double the recipe, only add half again as much butter, spices, and tomatoes. If you triple it, double the butter, spices, and tomatoes. You can make this vegetarian/vegan by using olive oil instead of butter. My recipe for Madras-Style Curry Powder is on page 303. Serve over brown rice.

½ cup unsalted butter
1 medium yellow or white
    onion, diced
6 teaspoons Madras-style
    curry powder
1 tablespoon garlic powder
¼ teaspoon cumin seed
1 pinch hulled green
    cardamom
¼ teaspoon fennel

4 medium golden potatoes,
    cubed
1 cup peas, fresh or frozen
1 cup corn kernels, fresh or
    frozen
1 cup green beans, fresh or
    frozen
1 (14-ounce) can of diced,
    stewed tomatoes

1 Melt butter in a large, deep frying pan.
2 Add onion and cook a few minutes.
3 Add curry powder, garlic powder, cumin, cardamom, and fennel. Stir well.
4 Add potatoes, peas, corn, green beans, and tomatoes.
5 Bring to a boil, then reduce heat and simmer until the potatoes are tender (about 45 minutes to an hour).

Dal Makhani à la AJ

Total time: 1½ hours   Yields 4 servings

In India, *dal* can mean any number of different beans and legumes, and *makhani* means butter. *Dal Makhani*, a signature dish of the Punjab region of Northern India, is a rich, buttery dish of beans often made with cream. Highly nutritious, *Dal Makhani* is sometimes called the king of all *dals*. My former husband AJ came up with this version on our daughter's 24th birthday. His version uses *sabut masoor dal* (brown lentils), and lots of butter, but no cream. He used my garam masala (page 294) and Madras-Style Curry Powder (page 303). This recipe goes well as a side dish with my Turkey Curry (page 235), or served over rice as a main dish. When you serve it, garnish with chopped fresh cilantro and yoghurt, cream, or sour cream, and serve with rice, naan, or chapatis.

1 cup whole brown lentils, sorted and rinsed
3/4 cup unsalted butter
1 medium yellow onion, diced
2 large cloves garlic, chopped
2 teaspoons garam masala
2 teaspoons turmeric powder
1 teaspoon Madras-style curry powder
1 teaspoon cayenne

2 small tomatoes, diced, or 2 tablespoons tomato salsa or 1 tablespoon tomato paste
2 tablespoons candied ginger, diced
1 tablespoon fresh ginger, sliced into thin strips (no need to peel)
1 cup hot water

1 Preheat oven to 325°.
2 Place lentils in a medium saucepan with enough water to cover one inch above the lentils. (Don't use the 1 cup of hot water—you'll use that later.)
3 Bring lentils to a boil over high heat, then lower heat to medium and simmer while you prepare the butter/spice/onion mixture.
4 Melt butter in a large saucepan over high heat.
5 Add onions and garlic and cook for about five minutes, or until onions are transparent and barely start to brown.
6 Stir in garam masala, turmeric, curry powder, and cayenne.
7 Add tomatoes, candied ginger, and chopped fresh ginger. Stir well.
8 Reduce heat to low while the lentils continue to cook.
9 When lentils are still hard but starting to get tender on their edges (20 to 30 minutes), add onion/butter/spice mixture. Stir well.
10 If mixture isn't liquid enough, add the 1 cup hot water and stir well. (The water needs to be hot so the mixture keeps cooking.)

11 Cover, increase heat to high, and bring to a boil.

12 Place covered saucepan in preheated oven and bake for 45 minutes or until lentils are quite tender.

Delicate Bean Soup

Total time: 3 hours   Yields 8 servings

T his soup, another of my own recipes, is a good illustration of how just changing the spices while using the same main ingredients can make a profoundly different dish. This recipe uses the same beans as Nine-Bean Soup (page 49), but is more subtly and delicately flavored—while still as satisfying.

2 cups Dry Bean Soup Mix
   (page 39)
1 medium white onion,
   chopped
1 cup chopped carrots
1 cup chopped celery

2 teaspoons Quatre Épices
   (page 310)
2 teaspoons cumin seed
1 teaspoon garlic granules
1 medium bay leaf
2 teaspoons chili powder

1   Rinse beans. If not using the Bean Soup Mix, sort the beans as well.
2   Place beans in a large stock pot and cover with water.
3   Bring water to a boil. Boil for three minutes. Turn off heat, cover, and let beans sit for one hour.
4   Drain and rinse beans once again. Add six cups water.
5   Add onions, carrots, celery, Quatre Épices, cumin, garlic, bay leaf, and chili powder.
6   Bring to a boil again, then turn to medium low, cover, and simmer for two to three hours or until the beans are tender. While cooking, add more water if needed.

Dry Bean Soup Mix

Total time: 5 minutes   Yields 18 cups dried mix

T his soup mix (my own) uses a variety of dry beans that work well together. You make this mix ahead of time, then store it until you need it. This mix makes a variety of hearty and wonderful bean soups. If you don't like the beans in this mix, experiment with your own favorite beans or some heirloom varieties. For example, try the lovely, meaty Sea Island Red Peas from Anson Mills. To make this mix into soup, use your own bean soup recipe, or see Delicate Bean Soup (page 38) or Nine-Bean Soup (page 49). Keeps for six to eight months.

2 cups dry kidney beans	**2** cups dry white beans
2 cups dry cannellini beans	**2** cups dry split peas, yellow
2 cups dry red beans	**2** cups dry split peas, green
2 cups dry pinto beans	**2** cups dry black-eyed peas
2 cups dry lima beans	

1   Sort the beans. You're looking for broken beans, rocks, and any other thing that should be removed. Beans are a natural product, so sometimes rocks sneak into the package. Normally you'd also rinse the beans, but that's only right before cooking them.
2   Combine kidney, cannellini, red, pinto, lima,and white beans with yellow and green split peas and black-eyed peas.
3   Mix well and store in a dry, airtight container and store in a cool, dark place.

Eggplant Parmigiana

Total time: 1 hour   Yields 6 to 8 servings

Eggplant comes into season in late October, just when the days are growing cooler in the northern hemisphere and a warm, hearty casserole is a welcome meal. Eggplant parmigiana is a popular dish for just these reasons. My version arose out of having eggplant but no eggs, forcing a tasty improvisation that is vegetarian to boot (if you're a vegetarian who eats cheese). And you don't even have to peel the eggplant! When researching eggplant, I was intrigued to find the Arabs brought eggplant from India to Italy in the fifteenth century, where its popularity took root, so to speak. Unknown to me, when I invented this recipe, I was recreating a version much like Ippolito Cavalcanti's eggplant parmigiana, which he describes in his cookbook, *Cucina Teorico-Pratica col corrispondente riposto ed apparecchio di pranzi e cene con quattro analoghi disegni* (Di G. Palma, 1839). Serve with a tossed green salad and garlic bread.

1 quart spaghetti sauce
1 quart stewed tomatoes
2 cloves garlic, sliced
1–2 cups olive oil

2 medium eggplants, sliced into ¼-inch rounds
1 cup fine bread crumbs (or finely crushed stuffing mix)
1 cup grated Parmesan cheese

1 Combine spaghetti sauce, tomatoes, and garlic in a medium saucepan and start heating.
2 While the spaghetti sauce heats, put about ¼ to ½ cup of the olive oil in a large frying pan and heat at medium high.
3 Fry the slices of eggplant in olive oil until they darken and turn soft and slightly limp. Remove slices from pan as they reach this state and keep adding new ones. As you remove the cooked slices, press them into the bread crumbs. Add olive oil to frying pan as needed.
4 When you finish frying the eggplant, put about ¼ to ½ cup of the tomato mixture into the bottom of a large casserole dish.
5 Cover the tomato mixture with a single layer of eggplant slices.
6 Sprinkle generously with Parmesan cheese.
7 Cover with tomato sauce and another layer of eggplant slices and Parmesan. Keep layering until the dish is full or until you run out of eggplant, whichever comes first.
8 Top with tomato sauce and Parmesan cheese.
9 Cover and bake at 350° for about 25 to 30 minutes.

Gazpacho

Total time: 20 minutes plus 4 hours chill time

Yields 4 servings

A summer staple for many, this healthful cold soup, which Andalusia (Andalucía), Spain claims as its own, is one of my very favorite soups ever. I prefer red bell pepper, but you can use any color you like. You can use red wine vinegar or apple cider vinegar if you don't have sherry vinegar. Instead of (or in addition to) the lime slices, you can garnish with chopped cilantro or a drizzle of fresh cream.

4 large Roma tomatoes, cored, seeded, and coarsely chopped
1 stalk celery, coarsely chopped
1 small cucumber, peeled and sliced
½ small red onion, coarsely chopped

2 tablespoons sherry vinegar
½ bell pepper, sliced
2 tablespoons olive oil
½ teaspoon sea salt
½ teaspoon ground cumin
1 clove garlic
4 slices lime

1 Combine tomatoes, celery, cucumber, onion, vinegar, bell pepper, olive oil, salt, and cumin (everything but the garlic and lime).
2 Purée to your desired consistency.
3 Add garlic clove and chill 4 hours.
4 Just before serving, remove garlic clove. Serve in four individual-serving-sized bowls. Garnish each bowl with a lime slice.

Gingered Carrots

Total time: 10 minutes   Yields 1 serving

Carrots are one of the vegetables where the cooked version is more nutritious than the raw. For example, carrots contain vitamins A, E, and K, which are heat stable. And cooking carrots frees up more nutrients by breaking down the carrot's cell walls. This little dish with its faint bite of ginger is quick and kind of fun.

2 large carrots, shredded $\frac{1}{8}$ teaspoon ground ginger
1 tablespoon butter $\frac{1}{4}$ teaspoon honey

1   Melt butter in a small skillet.
2   Add carrots and sauté, stirring often, for 3 to 5 minutes or until the shreds wilt.
3   Sprinkle with ginger and honey and toss to mix well.

Greek-Style Lemon Potatoes

Total time: 1 hour   Yields one 13- x 9-inch panful

When researching the history of another recipe for this cookbook, I came across Christine Cushing's YouTube channel. Many of her videos focus on Greek cookery. In one video, she shows how to bake these Greek-style potatoes. This recipe is almost identical to my own Herbed Potatoes (page 46), but with the surprising addition of lemon. I tried her recipe, loved it, and, as usual, adapted it to my own tastes. This recipe falls under the category of Greek *lathera* recipes (vegetables made with lots of olive oil; see page 44 for more on *lathera*). You can make this recipe with any kind of potato, but I'm particularly fond of Yukon Golds (they're tender, not mealy; thin-skinned; with creamy, almost buttery flesh; and their gold color adds a festive look to any dish). For a Cretan flair, try ½ cup fresh orange juice instead of lemon juice. (As in Florida and Southern California, oranges are readily available in Crete.) These potatoes reheat well in the oven.

½ cup olive oil
1 tablespoon fresh rosemary
zest and juice of 1 lemon
2 teaspoons dried oregano

6 medium Yukon gold
   potatoes, washed, cut in
   half lengthwise, then cut
   into thin half-moon slices
   (no need to peel)

1   Preheat oven to 350°.
2   Spread a few tablespoons olive oil over bottom of a 13- x 9-inch baking pan.
3   Sprinkle fresh rosemary over oil.
4   Place potatoes in pan and pour lemon juice and remaining olive oil over potatoes.
5   Sprinkle potatoes with oregano. Turn potatoes so they are well coated, then spread them out.
6   Roast potatoes until tender and golden brown, about 35-45 minutes. You can turn them every 15 minutes if you're worried about the potatoes sticking, but it shouldn't be necessary.
7   Remove from oven and serve hot.

Greek-Style Green Beans

Total time: 45 minutes   Yields 6 servings

Called *fasolakia lathera*, or green beans cooked in oil, by the Greeks, this classic recipe makes an excellent addition to any meal. *Lathera* are a type of vegetable dish made with lots of olive oil and usually also tomatoes. It's typical of the healthful Mediterranean diet, which is high in fiber, rich in "good" fats, low in "bad" fats, and filled with antioxidant-rich fruits, vegetables, nuts, and grains that nourish and replenish the heart and soul. One advantage of Mediterranean cooking is that herbs and spices are used to flavor food instead of salt. This recipe is best with fresh tomatoes, though you can substitute tomato paste.

½ cup olive oil

3 pounds potatoes, cut into ½-inch cubes (no need to peel)

1½ pounds green beans, fresh or frozen

1 medium yellow onion, coarsely chopped

1 cup fresh basil or cilantro, finely chopped

2 teaspoons oregano, fresh or dried

1 teaspoon cumin, whole or ground

1 bay leaf

6 small tomatoes, coarsely chopped, or 6 ounces tomato paste and 2 tablespoons water

1   Place the olive oil and potatoes in a coverable baking dish.
2   If green beans are fresh, wash them, cut off stem ends, cut into 3-inch lengths, and add to baking dish. If green beans are frozen, just add to baking dish.
3   Add onions, basil, oregano, cumin, and bay leaf.
4   Stir in tomatoes and water. If using a 6-ounce can of tomato paste, stir in tomato paste. Then put the 2 tablespoons water into can, swirl to get remaining paste, and add water from can to baking dish. (If using tomato paste from a larger can, add tomato paste and the two tablespoons of water to baking dish.)
5   Cover and bake at 350° for about 40 minutes. Stir every 10 to 15 minutes. When onions become semi-translucent and potatoes are tender, remove from oven and serve.

Green Beans Almondine

Total time: 30 minutes   Yields 3 cups

T his classic dish, one of my daughter's favorites, is often served during the winter holidays in America. The tartness of the lemons and the butter's round fullness pair well with the crisp snap of the green beans. Because it is fast and simple, yet healthful and delicious, there is no reason not to prepare this dish any time of year. Fresh green beans taste unpleasantly like grass, and overdone green beans are unappealingly limp and mushy. This recipe uses what I think is the best method for cooking the beans without under- or overcooking them, a method I worked out through experimentation.

1½ pounds fresh green beans   **2** tablespoons unsalted butter
½ cup slivered almonds   **1** teaspoon fresh lemon juice

1 Prepare green beans by rinsing them, then cutting off the ends.
2 Start steaming green beans (they steam fast, so be ready to move quickly).
3 While steaming the beans, melt butter in a medium skillet. Sauté almonds in butter until lightly browned (perhaps a minute or so); do not burn.
4 Remove skillet from heat and add lemon juice to almonds.
5 When the green beans are just tender (no longer grassy tasting, and with a bit of crunch still), toss with almonds, butter, and lemon juice. Serve immediately.

Herbed Potatoes

Total time: 1 hour 15 minutes   Yields one 13- x 9-inch pan

This simple savory dish, my own recipe from the 1990s, makes a good side dish for a variety of other foods. Although I specify yellow potatoes, it's delicious made with red potatoes or a blend of red and yellow potatoes. You can use any other variety, though the mealy russets don't have the tender texture that the waxier red and yellow potatoes have. These potatoes are vegan if you use only olive oil instead of the combination of olive oil and butter.

5 pounds yellow potatoes, thinly sliced
5 tablespoons olive oil or 4 tablespoons olive oil and 1 tablespoon unsalted butter, melted

1 tablespoon Italian seasonings
1 teaspoon granulated garlic powder
½ teaspoon cayenne
¼ teaspoon ground black pepper

1 Place a tablespoon or so of the oil in the bottom of a 13- x 9-inch baking pan—just enough to lightly coat the bottom. (Alternatively, you can use cooking spray.)
2 In a small bowl, combine remaining oil with Italian seasonings, garlic, cayenne, and pepper.
3 Place a layer of sliced potatoes in baking pan, then coat with some of the oil/seasoning mix.
4 Continue layering and coating until all the potatoes are in the pan. The pan will be quite full.
5 Bake at 350° for 45 minutes or until potatoes are quite tender.
6 Remove from oven and cool a few minutes before serving.

Mushroom Soup

Total time: 1 hour   Yields 6 servings

T his rare and unusual recipe makes a clear, delicate, and elegant soup. The recipe isn't my own—someone shared it with me decades ago—but I've never seen another recipe like it. The butter and Parmesan are essential parts of this soup's flavor, so this recipe is vegetarian, but not suitable for vegans.

- **1** pound fresh button mushrooms, cleaned and sliced vertically
- **2** tablespoons unsalted butter
- **2** tablespoons olive oil
- **1** clove garlic
- **1** medium yellow or white onion, diced
- **3** tablespoons tomato paste
- **2** tablespoons dry vermouth
- **3** cups chicken stock
- **3** large egg yolks
- **2** ounces fresh Parmesan cheese, grated
- **2** tablespoons fresh parsley

1 In a large saucepan, combine mushrooms, butter, olive oil, garlic, onion, tomato paste, vermouth, and chicken stock. Simmer 15 minutes.

2 While the mushrooms cook, in a small bowl, combine egg yolks, Parmesan, and parsley.

3 Add a little hot broth to the egg mixture, enough to warm the mixture without cooking or curdling the eggs, then add egg mixture to soup. Adding a little hot mixture to eggs before adding eggs to the rest of a hot mixture helps prevent eggs from curdling.

4 Simmer another 30 minutes.

New England Clam Chowder

Total time: 1 hour   Yields about 2½ quarts

Mike Grimmer, a classmate at Santa Clara University, shared this recipe with me in the 1970s; I modified long ago. If you have *Delectable Desserts*, the first volume in this cookbook series, you may remember my mention of his sister, Pat Grimmer, who shared her perfect Snickerdoodles cookie recipe. Serve with liberal amounts of sourdough or French bread and, on the side, cayenne and a bottle of hot pepper sauce for those who like their clam chowder that way.

3 medium potatoes, cut into 1-inch cubes (no need to peel)

½ cup unsalted butter, divided

1 medium onion, diced

½ cup celery, sliced

1 teaspoon dried tarragon

3 teaspoons dried basil

1 bay leaf

1 quart whole milk

1 cup sour cream

½ pound mushrooms, cleaned, trimmed, and sliced

3 tablespoons fresh parsley

18 ounces canned clams and juice

1 Boil potatoes about 20 minutes, until still firm but just starting to get tender. Drain most of the cooking water (but leave about 1 cup) and set potatoes aside, still in their pot.

2 Melt ¼ cup of butter in a skillet. Sauté onions in butter until translucent.

3 Stir in celery and turn heat to very low.

4 Crush tarragon and basil and stir into onions and celery.

5 Add bay leaf to onions and celery.

6 Now let's return to the potatoes, who might be feeling lonely by now. Add milk and sour cream to potatoes. Heat slowly, but don't boil. Keep on heat while you prep the mushrooms.

7 Melt remaining ¼ cup butter in another skillet and sauté sliced mushrooms until they just start to get limp.

8 Add mushrooms, butter and all, to the pot of potatoes. Give it all a stir, then bring to a simmer.

9 Add onion/spice mix to the pot of potatoes. Stir in well, continuing to simmer.

10 Add parsley.

11 Stir in clams with their juice. Simmer about 30 minutes or until potatoes are tender. Fish out bay leaf before serving.

Nine-Bean Soup

Total time: 3½ hours   Yields 8 servings

This bean soup is thick and satisfying. It tastes wonderful served with brown rice or corn bread. For a gluten-free version, either use a gluten-free liquid smoke, or omit the liquid smoke.

2 cups Dry Bean Black Bean Soup Mix (page 39)
1 medium white onion, coarsely chopped
½ cup olive oil
½ teaspoon liquid smoke flavoring

1 tablespoon garlic powder
3 tablespoons Herbes de Provence (page 298)
1 teaspoon cayenne
1 bay leaf
1 3-inch square nori (sheet of dried seaweed)

1 Rinse and sort beans.
2 Place beans in a large stock pot and cover with water.
3 Bring water to a boil. Boil for three minutes. Turn off heat, cover, and let beans sit for one hour.
4 Drain and rinse beans once again. Add six cups of water.
5 Add onions, olive oil, smoke flavoring, garlic powder, Herbes de Provence, cayenne, bay leaf, and nori.
6 Bring to a boil again, then turn to medium low. Simmer for 2 to 3 hours or until beans are tender. While cooking, add more water if needed.

Potato Cheese Soup

Total time: 1 hour   Yields about 10 cups

A fast, economical soup, very satisfying, with a unique taste. You can use any variety of potato, though I like this recipe best with russets. Delicious with fresh French or sourdough bread. If you don't care for cilantro, you can substitute parsley. It'll be just as tasty. For a gluten-free version, use brown rice flour instead of all-purpose flour, and make sure you use a gluten-free Worcestershire sauce. In the US, Lea & Perrins Original Worcestershire sauce is gluten free. (Lea & Perrins in other countries is not gluten free.) Two other brands of Worcestershire sauce that are also gluten free are French's, and The Wizard's Gluten-Free Vegan Worcestershire Sauce.

2 cups diced russet potatoes
1 medium yellow onion, coarsely chopped
½ cup diced celery
4 cups water
¼ cup unsalted butter
¼ cup all-purpose flour or brown rice flour
2 cups whole milk
2 teaspoons Worcestershire sauce

1 teaspoon dry mustard
4 ounces sharp cheddar cheese, grated
1 teaspoon fresh cilantro, chopped
1 can (14 ounces) stewed tomatoes
2½ teaspoons salt
1 teaspoon pepper
¼ teaspoon dill weed, fresh or dried

1   Combine potatoes, onion, celery, and water in a Dutch oven and bring to a boil.
2   Cover and simmer 15 minutes.
3   While the potato mixture is cooking, melt butter in a small skillet.
4   Blend flour into butter to make a pale roux.
5   Add milk and Worcestershire sauce to roux; set roux aside.
6   After potatoes have cooked for 15 minutes, add roux to potatoes.
7   Add mustard, cheese, cilantro, stewed tomatoes, salt, pepper, and dill weed to potatoes.
8   Cook for another 5 minutes, stirring, until thickened.

Potatoes au Gratin

Total time: 2 hours   Yields one 13- x 9-inch panful

Potatoes and cheese—a perfect combination. Some people make this dish with diced or thinly sliced onions, which is a tasty variation. Some versions of this recipe just have you sprinkle grated cheese in layers, but the cheesy sauce for this recipe is delicious and versatile. (You can use it to make macaroni and cheese, for example.) Use any kind of potato you like; I like to use a mix of red and yellow potatoes. Slice the potatoes as thickly or thinly as you like. Because thinner potatoes cook faster, they can almost vanish in this recipe, so I prefer a slightly thicker slice.

Cheese Sauce

½ cup unsalted butter   4 cups whole milk
6 tablespoons flour   4 cups grated cheddar cheese

Potato Casserole

4 pounds potatoes, sliced

1. Preheat oven to 350°.
2. Thoroughly butter the inside bottom and sides of a 13- x 9-inch baking dish.
3. Melt butter over medium heat in a medium saucepan.
4. Add flour to butter and stir well. Cook 1 to 2 minutes.
5. Slowly drizzle in milk, stirring constantly, until milk and flour/butter mixture are completely mixed.
6. Cook, stirring frequently, until it thickens (about 8 minutes).
7. Quickly add cheese and stir well until cheese is melted.
8. Place a layer of sliced potatoes in baking dish and pour some cheese sauce over it. Add another layer of potatoes, more cheese sauce, more potatoes, and so on, ending with the last of the cheese sauce.
9. Take a piece of aluminum foil that is large enough to cover the baking dish, and spray with cooking spray (or butter it). Then cover dish with the aluminum foil. (The spray is to help prevent the potatoes from sticking to the foil.)
10. Bake 1 hour covered with foil, then uncover and bake another 20 to 30 minutes or until potatoes are tender.

Riviera Fish Soup

Total time: 30 minutes   Yields 4 servings

I 've had this recipe for so long (since the late 1970s) that I don't remember from whom I received it, the circumstances, or even why it's called *Riviera* Fish Soup. It's tasty, though. A quick Google search shows that many people have published similar recipes online, but none quite like this. If you don't have turbot or rockfish, you can substitute any other firm, white-fleshed fish fillets, such as cod. Serve with a fresh green salad, hunks of fresh French bread, and lots of softened butter for the bread.

1 tablespoon olive oil
1 small onion, sliced
1 clove garlic, crushed
¼ cup sliced celery
2 tablespoons chopped fresh parsley
½ teaspoon Italian seasonings

1 can (10 ounces) tomato soup
2 tablespoons tomato paste
1¼ cups hot water
1 can (about 6½ ounces) clams, minced, juice reserved
1 pound turbot or rockfish fillets

1   Warm olive oil in a skillet and add onion, garlic, and celery. Sauté until onions are translucent (about 5 minutes).
2   Stir in parsley, Italian seasonings, tomato soup, tomato paste, hot water, clams, and the reserved clam juice. Bring to a boil.
3   Add fish and simmer until fish is cooked through (about 5 minutes).

Sautéed Cabbage

Total time: 10 minutes   Yields about 3 cups

When my daughter made this dish, it was love at first bite. Yes, it only has two ingredients and three seasonings. Yet often the simple dishes are surprisingly satisfying. This recipe only takes a few minutes from start to finish, from chopping the cabbage to dishing it up. Give it a try! This dish is also tasty cold.

½ cup salted butter
1 small green cabbage, cored
    and coarsely chopped
    (about 4 cups)

1 teaspoon smoked chile flakes
¼ teaspoon salt
½ teaspoon freshly ground
    black pepper

1   Melt butter in a deep 12-inch sauté pan over medium heat.
2   Spread cabbage evenly in pan. Stir until cabbage is thoroughly coated with butter.
3   Add chile flakes. Stir until flakes are evenly distributed throughout the cabbage.
4   Keep stirring until cabbage starts to wilt (about 5 minutes). At this point, use your judgment and preferences for how cooked you want the cabbage to be. The longer you cook it, the softer the cabbage gets. I like to leave a soft crunch in the cabbage, but you may prefer it crunchier (so cook it less) or softer (cook it more).
5   When cabbage is cooked the way you like, remove from heat, add salt and pepper, and serve immediately.

Sorrel Soup

Total time: 1 hour plus 3 hours chill time   Yields about 4 cups

Sorrel (*Rumex acetosa*) is lovely plant with green, arrowhead-shaped leaves. Used in European cooking for centuries, sorrel gets its sourness from oxalic acid. This recipe, shared by my friend Jolie Mason in the 1990s, makes a delicate soup suitable as a light snack or for whetting the appetite. You can substitute 1 pound fresh spinach for the sorrel and ¼ cup fresh lemon juice for the sourness; add the lemon juice when you add the seasonings. Serve cold, topped with small dollops of sour cream.

2 small russet potatoes, thinly sliced
3 cups water
¾ teaspoon salt
1 pound fresh sorrel, finely chopped

2 large eggs, beaten
¾ teaspoon dried dill weed
¼ teaspoon freshly ground black pepper
2 green onions, minced
sour cream for garnish

1   Combine potatoes with water and salt. Cook until potatoes are just tender.
2   Drain potatoes, reserving cooking water.
3   Cook chopped sorrel in a dry skillet until it is wilted (about 3 to 5 minutes).
4   Place eggs in a large bowl. Whisking the eggs, slowly drizzle in the hot potato cooking water. Beat well.
5   Add potatoes, sorrel, dill weed, pepper, and green onions to eggs and water.
6   Chill until very cold (about 3 hours).

Steamed Artichokes with Garlic-Lemon Mayonnaise Dip

Total time: 1¼ hour   Yields 4 servings

As a native Californian, I grew up eating steamed artichokes. An artichoke is basically a giant unripe flower bud whose petals have a meaty edible base. My favorite way to prepare and at them is my own method, using apple cider vinegar and garlic to subtly flavor the artichokes as they steam. (If garlic's not your thing, you can leave it out.) It's a pleasure to eat the artichoke petals while they are almost too hot to handle. You can make the mayonnaise dip a day ahead; the flavors will deepen. Serve the freshly steamed artichokes with dollops of garlic mayonnaise in small, individual dishes, one artichoke and one small dish of mayonnaise for each person. Have a large bowl or paper bag on hand for the inedible portions of the discarded petals. To eat, pull off each petal, dip the base in mayonnaise and use your teeth to scrape off the meat. Discard the rest of the petal. When you get to the center, scrape out the fluffy, spiky stuff in the middle and eat the heart with or without dip. The stem is also edible.

Artichokes

4 large artichokes
½ cup apple cider vinegar

4 cloves garlic, coarsely chopped

Garlic-Lemon Mayonnaise Dip

1½ cups vegan mayonnaise
4 cloves garlic, minced

¼ cup lemon juice

1 Trim ½ inch from ends of artichoke stems. Place artichokes vertically, stems pointing downward, in a steamer basket in a pan of water. Make sure water does not touch the artichokes.
2 Add vinegar and the first four garlic cloves to the water.
3 Cover and bring water to a boil. Steam artichokes for 45 minutes or until done. If you need to add more water while steaming, use boiling water so you don't slow down the steaming. To test for doneness, carefully pull out an outer petal. If it pulls out easily and the meat at the base of the petal is tender, the artichokes are done.
4 While artichokes are steaming, prepare mayonnaise dip. Combine mayonnaise with the remaining four garlic cloves and with the lemon juice. Stir well. Chill in refrigerator until artichokes are done.

Sweet Potato Tempeh Curry

Total time: 1 hour   Yields 4 servings

My local organic farm box arrives with a lot of sweet potatoes in late winter. You can only bake them so many times, topped with melted butter, cinnamon, and nutmeg, before you long for something else. In desperation, I invented this recipe in early January 2015. If you leave out the butter, this delicious recipe is vegan. Tempeh is a firm cake of whole soybeans that have been cultured and fermented. The fermentation process makes it more digestible and produces a higher proportion of protein, vitamins, and fiber than is found in tofu. This recipe is satisfying served alone or over brown rice.

¼ cup avocado oil

2 tablespoons unsalted butter

1 medium yellow onion, cut into 8 wedges, then each wedge cut in half

2 cups sweet potatoes, cubed (no need to peel)

1 cup Nantes carrots, sliced thickly

1 teaspoon ground cinnamon

¼ teaspoon hulled green cardamom, pounded

¼ cup sweet curry powder (page 314)

1 8-ounce package tempeh, cut into small cubes

1 can (28 ounces) diced tomatoes

1 cup water

1 In a large saucepan, heat oil until simmering, then add butter and stir until it melts.

2 Add onion to oil and butter and cook, stirring, until onions are just going translucent (about 3 minutes).

3 Stir in sweet potatoes. Cook a few minutes without stirring, until sweet potatoes start to lightly brown. Turn sweet potatoes. Continue cooking until pieces are brown on all sides.

4 Stir in carrots, cinnamon, cardamom, and sweet curry powder.

5 Add tempeh and stir so pieces are coated with oil and spices.

6 Stir in diced tomatoes and water.

7 Cook until carrots are *al dente* and sauce is thickened, about 10 minutes.

Tempeh Chili

Total time: 1 hour   Yields 6 servings

E veryone I've served this recipe to, including inveterate, dyed-in-the-wool meal lovers, loves this chili. Many express surprise when I tell them it's vegetarian (vegan if you skip the grated cheese garnish). It's a deeply satisfying, thick, savory stew that tastes great served over brown rice. The original recipe came from the back of a White Wave tempeh package in the early 1990s, though I've refined and modified it over the years. The cumin is a key flavor; don't leave it out. Cumin seed is best, but ground cumin is also fine. The recipe keeps well and is even tastier the next day. Great for potlucks, and it doubles, triples, and quadruples well. Garnish with diced red onion and grated cheddar or Monterey Jack cheese.

8 ounces tempeh
¼ cup water
1 tablespoon sesame oil
2 tablespoons chili powder
1 tablespoon garlic powder
2 teaspoons Italian seasonings
1 tablespoon whole or ground cumin
1 teaspoon mustard powder or seed
¼ teaspoon ground black pepper

6 tablespoons olive oil
1 small yellow onion, coarsely chopped
1 can (28 ounces) whole stewed tomatoes
1 can (15 ounces) kidney beans, drained and rinsed
1 can (15 ounces) pinto beans, drained and rinsed
1 can (15 ounces) black beans, drained and rinsed

1 Break tempeh into small chunks and place in a small bowl.
2 Combine water, sesame oil, chili powder, garlic powder, Italian seasoning, cumin, mustard powder, and pepper. Sprinkle over tempeh. Do your best to coat all pieces. The tempeh will rapidly absorb all liquid. Set aside.
3 Heat olive oil in a deep stock pot. When oil is hot, add onion and sauté briefly (3 to 5 minutes).
4 Add tempeh mix and sauté 5 minutes.
5 Add tomatoes and beans to tempeh and onions. Bring to a boil. Lower heat and simmer over medium low heat (or bake in oven at 350°) for 30 to 45 minutes.

Tofu and Kimchi Soup

Total time: 45 minutes   Yields about 5 cups

In our household, kimchi is a staple, and I often make my own (page 248). When I was putting the finishing touches on this cookbook, my daughter found this recipe, which is Chris Morocco's, published in the January 2017 *Bon Appetit*. We both agreed it's a new favorite. (Until, that is, I developed a sudden allergy to commercial gochujang. But my daughter improvised by making a homemade gochujang with gochugaru, a tasty Korean hot red pepper; that version didn't cause a reaction.) The original recipe calls for firm tofu, but we prefer soft. My daughter used tamari instead of the called-for soy sauce because we prefer the taste and it's gluten free. She also added toasted sesame oil, which we both love. For a vegan version, substitute vegetable broth for the chicken broth. If you can't find daikon (a mild white radish that looks a bit like a thick carrot), try regular radishes. The kimchee and gochujang are vital to this soup's flavors.

1 tablespoon avocado oil
1 tablespoon toasted sesame oil
6 scallions, chopped; separate white and pale green parts from dark green parts
4 garlic cloves, sliced
1 one-inch piece ginger, diced (no need to peel)
4 cups chicken broth

3 tablespoons gochujang (Korean hot pepper paste)
3 tablespoons tamari
1 small daikon, thinly sliced and cut into triangles (like pizza slices)
½ cup kimchee
1 (16-ounce) block soft silken tofu, cut into 1-inch cubes

1   Heat avocado and sesame oils in a large saucepan over high heat.
2   Add white and pale-green parts of scallions, garlic, and ginger. Cook, stirring often, until softened and fragrant, about 3 minutes.
3   Add broth and bring to a boil.
4   Reduce heat to medium; keep soup simmering.
5   Stir in gochujang and tamari.
6   Add daikon. Continue to simmer until daikon is tender, 15 to 20 minutes.
7   Add kimchee and tofu. Simmer until tofu is heated through, about 5 minutes.
8   To serve, sprinkle reserved green parts of scallions over top of each bowl of soup.

Turmeric Roasted Cauliflower

Total time: 40 minutes   Yields 4 servings

My first attempts at coming up with my own version of turmeric-roasted cau-liflower were inedibly bitter. I was using only turmeric and oil; it was just too much unrelenting turmeric. After searching Aunt Google for answers, I realized my mistake. To dial back the full-on turmeric flavor and texture, you need other spices and less turmeric than I was using. This recipe would also be delicious with 2 to 3 tablespoons of my Madras-style curry powder (page 303) instead of the other spices, but then that would be *curried* roasted cauliflower, not *tumeric* roasted cauliflower. And I wanted a more turmeric-forward flavor. This vegan, gluten-free recipe, adapted from TwoPeasAndTheirPod.com, fits the bill. Taste great hot or cold. If using two cau-liflowers, triple the oil and spices.

1 large head (about 2 pounds) cauliflower, cored and cut into 1-inch florets
3 tablespoons olive oil
1 teaspoon ground turmeric

1 teaspoon cumin seed
¼ teaspoon smoked paprika
¼ teaspoon garlic powder
1 teaspoon Himalayan salt

1   Preheat oven to 375°. Prepare a baking sheet by lining it with parchment paper or a silicone baking mat.
2   Place cauliflower florets in a large mixing bowl.
3   In a separate small bowl, combine olive oil, turmeric, cumin, paprika, garlic powder, and salt. Mix well.
4   Toss olive oil/spice mixture with cauliflower until florets are evenly coated. Take your time. It will seem like there isn't enough oil and spice mix to go around, but there is. You don't want the florets soaking; you just want them lightly yellow. Just keep tossing until they reach that stage.
5   Evenly spread florets over prepared baking sheet.
6   Roast 25 to 30 minutes or until cauliflower is tender and starting to lightly brown. Check after 15 minutes. Watch carefully and adjust oven temperature if cauliflower browns too quickly.

Tuscan-Style Soup

Total time: 45 minutes   Yields 2½ quarts of delicious soup

This delicious recipe is based on a recipe I found on Food.com. Of course, I've made many changes to suit my tastes. You can use red, yellow, or russet potatoes. The kale is my favorite part of this soup. Serve with sliced sourdough bread.

3 tablespoons olive oil
1 pound ground turkey or pork sausage
1 tablespoon Italian seasoning (page 300)
1 teaspoon fennel seed
¼ teaspoon hot pepper flakes
⅛ teaspoon cayenne powder
2 quarts chicken broth or water
10 small potatoes, cut in ¼ inch slices (do not peel)

1 large yellow onion, coarsely chopped
4 garlic cloves, minced
4 cups red kale, coarsely chopped (this will seem like a mountain of kale, but it will cook down)
1 cup heavy cream or half-and-half

1 Put oil in a large stock pot and heat until shimmering.
2 Add turkey, Italian seasonings, fennel, hot pepper flakes, and cayenne. Cook, stirring as needed, until turkey is browned.
3 Add chicken broth, potatoes, onion, and garlic. Bring to a boil, then lower heat and simmer until potatoes are tender (about 20 minutes).
4 When potatoes are tender, add cream and kale and heat another 5 minutes.

Winter Squash Soup

Total time: 1 hour 30 minutes   Yields 2 servings

T his soup, which you can make with a variety of winter squashes, is a hearty bowl of delectation from my friend AJ's kitchen. Use as either a vegetable side dish or as a main dish in winter. You can make this recipe vegan by using olive oil instead of butter. Skinning winter squash is a tough job, so consider buying it pre-cut. The first time he made it, AJ used my Madras-Style Curry Powder (page 303), but you can use any savory curry power you wish.

2 tablespoons unsalted butter	**1** cup peeled and seeded
2 tablespoons sesame oil	winter squash, chopped
1 medium onion, chopped	into 1-inch cubes
2 tablespoons curry powder	**½** cup water
1 teaspoon ground ginger	**1** cup baby corn kernels
1 tablespoon ground coriander	**¼** cup tomato sauce or diced
1 dash ground cloves	tomatoes
¼ teaspoon salt	

1 Combine butter, oil, onion, curry powder, ginger, coriander, and cloves in a medium saucepan. Heat 5 minutes.
2 Add salt, squash, water, corn, and tomato sauce.
3 Cook, covered, for 1 hour or until squash is quite tender.

Beverages

Many recipes in this chapter are originals: fortuitous combinations of ingredients discovered when experimenting (such as the surprisingly delicious combination of limeade and blueberries in Surprise Blueberry Smoothie on page 79). Some recipes are versions of a well-known and beloved classic, like my friend AJ's Rich, Dark Hot Chocolate on page 56.

Most of these recipes are easy to make and all are family friendly. You can package the ingredients for some of these recipes as gifts or as make-ahead mixes for yourself, such as the Bittersweet Hot Cocoa Mix on page 67.

Enjoying Smoothies

This chapter contains a number of original smoothie recipes, most of which rely on yogurt for body. Smoothies are a wonderful way to combine healthful ingredients in a tasty manner; because of my smoothies, my family consumes a lot more fruit than they would otherwise. Use plain yogurt with active cultures and no added sugar or flavors; when used in smoothies, the plainness of the yogurt balances the sweeter ingredients.

If you want to make smoothies a regular part of your life, invest in a sturdy blender (I recommended getting a Vitamix; I bought a refurbished unit in 1998 and it was still going strong in 2020) and keep plenty of fruit (fresh or frozen) and plain yogurt on hand. Try some of my recipes and experiment on your own. Do you have some fruit on hand that nobody is eating? Perhaps some fruit juice? Toss it all into the blender with whatever else seems tasty.

When making smoothies, watch your fluid balances. If you don't use enough of fluid, the smoothie is too thick (and hard on the blender). Too much of fluid, and the smoothie is too thin.

The proportions I use are

- 1 cup fluid (for example, juice, milk, almond milk, rice milk, coconut water, or water)
- 1 cup plain, unsweetened yogurt
- 1 to 2 cups fruit (fresh, frozen, or a combination; if using frozen, it helps to leave the fruit out about 15 minutes before blending)
- 1 to 3 teaspoons maple syrup or honey as a sweetener, though often the fruit adds enough sweetness

In my experiments, I've found that some combinations that seem like they would work well aren't so tasty, while others that seem unlikely to succeed are delicious. Be willing to continue experimenting even when something doesn't work out. When you find a combination that you like, write it down so you can duplicate it.

Smoothies are very much an in-the-moment pleasure; they don't keep well in the refrigerator. However, if you have some left over, freeze it in small freezer containers. Look for 1-cup plastic freezer containers with screw-top lids in the canning supplies department of your grocery or hardware store; if you find them, purchase a set or two, as they are also handy for freezing leftover egg yolks and whites (see page 323), as well as other small quantities of fluids or food. Later, you can release the frozen contents by running hot water over the container for a few seconds, then use in a new smoothie.

About Cocoa Powder and Chocolate

Have you ever wondered what the difference is between natural and Dutch process cocoa powders? When to use one or the other? Or between cocoa and chocolate? Knowing the difference can help you use various chocolate products with confidence.

In a nutshell, natural cocoa powder is ground cacao beans with nothing further done to them (simplifying greatly). It's slightly acidic. Dutch process cocoa powder has been treated to neutralize cocoa's natural acidity and make it less bitter. It's a richer, deeper brown than natural cocoa.

Because of baking chemistry, use **natural cocoa powder** in recipes that call for baking soda. Use **Dutch process cocoa powder** in recipes that call for baking powder. If a recipe calls for an acidic ingredient, such as sour cream or buttermilk, or if it calls for both baking powder and baking soda you can use either type of cocoa powder. I got into a lot more detail in *Delectable Desserts*, the first book in the cookbook series.

Apple Cider Vinegar Drink

Total time: 5 minutes   Yields 1 serving

You can buy commercial apple cider vinegar drinks, all of which have question-able ingredients and too much sweetening, or you can make your own and know exactly what goes into it. Why drink an apple cider vinegar drink? You'll have to refer to the experts for possible health benefits; I just like how the vinegar cuts the sweetness of juices. This is my own recipe. I use organic apple cider vinegar be-cause apples are consistently on the Environmental Working Group's Dirty Dozen list (a guide to pesticides in produce. (The dirty dozen are the top twelve most pesticide laden fruits and vegetables.) I sometimes make this drink in a small bottle and keep it at my desk until I've finished it. For juices, experiment with your favorites, such as grape juice or pineapple-orange-banana juice. You could even use a vegetable juice, such as carrot juice. You could add honey, sugar, or some other sweetener, but for me, the juice is sweet enough.

¾ cup juice
3 tablespoons filtered water

2 tablespoons organic apple cider vinegar

1   Combine juice, water, and apple cider vinegar. Mix well.

Apricot Nectar Smoothie

Total time: 5 minutes   Yields 4 cups

This smoothie uses apricot nectar, which I keep on hand as a home remedy for mild intestinal upsets. The yogurt is for restoring intestinal flora, bananas are for potassium, and milk for magnesium and calcium. The ice helps with hydration. This is not medical advice; consult a medical professional if you have any health concerns.

1 cup ice, preferably made from pure, filtered water
½ cup whole milk

1 cup plain, unsweetened yogurt with live, active cultures
12 ounces apricot nectar
2 bananas

1   Place ice in a blender, then add milk, yogurt, apricot nectar, and bananas.
2   Blend until well mixed (about 1 minute).
3   Serve immediately.

Bittersweet Hot Cocoa Mix

Total time: 10 minutes   Yields 1 quart of dry mix

I created this hot cocoa mix so I could have hot chocolate just the way I like it—dark, bittersweet, with just a hint of spices, and free of undesirable ingredients. The two cocoas balance each other; pure Valrhona, a Dutch process cocoa, would be too dark on its own, and pure natural cocoa wouldn't be rich enough. You can use any Dutch process cocoa powder, but Valrhona's cocoa is fair trade—another reason to love the brand. (See appendix A for a discussion of the differences between natural and Dutch process cocoas.) The cornstarch gives a richer, creamier texture (which makes up for the dry milk), but some people are allergic to cornstarch. You can leave it out if you need to. (Also, if you're allergic to cornstarch, use only organic powdered sugar—regular powdered sugars are mixed with cornstarch.) For a dairy-free version, use rice milk powder instead of the dry milk and omit the powdered cream. If you like your cocoa sweeter, increase the amount of sugar. Attractively packaged, this cocoa mix makes a fun gift.

3 cups dry milk
1 cup heavy cream powder
2 tablespoons cornstarch
1 cup Valrhona cocoa or
  another Dutch process
  cocoa

½ cup natural cocoa
2 cups powdered sugar
¼ teaspoon cayenne
⅛ teaspoon ground ginger
⅛ teaspoon ground nutmeg
⅛ teaspoon salt

1 Combine powdered milk, powdered cream, cornstarch, Valrhona cocoa, natural cocoa, powdered sugar, cayenne, ginger, nutmeg, and salt. Mix well and store in an airtight container.

2 To make a cup of hot cocoa, put ¼ to ½ cup mix into a 12-ounce mug. Fill with boiling water. Stir well to break up lumps.

Blueberry Power Smoothie

Total time: 5 minutes   Yields 3 cups

Blueberries are delicious little rounds packed with antioxidants and healthful nutrients. Kefir is a cultured milk drink and is something like a drinkable yogurt. (Though kefir has about three times as many probiotics as yogurt.) It makes a great base for smoothies.

1 cup whole milk
1 cup plain unsweetened
    yogurt

1 cup blueberries, fresh or
    frozen
1 tablespoon kefir
1½ tablespoons maple syrup

1   Combine milk, yogurt, blueberries, kefir, and maple syrup.
2   Blend on low to medium speed until well blended (a few minutes).

Fruit-Flavored Kefir

Total time: 5 minutes   Yields 5 cups

This recipe doesn't tell how to make kefir from scratch (though that's pretty easy). Instead, it tells you how to jazz up your favorite plain kefir so it's as delicious as the commercial flavored kinds. Kefir is convenient—you can just pour some into a cup or glass. And plain kefir is naturally low in sugars. Some people find plain kefir too tart, though, and buy flavored, sweetened kefirs. If you like those flavored kefirs, but don't like the added sugars and other unwanted and unnecessary ingredients, give this recipe (which is my own) a try. Experiment with your favorite fruits; I'm particularly fond of raspberries and peaches. Raspberries, strawberries, blackberries, and peaches are all low in natural fruit sugars, so they're diabetic friendly as well. When I make this recipe, I serve myself some immediately, then pour the rest back into the kefir container, shake well, and store in refrigerator for up to a few days.

4 cups (32 ounces) plain kefir   1 cup fruit, fresh or frozen

1   Pour kefir into a sturdy blender.
2   Add fruit.
3   Blend until fruit is well incorporated.

Ginger Ale Elegance

Total time: 10 minutes   Yields 1 serving

T his is my variation on the classic root beer float.

2 scoops coffee ice cream   2 cups ginger ale

1   Place scoops of ice cream in a tall glass, then slowly pour ginger ale into glass. It will foam, so you may not be able to add all the ginger ale at first. Add more ginger ale as you consume the float.

Grapefruit Juice Smoothie

Total time: 5 minutes   Yields 6 cups

As with many recipes, I created this recipe by experimenting with a number of odds and ends. The combination of ingredients may sound odd, but the flavor is delicious—tart and sweet at the same time, and quite refreshing. The recipe makes a lot—you may need to blend it in two batches. A note about strawberries: Strawberries are consistently at the top of the Environmental Working Group's dirty dozen—a list of twelve conventionally grown (that is, non-organic) fruits and vegetables with the highest levels of pesticide residue. To find out more, visit ewg.org.

3 cups grapefruit juice
10 large organic strawberries, hulled
2 cups vanilla yogurt

2 tablespoons frozen pineapple juice (not reconstituted)
1½ tablespoons maple syrup

1   Combine grapefruit juice, strawberries, yogurt, pineapple juice, and maple syrup in a sturdy blender.
2   Blend well. Serve immediately.

Green Tea Latte

Total time: 10 minutes   Yields 2 cups

You're surely familiar with *caffè latte* (Italian), or *café au lait* (French), both of which mean coffee (*caffè*, *café*) with milk (*latte*, *au lait*). This recipe combines matcha (a green tea powder) with milk; so, a green tea latte. This is my own recipe, created after a bit of experimentation. For the best taste, use a good-quality matcha powder from Japan. Buy pure matcha powder; it should be a lovely rich green, not brown or brown-ish green. You can also use sweetened matcha powder; if you do, don't add sugar. This recipe makes enough for two 8-ounce mugs or one 16-ounce glass. You can make it hot or cold. It doubles nicely.

2 cups whole milk   2 tablespoons granulated sugar
1 tablespoon matcha powder

1   If you want a hot green tea latte, heat milk until hot, but not scalding.
2   Combine matcha and sugar in a small dish and stir well.
3   Pour milk into a blender, then add matcha/sugar mix.
4   Blend until well mixed, then serve.

Masala Chai

Total time: 50 minutes   Yields 2 quarts

My friend Karen's first taste of masala chai (hot spiced tea and milk) was from this recipe, which I've perfected over many years. She says I've spoiled her; she's never found anything as good anywhere else. In the US, the word chai is used to refer to what is more properly called masala chai. Masala means spices and chai means tea. The drink originated in East India (or, some say, what is now Thailand) many thousands of years ago as an Ayurvedic beverage (sans tea). It's now popular worldwide. The word for tea in many languages is some variation of te (tea, thé, té, tee, thee, der Tee) or some variation of cha (chai, cha, shai, tsai, ceai, chah). All those words for tea came from two pronunciations of the Chinese character for tea (茶). To make my masala chai, you can find the needed spices, organic and fair trade, at MountainRoseHerbs.com. For a high-quality whole-leaf tea, try Vahdam's Darjeeling or Assam (available on Amazon). For a richer chai, substitute 2 cups half-and-half or heavy cream for 2 cups of the milk. For a caffeine-free version, leave out the black tea. For step 1, my oldest brother, Norman, steeps the spices overnight, then adds warm milk in the morning. Serve hot, though it's also delicious cold.

1 quart water
1 teaspoon hulled green
    cardamom (*Elettaria
    cardamomum*), crushed
1 three-inch stick cinnamon,
    broken into pieces
8 whole cloves
1/4 teaspoon ground ginger or
    1/4 teaspoon grated fresh
    ginger

1 teaspoon whole mace blades,
    crushed
4 smoked black peppercorns
8 pink or white peppercorns
1 star anise, broken
2 to 3 teaspoons loose-leaf
    black tea (try Assam, Ceylon,
    Darjeeling, or Keemun)
1/8 cup granulated sugar
1 quart whole milk

1 Put water in a two-quart non-reactive saucepan. Add cardamom, cinnamon, cloves, ginger, mace, black and white peppercorns, and anise. Bring to a boil. Cover and simmer for 15 to 30 minutes.
2 Put milk in a separate four-quart non-reactive saucepan. Add sugar and warm gently (to avoid scalding the milk).
3 Remove milk from heat when it's hot but not scalded.
4 After spices simmer 15 minutes, add black tea to the water and spices, cover again, and remove from heat. Steep until quite dark (15 to 30 minutes).
5 Strain the water/tea/spice mixture into milk. Mix well, then serve. Discard spices and spent tea leaves into your compost.

Mocha Mix

Total time: 10 minutes   Yields 5 cups of dry mix

Homemade coffee, hot cocoa, and mocha mixes have been around for decades. But the homemade recipes and most commercial brands use ingredients that we don't want to consume, such as corn syrup, partially hydrogenated fat, and propylene glycol monostearate. (Propylene glycol, an ingredient in antifreeze, is "generally recognized as safe" by the United States Food and Drug Administration, but it has a small upper limit of safe consumption that most Americans exceed by almost half again as much as they should consume.) Surely, I thought, we can make our own mix from scratch with better ingredients. My version of many common recipes uses Hoosier Hill Farm's heavy cream powder instead of non-dairy creamer. I also used Mount Hagen's organic, fair-trade dried coffee; organic sugar; and organic natural cocoa. I experimented with using Valrhona's Dutch process cocoa, but its strong chocolate flavor overwhelms the mix. Experiment to see what you like. Leave out the coffee for a very nice hot cocoa mix. This recipe makes lovely gifts.

1 cup granulated sugar
1 cup dry milk
2 cups heavy cream powder
¾ cup natural cocoa
¼ cup instant coffee granules
1 tablespoon powdered vanilla

1   Combine sugar, milk, cream, cocoa, coffee, and vanilla, stirring well after each addition. Gently press the back of your mixing spoon against any lumps to smash them. Stir until well blended and no lumps remain. If it's too lumpy, whir the ingredients in a blender or with an immersion blender.
2   Store in an airtight container.
3   To serve, mix ¼ cup powder with 8 to 12 ounces hot water or hot milk. Stir until dissolved. For an extra bit of richness, add a dollop of whipped cream or foamed milk.

Refreshing Fruit Shake

Total time: 15 minutes   Yields 1 serving

Maple syrup is a key ingredient in this wonderful flavor combination. I recommend you don't change it. Aside from that, you can substitute different fruits to make your own unique blends. Stone fruits (nectarines, peaches, plums, with the pits removed, of course) are excellent in this shake, an original from my friend AJ.

6 ice cubes
1/2 cup whole milk
2 tablespoons vanilla ice cream
2 tablespoons seedless
   strawberry jam
1/4 cup sliced bananas

1/4 cup kiwifruit
1 1/2 cups sliced fruit, your
   choice
1 pinch vitamin C powder
1/2 teaspoon lemon juice
1 teaspoon maple syrup

1 Place ice, milk, ice cream, jam, bananas, kiwifruit, sliced fruit, vitamin C powder, lemon juice, and maple syrup in a blender.
2 Blend, serve, and enjoy.

Rich, Dark Hot Chocolate

Total time: 15 minutes   Yields a scant 3 cups

A little of this rich, dark hot chocolate goes a long way. If you want to be precise, hot chocolate is made with chocolate. It can include cocoa powder, but *must* have chocolate. Hot cocoa is made only with cocoa powder, no chocolate. This hot chocolate recipe, invented by my friend AJ, calls for Ghiradelli's Double Chocolate Premium Hot Cocoa mix, though Ghirardelli does not buy fair-trade chocolate, so you can substitute my Bittersweet Hot Cocoa Mix (page 67) for the Ghiradelli if you prefer. Most chocolate chips are gluten free, but if you need to avoid gluten, check the ingredients of whichever brand you're using. This beverage is delicious topped with whipped cream.

Hot Chocolate

1 cup semisweet chocolate chips
1 cup whole milk
1 cup half and half

2 heaping tablespoons cocoa
3 heaping tablespoons Ghiradelli Double chocolate Premium Hot Cocoa mix

Topping

½ cup heavy cream
1 teaspoon powdered sugar

¼ teaspoon vanilla extract

1 Combine chocolate chips, milk, half and half, cocoa, and hot chocolate mix in a medium saucepan.
2 Heat until just starting to scald (180°), stirring occasionally. (At the scalding point, tiny bubbles start to form around the edges.) **Do not boil**!
3 When milk is barely at the scalding point, beat with a hand mixer or immersion blender until frothy (this is to emulsify the chocolate chips). Be careful not to spatter the milk.
4 Whip cream with powdered sugar and vanilla so it forms soft peaks.
5 Pour hot chocolate into cups and top with whipped cream.

Simple Hot Cocoa

Total time: 5 minutes   Yields 2¼ cups

T his is my stripped-down, quick hot cocoa recipe. You don't have to add the cayenne or butter, but they add to this recipe's intensity and richness.

1 tablespoon Valhrona cocoa   2 tablespoons water
2 tablespoons sugar   1 teaspoon butter
1 pinch cayenne   2 cups whole milk

1   Combine cocoa and sugar in a dry saucepan.
2   Add cayenne.
3   Add water and stir until you have a paste.
4   Start heating. Add butter and stir until melted.
5   Gradually stir in milk.

Summertime Smoothie

Total time: 5 minutes   Yields 2 servings

I invented this delicious smoothie on a hot summer day when I had a number of leftover this-and-thats hanging about. The unsweetened cranberry juice adds the power of antioxidants to the drink, and tones down the sweetness a bit, while the sweeter ingredients help keep the drink from being too tart. The result is light and refreshing.

1 cup limeade
2 scoops peppermint ice
    cream
1½ cups apple juice
1 banana

½ cup frozen pineapple
    chunks
½ cup pure (unsweetened)
    cranberry juice

1   Combine limeade, ice cream, apple juice, banana, pineapple, and cranberry juice in a large, sturdy blender.
2   Blend until well blended (a few minutes).
3   Serve immediately.

Surprise Blueberry Smoothie

Total time: 5 minutes   Yields 4 servings

I made this smoothie when in an experimental mood. I didn't expect it to be quite as delicious as it turned out; hence the "surprise." I wasn't sure the limeade would be a good addition, what with the milk products, but it married well with the blueberries.

1 cup limeade
1 cup whole milk
1 cup yogurt

1 cup frozen blueberries
1 tablespoon maple syrup

1 Combine limeade, milk, blueberries, and maple syrup in a large, sturdy blender.
2 Blend well.
3 Serve immediately.

Tropical Ambrosia

Total time: 9 hours   Yields about 4 quarts

I adapted this recipe from a tiny brochure published by Try-Foods International in the 1990s. This recipe makes a whopping large amount, and so is suitable for a party. Try mixing it with iced tea, using it to make popsicles, and just drinking it straight. Freshly juiced apples, oranges, and lemons are best.

¼ cup chopped fresh ginger   4½ cups orange juice
3 cups water   4½ cups apple juice
2 cups granulated sugar   2½ cups lemon juice
10 whole cloves

1   Combine ginger, water, sugar, and cloves in a saucepan and bring to a boil.
2   Simmer five minutes.
3   Cool and steep 6 to 8 hours.
4   When ginger mixture has finished steeping, combine ginger mixture with orange juice, apple juice, and lemon juice.
5   Remove cloves and serve hot or cold as described below.

Serving Suggestions

1   Serve hot by warming the desired amount until just steaming. Pour into mugs. Float apple slices studded with cloves in each mug.
2   Serve cold with or without ice as a beverage.
3   Serve cold as an Arnold-Palmer-style drink by combining with equal quantities of iced tea.
4   Serve as a cold punch: pour over a block of ice in a punch bowl (don't worry about dilution; this mixture can take it). Float orange slices studded with whole cloves on top.
5   Freeze in ice cube trays or popsicle molds. Use the ice cubes in iced tea or in punch.

Tropical Smoothie

Total time: 5 minutes   Yields 3 servings

T his is another of my spontaneous smoothie combinations that came out particularly well.

1 cup tangerine juice   **1** cup pineapple chunks, frozen
¼ cup apricot nectar   ¼ cup cream of coconut
1½ cups mango-passion juice   ¾ cup mango chunks, frozen

1   Combine tangerine juice, apricot nectar, mango-passion juice, pineapple, cream of coconut, and mango in a large, sturdy blender.
2   Blend on low to medium speed for a few minutes until well blended.
3   Serve immediately.

Turkish Coffee

Total time: 10 minutes   Yields 1 serving

Turkish coffee is traditionally made in an ibrik (also called a cezve or a briki). An ibrik is a tiny pot, often copper, with a long handle and sometimes a nipped-in waist. If you don't have an ibrik, a small saucepan is also suitable. If you grind the coffee yourself, consider grinding the cardamom with the coffee beans. This coffee is wonderful with tea-time desserts.

½ cup water
1 tablespoon coffee, very finely ground
1 teaspoon granulated sugar

2 small whole green cardamom pods, very finely ground

1   Combine water, coffee, sugar and cardamom in an ibrik or small, high-sided saucepan.
2   Slowly bring to a boil.
3   When froth starts to form, remove pot from heat briefly and stir froth into coffee. (Some people spoon the froth into the cup they will be serving the Turkish coffee in.)
4   Return to heat and heat until froth rises again.
5   Again, remove briefly from heat and stir in froth.
6   Heat a third time until it froths again. Some people say let the froth rise three times; others say do this four or five times or until you have a fair amount of froth. It depends on your tastes. Experiment!
7   Serve, dregs and all, in a demitasse cup.

Vanilla Cream Soda

Total time: 5 minutes   Yields 1 cup

According to Wikipedia, E. M. Sheldon's cream soda recipe, published in 1852 in volume 10 of the *Michigan Farmer*, called for making a syrup of sugar, egg, milk, cream of tartar, Epsom salts, and tartaric acid. No vanilla. You'd then add some of that syrup to water and baking soda, which E. M. Sheldon urged you to "drink during the effervescence." The first commercial cream soda, Dr. Brown's in 1868, did include vanilla, which science tells us contributes to our perceiving a creamy flavor. Nowadays, when you purchase commercially made cream soda, it's carbonated, flavored, sweetened water with no dairy. Sometimes you'll find it at a soda counter or restaurant made with milk, half-and-half, or cream. I love the taste of commercial cream sodas, but I never buy them because they're usually made with high fructose corn syrup. So I was delighted to find many cream soda recipes online. For extra flavor, use your own homemade vanilla extract (page 315). To multiply this recipe, use the same proportions. You can also make other cream sodas using this recipe; just swap in another flavor of syrup for the maple syrup. For example, if you want an orange cream soda, use orange syrup. If you want cream in your cream soda, add 2 tablespoons heavy cream.

1 tablespoon vanilla extract   **8** ounces sparkling water
2 tablespoons maple syrup

1   Combine the vanilla, maple syrup, and sparkling water.
2   Stir well and serve.

Breads

Between 1947 and 1965, nutritionist Adelle Davis, an early advocate of wholesome food, published a series of books criticizing the food industry and encouraging people to gain a greater awareness of and responsibility for our food needs. Her recommendations included making meals from whole, unadulterated foods, such as homemade whole grain breads, as well as minimizing the consumption of sugar, soft drinks, and heavily processed foods.

Some might say Adelle was ahead of her time, but she was with her times in terms of what science knew then. It just took 50 years for what she knew about the relationship between nutrition and health to percolate into general awareness. As with many pioneers, she wasn't always right, and sometimes she was terribly wrong. But the basics of her nutritional advice are still valid.

My mother fed my brothers and me according to Adelle's guidelines. She often baked fresh homemade bread, and didn't allow us much of what most children were taking for granted, such as highly sugared cereals, white bread, and soft drinks (though our mother allowed us non-caffeinated sodas on rare occasions).

At the time, my mother was more an anomaly than the norm, and so I sometimes felt self-conscious about my food, especially at school lunch times when I pulled out my brown paper lunch bag filled with an apple and a peanut butter sandwich made with homemade whole-wheat bread. Nevertheless, I'm glad she fed us the way she did; it instilled a life-long appreciation of and taste for good, healthy foods.

Since you are reading this chapter, I assume that you, too, enjoy breads (and other foods!) prepared from scratch. You probably have your own favorite bread recipes. In this chapter, you'll find recipes that are out of the ordinary in some way. All are delicious. Many are also unusual—either regional specialities or my family's recipes.

About Yeast-Raised and Quick Breads

A yeast-raised bread gets its lift from yeast. Usually you'll need to let the bread rise, knead it, and let it rise again before you can bake it.

A quick bread is one that rises because of non-yeast leavenings such as baking powder or baking soda (or both). For quick breads, you only need to combine ingredients as directed, then pop the bread into the oven. This is why they are called quick breads. Not only is no waiting necessary, sometimes waiting can cause the power of the leavening to dissipate.

Another difference between yeast-raised and quick breads is the flour you use. Setting aside the variations in ingredients for gluten-free breads, yeast-raised breads do best when you use bread flour (called strong flour in some countries). Quick breads do better with all-purpose flour.

Quick breads are easy and require little understanding of leavening for them to work. Yeasts are a bit more complicated.

Types of Yeast

Long ago, if you wanted to make bread, you couldn't pop over to your corner grocery store and buy a packet of yeast. Instead, you'd cultivate your own wild yeast and make bread from a home-grown sponge. (A sponge is a bubbly mix of flour, water, and yeast.) The yeast comes from bacteria occurring naturally in the air and flour.

These wild yeast cultures are still used today, and in recent years there's been a resurgence of interest in cultivating wild yeast to bake bread. Such yeast cultures are called starters. One type of wild yeast starter is sourdough, which is used when making sourdough bread, pancakes, muffins, and a variety of other foods. Sourdough gets its name from its distinct tanginess.

Wild yeast starters are individual—there isn't just one wild yeast, there are many, and many are specific to a locality. That's why not all wild yeast breads are sour, and why San Francisco's sourdough bread is legendary.

In addition to, or instead of, using a wild yeast starter, you can purchase commercial yeasts (called baker's yeast, available in wet or dry forms) to make yeast-raised bread. The wet forms of baker's yeast are called cake yeast and are perishable; the dry forms of baker's yeast, called active dry yeast, keeps well in the refrigerator for about a year, and stores almost indefinitely in the freezer (in an airtight, waterproof container). You can buy other types of commercial yeasts to make wine and beer.

Most of the yeast-raised bread recipes in this chapter use active dry yeast; one recipe tells you how to create your own sourdough starter and sourdough bread.

Proofing Commercial Yeast

Being a living organism, yeast doesn't last forever. And it would be a shame to go through all the effort of making bread or another yeast-raised item, only to find that the yeast just wasn't up to it. So if your yeast is getting old, you can use a process called proofing to test whether it's still viable. (Don't use this process on rapid rise or instant yeast—you'll use up that yeast's leavening power.) You can proof your yeast right before you make a recipe, and then immediately use the proofed yeast (assuming it proved) in your recipe. If you aren't using the proofed yeast immediately, and are only testing your yeast, throw the proofed yeast out—don't keep it for a future time.

To proof yeast,

1   Take ½ cup lukewarm water (no hotter than 90°), a pinch of sugar (brown or white, doesn't matter), and one package of active dry yeast (2¼ teaspoons).
2   Dissolve sugar in water, then add yeast. Within a few minutes, the yeast should begin to form tan lumps of foam on the water's surface. That means you can use it in your recipe. If it doesn't foam, throw it out and use other yeast.

Testing Baking Powder

Baking powder can get old, and when it does, it won't provide the same leavening power as when it's fresh. Baking powder has a long shelf life, but if your container has been in the cupboard longer than a year, it's a good idea to test it.

Unlike proofing yeast, where the proofed yeast can be used in a recipe right away, testing baking powder destroys the baking powder's leavening power. Even if it tests okay, you'll need to throw out the test batch and use fresh baking powder from the same container.

Testing baking powder is fast and easy: put ¼ teaspoon baking powder into a cup of hot water. If it bubbles or fizzes right away, it's good.

Beignets

Total time: 15 minutes plus overnight rising plus frying

Yields 4 dozen beignets

Beignets (pronounced ben YAYZ) are a New Orleans specialty (and cultural treasure, if you ask me). The world famous Cafe du Monde in New Orleans' French Market helped put beignets on the map. The word beignet has roots in the Celtic language (from "bigne," meaning "to raise") and the food may have originated in ancient Rome, where the Romans made *scriblita*, a dessert made, as beignets are, with a high-moisture dough and cooked in boiling animal fat. In recent years, there's been a disturbing trend of frying a cake-like dough in the shape of beignets and calling the result "beignets." Nay, nay, I say. Real beignets are light little hollow pockets of a thin, delicious, yeast-raised choux dough. They are *not* doughnuts. (Though Cafe du Monde muddies the waters by calling their beignet mix "French doughnuts.") If someone offers you a "beignet," but it's solid and doughnut-like inside, enjoy the treat, but enlighten them so they can discover the joy of authentic beignets. After searching for some time for a genuine beignet recipe (not the doughnut imposters), I found this recipe, which I've adapted, in Eli Jacobs' *Fry It Like a Pro* (Rascal Face Press, 2018). This recipe makes a huge number of beignets, so you can cut it in half or even a quarter if you like, because beignets don't keep well and are no longer magical when cold. However, leftover beignets are fantastic when used in my steamed bread pudding recipe (in the companion volume to this book, *Delectable Desserts*). The traditional way to serve beignets is hot out of the fryer, dusted with powdered sugar. And that's it. You can also drizzle with chocolate syrup (in addition to or instead or the powdered sugar) or serve with jam or ice cream or whatever strikes your fancy. Like sopapillas (page 106), some people eat beignets with savory foods, such as beans or chili.

½ cup granulated sugar
2¼ teaspoons (1 packet) active dry yeast
1½ cups lukewarm water (98°)
1 cup evaporated milk
2 eggs, lightly beaten
1¼ teaspoons salt

7 cups all-purpose flour
¼ cup unsalted butter, softened
cooking oil for frying
powdered sugar for dusting the beignets

1 In a large bowl, dissolve sugar and yeast in lukewarm water. Set aside for 10 minutes.
2 In a smaller bowl, combine milk, eggs, and salt. Stir well.
3 Add egg mixture to yeast mixture and stir well.
4 Add 3 cups flour to yeast/milk mixture. Stir gently.

5 Add butter and remaining 4 cups flour. Use the back of your spoon to smash the butter around. Mix until a dough forms. Don't over mix the dough, or your beignets will be tough.

6 Turn dough out onto a lightly floured surface and knead until smooth. The dough will have a lovely, silky feel.

7 Wash and dry the bowl you mixed the dough in. Very lightly oil bowl. Put dough back into bowl and cover bowl with plastic wrap.

8 Refrigerate 8 hours or overnight. The dough should rise a lot. If it doesn't rise at all, your yeast was likely old. There's nothing much you can do about that; you'll need to remake the dough.

9 After refrigerating the dough, turn dough out onto a lightly floured surface.

10 Prepare frying oil in your frying implement of choice. Use fresh oil (not old, reused frying oil) so you don't inadvertently flavor the beignets. Sunflower oil is lovely for frying beignets. Heat oil to 355°.

11 Roll out dough very thinly—$\frac{1}{8}$ inch or thinner. The beignets won't puff into pockets properly if the dough isn't thin enough.

12 Cut dough into 2-inch x 3-inch rectangles. (Rectangles are traditional.) Imprecision is okay; just aim for roughly uniform shapes and sizes. Or throw caution to the winds and try your own shapes—circles, triangles, whatever. Set dough scraps aside, cut into shapes, and fry them just as they are. Don't try to recombine and reroll dough scraps; the beignets will be tough if you do.

13 When oil reaches the right temperature, fry beignets, two to three at a time, until they puff (which should be immediately) and are a golden brown (about 3 minutes). They might not all puff; that's okay. They'll be delicious anyway. However, if *none* of them puff and your dough had risen properly, roll the dough out more thinly. Also check that the oil temperature is correct.

14 As you finish each batch, drain beignets on a large plate lined with paper towels, then serve immediately with a dusting of powdered sugar.

Bread Machine Potato Bread

Total time: 3½ hours   Yields one 2-pound loaf

My friend AJ gave me an Oster bread machine for Mother's Day 2019. I baked my way through the recipes in the booklet that came with the machine, and they all worked perfectly. I tried this potato bread recipe in August 2019, and ended up making it over and over again because it's so perfect for so many things, including sandwiches (especially grilled cheese sandwiches!), bread crumbs for the Barbecue Meat Loaf (page 171), my Steamed Bread Pudding (in *Delectable Desserts*), and just eating hot, slathered with butter. My aim for my cookbooks is to provide recipes that don't require special machines to make. And most don't, not even this one. You could make this bread as a conventional loaf.

1⅜ cups water
2 tablespoons butter, cut up
1¼ teaspoons salt
4 cups bread flour

2 tablespoons sugar
¼ cup instant potato flakes
2 tablespoons dry milk
1¾ teaspoons active dry yeast

1 Put the bread machine's paddle into the bread pan. (I sometimes forget this step, to my sorrow and dismay.)
2 Add ingredients to the bread pan in the following order: water, butter, salt, flour, sugar, potato flakes, and milk. Give the dry ingredients a bit of a stir, but not enough to mix them with the water.
3 Make a shallow well in the dry ingredients and put the yeast into the well. You must never let the yeast get wet at this stage.
4 Put bread pan into bread machine and close bread machine's lid.
5 Choose the basic setting, set loaf size to 2 pounds, and select whatever crust color you like. (I like the light crust color.)
6 Start the machine and let it rip.

Cinnamon-Dusted Fair Doughnuts

Total time: 2 hours   Yields about 4 dozen doughnuts

Fair doughnuts—delightful, bite-sized, yeast-raised, fried doughnuts dusted with cinnamon sugar—became popular in the late 1950s, about ten years after the Tom Thumb doughnut machine was invented in 1949. They've remained a mainstay on the midway ever since. They're super easy to make, though it takes a little practice to get the holes right. Although you can use a deep fat fryer, these doughnuts only need about 1 to 2 inches of oil, so you can also use a cast iron skillet or Dutch oven. I adapted this recipe from melarky's (their capitalization) recipe on Instructables.com.

- 1 package (2¼ teaspoons) active dry yeast
- 2 tablespoons lukewarm water (100° to 105°)
- 3¼ cups all-purpose flour
- 1 cup whole milk, room temperature
- 4 tablespoons butter, softened
- 1 large egg, lightly beaten
- 2 tablespoons plus ½ cup granulated sugar
- 1 tablespoon ground cinnamon
- 2 quarts (or more) oil for frying

1 Combine yeast, water, and the 2 tablespoons sugar. Set aside. Make sure the yeast starts forming clumps, indicating it's good.
2 Combine flour, milk, butter, and egg. Add yeast mixture. Mix until dough is soft but not sticky.
3 Cover with a cloth towel. Let rise until doubled (about 1 hour).
4 While dough rises, in a small bowl, mix cinnamon with remaining ½ cup sugar. Set aside.
5 Turn out dough onto a lightly floured surface. Roll out to about ¼- to ½-inch thick. Use a 2½-inch cookie cutter to cut out doughnuts. Use a tiny sharp round something (about ¼ inch across) to create holes. (I use the bottom end of a small metal funnel. You can also use your finger or a straw, but I like the uniformity of the funnel.) If the hole is too small, it will close up when frying, so you might need to experiment. Keep cutting out until you run out of dough.
6 Set doughnuts on a baking sheet. Cover with a cloth towel and let them rise for 20 to 30 minutes.
7 Heat about 2 inches of oil until it's hot (between 360° and 375°).
8 Cook doughnuts a few at a time, turning once, until they're puffed and golden brown, about 2 minutes per batch. Drain on paper towels, then toss them with the cinnamon sugar. Serve hot.

Cinnamon Rolls

Total time: 1 hour 20 minutes   Yields 12 to 16 rolls

You can use the dough part of this easy recipe as the basis for other sweet breads. If you want, you can make the dough in a bread machine, then finish the recipe by hand. Pecans, walnuts, and almonds all taste great in this recipe.

Dough

2 teaspoons active dry yeast
3/4 cup lukewarm water
6 tablespoons granulated
 sugar
1 1/2 tablespoons unsalted
 butter, melted

1 large egg, lightly beaten
2 1/2 cups all-purpose flour
3/4 teaspoon salt
1 1/2 tablespoons dry milk

1 In a medium bowl, mix yeast and sugar with lukewarm water.
2 Stir butter into yeast water. Mix lightly.
3 Stir egg into yeast water.
4 In a separate bowl, combine flour, salt, and dry milk.
5 Stir wet ingredients into flour mixture.
6 Knead dough. Dough should be fairly sticky. If it's too dry, add a little more lukewarm water; if too wet, carefully add a bit more flour.
7 Set dough aside to rise for 30 minutes or until it looks right. While it's rising, prepare pan as described next.

Preparing the Pan

1/4 cup unsalted butter, melted
3 tablespoons ground
 cinnamon

2/3 cup packed brown sugar
1/2 cup chopped nuts

1 Pour melted butter in a 9- or 10-inch round cake pan.
2 Sprinkle bottom of pan with cinnamon, brown sugar, and nuts, in that order.

Making and Baking the Rolls

1/2 cup unsalted butter, melted
2 tablespoons ground
 cinnamon

1 cup packed brown sugar
1/2 cup chopped nuts

1 When dough has risen, roll it out on a floured surface to a half-inch thick rectangle (about 10 inches x 12 inches). You'll need extra flour for the surface and rolling pin—the dough will be quite sticky.

2 Baste rolled-out dough with melted butter. Sprinkle dough with cinnamon, brown sugar, and chopped nuts, in that order.

3 Carefully roll up dough along long edge until it is entirely rolled up. Gently press the edge into the roll to seal it.

4 Cut roll into slices about ¾ inch thick (about 12 to 16 slices).

5 Place rolls in pan, one of the cut sides down (so you are looking down at the spirals). The rolls should be touching, slightly pressing each other but not squashing each other.

6 Bake at 400° for 20 minutes or until golden brown.

7 Remove pan from oven. Immediately invert pan onto a plate and shake out rolls, letting the cinnamon, sugar, and nuts from the pan's bottom fall onto the rolls. Serve warm.

Corn Bread Mix

Total time: 10 minutes   Yields 8 cups of mix

This make-ahead mix is free of the extra chemicals that store-bought mixes have. For truly authentic cornmeal that doesn't require the addition of flour to make proper corn bread, check out Anson Mills (ansonmills.com). (Their website has flour-free, and therefore gluten-free, corn bread recipes.) For instructions on making corn bread from this mix, see Southern-Style Corn Bread (page 112).

4 cups all-purpose flour   3 tablespoons baking powder
4 cups cornmeal (any color)   2½ teaspoons salt

1   Combine flour, cornmeal, baking powder, and salt.
2   Mix well. Store in an airtight container.

Dill Bread

Total time: 2 to 3 hours   Yields 1 medium round loaf

My mother's recipe, this makes a moist bread with a large crumb. It's wonderfully hearty, yet delicate and light, with unmatchable flavor. This bread keeps very well. You can also easily double the recipe. You'll get the best results if you have all ingredients at room temperature. Although this is a yeast-raised bread, my mother always made it with all-purpose flour, not bread flour, and it comes out perfectly anyway. Serve warm with butter.

1 package (2¼ teaspoons) active dry yeast
¼ cup lukewarm water (105°)
2 tablespoons brown sugar
1 cup cottage cheese, softened
1 large egg, unbeaten
1 tablespoon minced onion

1 tablespoon unsalted butter, melted and slightly cooled
2 teaspoons dill seed
1 teaspoon salt
¼ teaspoon baking soda
2½ cups all-purpose flour

1   Butter a medium sized, round casserole dish.
2   In a medium bowl, dissolve yeast in lukewarm water.
3   Add brown sugar, cottage cheese, egg, onion, butter, dill seed, salt, and baking soda to yeast.
4   Stir in flour; dough will be very soft and slightly sticky. Add more flour if needed, but not so much the dough is no longer soft and sticky.
5   Place dough in prepared casserole dish and set aside in a warm spot to rise until doubled in size (30 minutes to an hour).
6   Take dough out of casserole dish, knead it, and shape into a ball.
7   Rebutter casserole dish heavily (the butter will melt into the baking bread), then place dough back into dish. Set aside dough to rise again in a warm spot (about 30 minutes).
8   When dough is risen the second time, bake in the casserole dish at 350° for about 35 minutes.

Dinner Rolls

Total time: 2½ hours   Yields 12 large rolls

T he rolls this recipe makes are perfect in texture and flavor. I adapted this recipe
     for truly fine dinner rolls from Marcy Goldman and Yvan Huneault's *The Best of
BetterBaking.com* (TenSpeed Press, 2002). This recipe requires a lot of time, but most
of that is waiting for the dough to rise. Although delicious served warm out of the
oven, these rolls are even better the next day.

$1^1/_2$ cups warm water (110°)
2 tablespoons active dry yeast
$^1/_3$ cup granulated sugar
2 large eggs, lightly beaten
$^1/_2$ cup unsalted butter,
    softened

5 cups bread flour, plus 1 to 2
    cups more as needed
$2^1/_2$ teaspoons salt
$^1/_4$ cup unsalted butter, melted
    (for brushing rolls)

1   Oil, butter, or spray a 13- x 9-inch baking pan. Also butter a large
       bowl (for dough to rise in).
2   Prepare a large, clean mixing bowl by rinsing it with hot water. This
       warms the bowl so that when you add warm water and yeast, the
       water stays at the right temperature. (No need to dry the bowl,
       since you will immediately add water and yeast.)
3   Stir water, yeast, and sugar together in prepared mixing bowl until
       yeast dissolves. Let sit a few minutes to get the yeast working.
4   Add eggs and butter to yeast. Mix a few minutes or until butter is
       fairly well mixed in. (It can still be chunky.)
5   Thoroughly combine 5 cups flour with salt, then add flour to yeast/
       egg/butter mix. (Mixing the salt with the flour first helps prevent
       adding too much concentrated salt into yeast mixture. Too much
       salt can kill yeast.)
6   Knead 10 to 15 minutes, adding more flour if needed. (8 to 10
       minutes if using a stand mixer.) Dough should be soft and not very
       sticky.
7   Turn dough out onto a lightly floured surface and form into a large
       ball. Place into prepared buttered bowl and cover with a clean
       kitchen towel. Place bowl in a warm place and let dough rise 45
       minutes or until almost doubled in size.
8   Gently knead dough a few seconds in bowl, then cover with towel
       again and let it rest in a warm place for 20 minutes.
9   Divide into 12 portions. Shape each portion into a smoothly rounded
       ball.

10 Arrange rolls in prepared baking pan so they are touching each other. Brush rolls with the ¼ cup melted butter and gently scatter a tiny bit of flour onto each roll.

11 Cover pan with towel and let rise in a warm place again for 20 to 30 minutes or until rolls are well risen.

12 After 15 to 20 minutes, start preheating oven to 350°.

13 Once rolls have risen, bake 30 to 35 minutes or until golden brown. Don't overcook. When you first pull these out of the oven, they should be a bit moist and doughy inside. You can serve them warm, though they will cook away the last of the doughiness as they cool.

Dutch Honey Bread

Total time: 1½ hours plus 24 hours   Yields one 9-inch loaf
standing time

Basically a tea bread, dark, spicy, and delicious. I've had this recipe since the 1970s. In 2019, my daughter gave me two stoneware tea loaf pans from King Arthur Flour as a birthday gift. I love them so much, especially for exactly this kind of recipe.

1 cup packed brown sugar	½ teaspoon ground ginger
½ cup unsalted butter, softened	½ teaspoon ground cinnamon
	½ teaspoon ground cloves
2 large eggs, lightly beaten	¼ teaspoon salt
1 teaspoon baking soda	¼ cup chopped nuts
½ cup honey	¼ cup chipped dried figs
½ cup buttermilk	¼ cup currants or raisins
2 cups all-purpose flour	

1 Prepare a 9- x 5-inch loaf pan by buttering it very well. You can also use a tea loaf pan (12 x 4 x 2½ inches).
2 Cream sugar and butter together.
3 Beat eggs into sugar and butter.
4 In a separate small bowl, stir baking soda into honey, then add buttermilk.
5 In a separate medium bowl, combine flour, ginger, cinnamon, cloves, and salt. Set aside ½ cup of this mix.
6 Alternating, starting with the flour mix, stir flour mix and buttermilk mix into creamed butter mix—a little flour, stir well, a little buttermilk, stir well. Do this until you've used up flour mix and buttermilk mix.
7 In a small bowl, combine the reserved ½ cup flour with nuts, figs, and currants, then fold results into batter.
8 Pour batter into prepared loaf pan. Let stand at room temperature for 20 minutes.
9 Bake at 350° for 45 to 50 minutes. If using a tea loaf pan, reduce baking time by about 10 to 15 minutes.
10 Remove from oven and cool 15 minutes, then remove from pan.
11 Wrap with a cotton tea towel and let sit for 24 hours.
12 Cut into thin slices to serve.

Frying Pan Blue Corn Bread

Total time: 1 hour   Yields 8 servings

When I was living in Tucson, I frequently gave rides to and from class to a friend and fellow graduate student. At the end of one semester, she gave me the *Pueblo Indian Cookbook* by Phyllis Hughes (Museum of New Mexico Press, 1972). That cookbook contained this Puebloan recipe. She also adopted one of my cats's stripey kittens who was half bobcat, and that's another sweet tale for another time. You can use yellow or white cornmeal if you don't have blue. Your chili powder's Scolville rating (a measure of heat intensity) will determine how spicy hot the corn bread is. Chile peppers range from 0 Scolville heat units (SHUs) to 2.2 *million* SHUs, and pepper growers are seeking to push that upper limit. For an idea of the scale, bell peppers are 0 SHUs. Jalapenos are 2,500 to 8,000 SHUs. Habaneros and Scotch bonnets are 100,000 to 350,000. The aptly named Carolina Reaper chile pepper is 2.2 million SHUs plus. I prefer this corn bread on the mild side, but you can use whatever level of heat you want. You may be tempted to add more chili powder, but the ingredients are finely balanced; too much chili powder ruins the corn bread.

6 tablespoons cooking oil
4 teaspoons chili powder
1½ cups whole milk
2 large eggs, lightly beaten
1½ cups all-purpose flour
1½ cups blue cornmeal

2 tablespoons baking powder
1 teaspoon salt
¼ cup granulated sugar
¼ cup chopped onion
⅓ cup grated cheese (cheddar or Monterey Jack)

1   Heat oil in a 10-inch cast iron skillet. Add chili powder to oil. Stir a few minutes.
2   Cool oil/chili mixture. You are cooling the mix so that, when you add the eggs, the eggs don't curdle or cook.
3   Add milk and eggs to cooled oil/chili mixture.
4   In a medium bowl, mix flour, cornmeal, baking powder, salt, and sugar.
5   Add onion and cheese to flour/cornmeal mix.
6   Stir milk mixture into dry ingredients and mix until well blended.
7   Return mixture to skillet and bake in a 400° oven for 35 minutes.
8   Remove from oven. Immediately cut into wedges and serve hot.

Northern-Style Sweet Corn Bread

Total time: Yields one 10-inch square panful or two
                                                              dozen muffins

According to *Bernard Clayton's New Complete Book of Breads* (Simon & Schuster, 2003), northerners (Americans living in the American northeast) prefer their corn bread sweet, thick (like cake), and made with flour and yellow cornmeal. That's this recipe. Southerners prefer their corn bread unsweetened, flat, and made with white cornmeal, no flour. The Southern preferences are historically accurate, but have changed (especially the flour/no flour part) in the past 70 years because the way corn is milled now means the recipes need flour. So Southerners use flour in their corn bread, like the Southern-Style Corn Bread (page 112). These are just generalities; exceptions abound, and I can imagine someone reading this saying they're a Southerner but they like savory, thick corn bread (or vice versa). I like my corn bread the way my mother made it: unsweetened (like Southerners) but thick (like Northerners).

¾ cup butter, softened
¾ cup granulated sugar
3 large eggs, lightly beaten
1½ cups cornmeal
2 cups all-purpose flour

3 teaspoons baking powder
½ teaspoon salt
2 cups whole milk
1½ cups peeled and diced
    apples or 1 cup blueberries

1   Prepare a 9- or 10-inch square baking pan or two 12-well standard muffin tins by buttering them well. (Standard muffin tins hold approximately ½ cup in each well.)
2   Cream butter and sugar until fluffy.
3   Add eggs and beat until blended.
4   Stir in cornmeal.
5   Combine flour, baking soda, and salt in a separate bowl.
6   In three rounds, stir ⅓ of the flour mix, then ⅓ of the milk mix. Stir gently after each addition.
7   Once all the flour and milk are incorporated, stir in fruit until pieces are just covered with batter.
8   Pour batter into prepared baking pan or muffin tins.
9   Bake at 375° for 40 to 50 minutes or until corn bread is browned and tests done with a toothpick. (20 minutes for muffins.)

Pecan Rolls

Total time: 3 hours   Yields 3 dozen sticky buns

T his fabulously tasty and very sweet recipe came from a co-worker in Tucson in the 1980s. She also shared the Ritz Cracker Pie recipe that you can find in *Delectable Desserts* (volume 1 of this cookbook series).

Dough

1 package (2¼ teaspoons) active dry yeast
¼ cup lukewarm water (105°)
¼ cup whole milk, scalded (brought to 180°), then cooled to lukewarm
¼ cup granulated sugar

1 teaspoon salt
1 large egg, lightly beaten
½ cup unsalted butter, softened
1½ cups all-purpose flour, plus 1½ to 2 cups more

Caramel Sauce

1 cup packed brown sugar
1 cup cream

½ cup unsalted butter

Topping and Filling

1½ cups pecan halves
½ cup granulated sugar
½ cup packed brown sugar

1½ teaspoons ground cinnamon
¼ cup unsalted butter, softened

1 **Start the dough**. In a 3-quart mixing bowl, dissolve yeast in lukewarm water. Let sit a few minutes to get the yeast working.
2 Prepare a bowl for rising by lightly buttering the bowl's inside.
3 Into yeast/water mix, stir in milk, sugar, salt, egg, butter, and the 1½ cups flour. Beat until smooth. Mix in enough of the remaining flour to make dough easy to handle.
4 Turn dough onto lightly floured surface. Knead until smooth and elastic (about 3 minutes).
5 Place dough in prepared bowl; turn to coat with butter on all sides. Cover. Set aside to rise in a warm place until double (about 1½ hours). Dough is ready if an indentation remains when touched.
6 **While dough is rising, make the caramel sauce**. Combine sugar, cream, and butter in a medium saucepan.
7 Heat to boiling, then reduce heat. Simmer 1 minute.
8 Remove from heat and cool.

9 **When dough has risen, make and bake the rolls**. Pour caramel sauce into a large, lightly buttered jelly roll pan. Scatter pecan halves over caramel, flat sides up. (When rolls are done, the pecans will be rounded sides up on the rolls.)

10 Mix granulated and brown sugars with cinnamon.

11 Punch dough down and divide in half. On a lightly floured board, roll each half into a rectangle, 18 inches by 9 inches. Spread each rectangle with two tablespoons of softened butter.

12 Divide sugar/cinnamon mixture evenly into two portions, then sprinkle each portion evenly over each rectangle.

13 Beginning along one of the long sides of rolled-out dough, tightly roll each rectangle into an 18-inch long cylinder. Pinch dough along long edge into roll to seal. Shape roll until even in width.

14 Cut each roll into 18 slices, each about 1 inch wide. Place slices on caramel in jelly roll pan.

15 Let rise until double (about 45 minutes).

16 When rolls have risen, bake at 375° 15 to 20 minutes or until golden brown.

17 When rolls are done, remove from oven and immediately invert onto large trays or baking sheets. Leave pan on top of the rolls a few minutes so the caramel can drizzle down from the pan onto the rolls, then remove pan and serve.

Perfect Savory Pie Crust

Total time: 10 minutes   Yields two 9-inch pie crusts

This recipe is the savory version of my perfect pie crust recipe in *Delectable Desserts,* the first volume in this cookbook series. If you want to make it sweet, replace the salt with 2 teaspoons sugar and a pinch of salt. My friend Jon Rioux says this truly is the perfect pie crust.

2 cups all-purpose flour
1 teaspoon salt
10 tablespoons unsalted butter, cold

2 tablespoons avocado oil or some other mild cooking oil
6 tablespoons ice-cold water

1   Combine flour and salt.
2   Cut in butter and oil until dough is the consistency of cornmeal.
3   One tablespoon at a time, sprinkle ice water over flour mixture, blending gently with a fork.
4   Keep adding water 1 tablespoon at a time until you can carefully and gently gather dough into a ball with your hands. The dough should be silky and not wet.
5   Divide dough into two equal balls. Roll out each ball with a well-floured rolling pin on a well-floured surface.
6   After putting pie crust in a pie pan, place pan in refrigerator for about 30 minutes so dough can relax. This relaxation period is the secret to not having your pie crust shrink quite so much when it bakes.

Protein-Rich Bread

Total time: 3½ hours   Yields three 8- x 4-inch loaves

I still have the original index card this recipe was written on. My friend AJ carefully calligraphed it and sprayed the card lightly with a plasticizing spray so it would repel stains. Based on the famous Cornell bread recipe created in the late 1930s by the late Clive McCay, a professor of animal nutrition at Cornell University, this recipe makes rich, hearty, delicious loaves providing, with the combination of the wheat germ, milk, and soy flour, more fiber and a more complete protein.

1 package (2¼ teaspoons) active dry yeast
½ cup lukewarm water (105°)
1 cup whole milk, scalded to 180°, then cooled to lukewarm
1 cup honey
½ tablespoon salt
⅓ cup salted butter, melted
1 large egg, lightly beaten

½ cup buckwheat flour
½ cup cornmeal
½ cup rolled oats
½ cup wheat germ
½ cup egg albumen (powdered egg whites)
1 cup soy flour
2 cups all-purpose flour
3 cups whole wheat flour

1 Grease three 8- x 4-inch loaf pans very well.
2 Dissolve yeast in warm water.
3 To yeast and water, add milk, honey, salt, butter, and egg. Let sit a few minutes.
4 In a separate bowl, combine buckwheat flour, cornmeal, oats, wheat germ, egg albumen, soy flour, all-purpose flour, and whole wheat flour. Stir so flours are well combined.
5 Pour liquid mix into flour and stir well.
6 Knead until dough is smooth and elastic (about 10 minutes), then cover and let rise until doubled in size (about 1 hour).
7 Knead again and shape into loaves. Place loaves into prepared loaf pans and let rise a second time in pans until doubled in size (about 1 hour).
8 Half-way though loaf rising time, preheat oven to 350°.
9 When loaves are risen, bake 45 to 60 minutes or until loaves test at 210° inside. If loaves start to brown too early (around 20 minutes), cover lightly with foil and continue baking.
10 Remove loaves from oven. Brush each loaf with melted butter. Cool before slicing.

Rich Cream Biscuits

Total time: 30 minutes   Yields about 12 biscuits

I found the original version of this recipe in Bernard Clayton's *The Complete Book of Breads* (Simon & Schuster, 1973). He said he adapted the recipe from Marjorie Kinnan Rawlings' *Cross Creek Cookery* (Charles Scribner's Sons, 1942). Over the years, I modified Mr. Clayton's version to better suit my taste. As I did so, I was unknowingly bringing the recipe closer to the original, which I discovered when I bought a copy of Ms. Rawlings' book in the early 2000s. One of the virtues of this recipe is that, unlike most biscuits, the dough can take a lot of handling and the biscuits still come out light and tender. Another virtue is that this recipe makes perfect biscuits every time. Serve warm with lots of butter, honey, and jam.

2 cups all-purpose flour
5 teaspoons baking powder
½ teaspoon salt
2 tablespoons unsalted butter

1 cup heavy cream (you can substitute whole milk, but the biscuits won't be as rich)

1   Preheat oven to 425°.
2   Combine flour, baking powder, and salt.
3   Work butter into flour mixture with your fingers or a pastry cutter until mixture resembles coarse meal.
4   Gradually add cream, starting with ½ cup, using a fork to mix it in. Keep adding cream until dough just holds together (like pie dough).
5   With a rolling pin, roll dough out to ½ inch thick. Fold it over, then fold it over again, then roll out again to ½ inch thick.
6   Cut dough with a 2-inch cookie cutter. (A smaller cookie cutter will result in crisper biscuits, which my daughter likes.) Gather scraps and roll out again; no need to fold this time.
7   Place biscuits on a baking sheet. (No preparation needed for the baking sheet.)
8   Bake 12 minutes or until golden brown. The biscuits will rise quite high—1½ to 2 inches.

Sopapillas

Total time: 1½ hours   Yields about 2 dozen

When I was living in Tucson, I loved to make a Southwestern favorite, sopapillas (pronounced soap-uh-PEA-yuhs). Sopapillas are like tiny beignets. As with beignets, the secret to getting the pocket is that you must roll the dough very thin. Thinner than that. No, thinner. It takes a little practice (but not a lot), then you have delicious bite-sized deserts. You can put a drift of powdered sugar on them, though I love them best broken open with honey drizzled inside. You can eat the versatile sopapillas as a savory accompaniment to anything you want—beans, salsa, barbecue sauce, the sky's the limit. In my many moves since Tucson, I lost my recipe, which didn't use oil or lard, but found an almost identical recipe in *Senor Vecino's Sopapillas and Navajo Fry Bread* recipe on YouTube. I've slightly adapted his recipe according to my experiences and what I remember of my original recipe. You can double this recipe, or make fry bread, though the dough needs to be much thicker for fry bread.

2 cups all-purpose flour	**1** tablespoon honey
1 tablespoon baking powder	**¾** cup whole milk
1 tablespoon granulated sugar	Oil or lard for frying
1½ teaspoons salt	

1   Combine flour, baking powder, sugar, and salt.
2   Stir in honey and milk. Mix until it forms a soft, sticky dough. You can use your hands.
3   Cover bowl and let dough rest for about 20 minutes.
4   After dough has rested, on a lightly floured surface, roll dough to a large ⅛-inch thick square. Even thinner if you can manage it.
5   Cut dough into squares measuring 1 inch by 1 inch. You can make them larger, but this is the size I make them.
6   Heat your frying oil of choice to 375°.
7   Drop sopapillas a few at a time into hot oil. They should puff immediately. Fry for about a minute, flipping them over at the halfway point. Like beignets, if they don't puff, that means the dough wasn't rolled thin enough. The sopapillas should be a light golden brown and you definitely don't want them too hard or crispy. They're supposed to be tender.
8   Drain each batch on paper towels. Continue until all the sopapillas are fried. Serve hot.

Sourdough Starter and Bread

Total time: Several weeks to make   Yields 1 round loaf
starter; 6 hours to make bread

This recipe explains each step of making sourdough starter and bread for the beginner or for those who need a refresher. Making sourdough might seem like it's not for the faint of heart, but in reality, it's just not for the impatient. If you make starter from scratch, it can take up to a full two weeks or more to get a good strong starter going. You can reduce that time if you have a friend who's willing to share their starter, or if you buy starter online. Once you take that first bite of your own, homemade, perfect loaf, you may decide it's worth it. Online, you'll find about as many ways to make sourdough starter and sourdough bread as there are bakers making sourdough bread, ranging from "there's only one right way" to "trust your baker's intuition." I vote for learning the basics, then trusting your intuition. After all, people have been making sourdough for thousands of years—how hard can it be? My loaves don't look gorgeous—I haven't applied myself to the art of scoring sourdough loaves—but they taste delicious and it's immensely satisfying to pull my own homemade sourdough loaves out of the oven. Once you're feeling comfortable with making sourdough bread, you can experiment with different flours or ingredients. For example, you could add fresh chopped garlic and fresh rosemary to your dough. For this recipe, I give measurements in grams, because weighing by grams is more precise, and sourdough relies on precise measurements for success.

Tools

    kitchen scale that can weigh in
        grams

    1-quart glass or plastic
        container for starter

Making Sourdough Starter

    Water (see instructions for
        amounts)

    Flour base: 800 grams all-
        purpose flour or 720 grams
        all-purpose flour mixed with
        80 grams whole wheat flour
        (the flours don't need to be
        bread flour)

1 **Day 1**: In a 2-quart container, combine equal weights of water and flour base. Try about 100 grams each water and flour. You can start with as little as 30 grams each, but these instructions are written for starting with 100 grams. The container shouldn't be airtight, and should have plenty of room to allow your starter to expand. Your starter won't expand right away, but one day it will. Stir well

and cover with a clean cloth. Set container in a warm, draft-free place. **Note**: Starter grows more readily in warmer temperatures. If your room is cold, find a warmish spot for the starter. Strter can do its thing in colder temperatures, though.; it just takes more time. Let sit 24 hours.

2   **Day 2**: Discard half the starter. **Don't toss the discarded starter down the sink (it's bad for the pipes).** Either compost it or throw it away. You can't cook with your discard yet. After discarding, add equal weights (100 grams each) of water and flour base to starter. Giving the starter more flour and water is called "feeding," and that's exactly what you're doing—feeding the precious organisms in your starter. Let sit 24 hours.

3   **Day 3**: Your starter may be bubbling and growing a bit. Now it's time to feed twice a day. Discard starter until you have about 100 grams of starter left. Add 100 grams each water and flour base and let sit 12 hours. Repeat in 12 hours.

4   **Days 4 and 5**: Every 12 hours, discard starter until you have about 100 grams left. Feed just as you did on day 3. On day 4, the starter may be smelling pretty high. Don't despair. This should be the turning point for your sourdough starter. Persevere! By day 5, your starter should have a pleasant, clean, earthy smell (though not everyone thinks it's pleasant). Also, your starter should be rising well.

Your sourdough starter is a collection of millions of living organisms. If you don't feed your starter on schedule, it will start to die. Bad organisms can take over and kill the weakened good ones. A hungry starter will have a sharp, almost acetone-like smell. That's okay. But if your starter starts to smell gaggingly bad or develops odd colors (red, green, orange, pink), throw it out and start again. Those colors mean undesired microorganisms have taken over. A dark liquid on top can be okay if you catch it soon enough. That dark liquid is a sign of a really hungry starter. Just pour off the liquid and feed your starter. Starter is forgiving; if you forget to feed your starter for a day (for counter starter) or a week (for refrigerator starter), just diligently feed it every day/week after that and it will recover. I neglected my vigorous starter for an entire year (in the refrigerator), and it came back roaringly strong once I started feeding it again.

---

5   **Day 6**: If your starter isn't showing a lot of activity (bubbles, rising), repeat the twice-daily feedings until it does. One way to test the vigor of your starter is to discard and feed as usual, then mark a line on the outside of the container. Beside that line, write the hour you fed the starter. Check starter every hour and draw a line at the point

it's risen to. Write the time next to each line. At some point, your starter will stop rising and start to collapse. If it takes six hours for your starter to reach that point, you have a six-hour starter. You're aiming for your starter to double in size in about six to eight hours after feeding. If your starter can't keep rising for that long, keep discarding and feeding every day until it can. **Note**: Once your starter is going, you don't have to keep composting the discard. The discard makes fabulous pancakes, waffles, and so on.

6   When starter is ready, you can do one of two things: feed it every day and keep it on the counter (if you bake daily), or put it in the refrigerator and feed it once a week (if you bake less often). Each time you feed it, discard half, then feed 100 grams each water and flour base. Are you eager to make some bread? Proceed to the next section.

Making One Sourdough Loaf

These instructions are for making one medium-sized round loaf, or boule. Boule (rhymes with tool) is French for ball; hence the name of the loaf shape.

150 grams sourdough starter
500 grams bread flour
250 grams water
5 grams salt
parchment paper
kitchen thermometer

5- or 6-quart cast iron Dutch oven with a lid or a 5- or 6-quart casserole dish with a lid; each needs to be able to survive a 500° oven
lame or a razor-sharp knife

1   If you don't have enough mother starter to remove 150 grams and still have enough left, feed your mother starter 180 grams each water and flour base and let sit on the counter 6 to 8 hours.

2   Once starter is ready, remove 150 grams starter from your mother starter. Put mother starter back where you normally keep it.

3   Put the 150 grams starter in a medium mixing bowl. Mix in 500 grams flour and 250 grams water. (No, I'm not forgetting the salt—that comes in a bit.) The dough should be soft and sticky. if it isn't, add a bit more flour or water as needed.

4   Place dough back in bowl and cover bowl. Rest dough 30 minutes to an hour. At this stage, your dough is **autolysing**. That means the flour is absorbing the water and starting to form gluten. Salt interferes with autolysing, which is why I said not to add it yet. However, if you already added the salt, don't worry. Some people add the salt with the flour. Either way, your bread will be fantastic. You've got this. The length of autolysing time isn't essential, and you can even skip the autolysing step.

5   After the autolysing stage, sprinkle salt over dough and knead it in.

6　You're now entering the **bulk rise stage**, during which the wild yeast does its thing.

7　This step is optional: about 20 minutes into the bulk rise stage, start a series of **stretches and folds**. Grab one part of the dough and stretch it in one direction, then fold the stretched portion back onto the rest of the dough. Stretch dough again in another direction, then fold. Do this several times. Put dough back in bowl, cover dough, and let rest 1 hour.

8　Repeat step 7 once every hour for 2 or 3 more times.

9　After 2 hours, start doing the **windowpane test**. If you're stretching the dough, you can do the windowpane test at the same time. Let dough relax a minute, then gently use your fingers to stretch out a small amount. You're looking for the dough to have sufficient strength from gluten that it can stretch thinly enough to become translucent without tearing. This translucency is called a windowpane. (Google "sourdough windowpane" for videos.)

10　During the bulk rise stage, you're also looking for your dough to double in size. The time it takes for dough to double depends on your room temperature and sourdought starter. The warmer the room and stronger the starter, the faster dough rises. In summer, it can take just a few hours; in winter, it can take half a day or more.

11　When you get the windowpane effect and your dough has doubled, you're ready to shape your loaf to prepare it for a second rise.

12　**Shaping the loaf** is hard to describe and easier to see; I recommend you look for a good video online. Take dough from bowl and place on a lightly floured surface. Using both your hands, pull loaf toward you and rotate loaf as you pull, pulling your hands tightly around the loaf and tucking the dough underneath as you do. As you pull and turn, gently shape dough into a tight, round loaf, pulling dough down and under to get a taut, smooth surface.

13　**Second rise**. Set shaped dough, seam side up, in a bowl lined with a lightly floured cloth. (The dough will go into the baking pot seam side down.) You use a round mixing bowl or a Banneton. A Banneton is a rattan basket. The rattan forms those nice ridges in the dough. If using a Banneton, dust basket lightly with flour or corn meal. Cover bowl or Banneton and let dough rise until it's light and airy, 30 minutes to 2 hours.

14　About 30 minutes before dough is ready, put cast iron Dutch oven (with lid on) into a cold oven and **turn oven to 450°**. If you're using a casserole dish to bake the bread, don't put the casserole dish into the oven. Instead, just start preheating oven to 450°. Some people skip the preheating stage and report that their loaves come out fine.

Important! You don't ever want to shock cast iron, so never expose your cast iron to a sudden extreme temperature change. For example, don't run cold water on a hot cast iron skillet; don't put a room-temperature cast iron Dutch oven into a super hot oven. Otherwise, your cast iron can warp, crack, or even break, and many sad faces will be made.

15 When loaf has risen, you're ready to **bake your loaf**. Gently turn loaf, seam side down, onto a square of parchment paper lightly dusted with flour or cornmeal. Quickly and lightly **slash loaf with a super sharp knife** or with a lame (pronounced lahm). Don't slash too deeply. Some people make an art of slashing their loaves. Again, the internet is a good source for videos on what this looks like. I usually draw a box on top with four overlapping lines, which gives my loaves a cute hat effect. One long slash will also work. The slash is important—it gives your loaf a place to expand. Though I've sometimes forgotten the slash and my loaves came out fine.

16 Open the oven. If you're using a Dutch oven, use good oven mitts to **carefully** pull out the now-super-hot Dutch oven and remove its lid. Holding edges of parchment, lower loaf and paper into Dutch oven (parchment paper still under loaf). Put lid back on, put Dutch oven back into oven, and close oven. If using a casserole dish, do the same—lower loaf into casserole dish, cover, and put in oven. You really, really need that parchment paper. I didn't use it once and spent a long time scouring my Dutch oven.

17 Bake for 20 minutes.

18 After 20 minutes, remove Dutch oven lid and set aside. (You no longer need it.) Your loaf should be a pale, underdone cream color. Loosely cover loaf top with aluminum foil to prevent scorching. Reduce heat to 400° and bake about 20 more minutes or until loaf is 210° internally when tested with a kitchen thermometer. When your loaf is done, the top of the loaf should be a gorgeous toasted brown.

19 Remove Dutch oven from oven and immediately (and carefully!) decant loaf. Set loaf to cool on a wire rack.

20 **Important**! No matter how tempting it may be, do *not* cut your loaf until it's cooled to about body temperature. Because of starch retrogradation, your loaf isn't done until it's cool; it'll be gummy if you cut too soon. (Though if you made rolls or a baguette instead of a loaf, slice away.) Store loaf in a paper (not plastic) bag, and on the counter, not in the refrigerator.

Southern-Style Corn Bread

Total time: 30 minutes   Yields one 8-inch square pan

This recipe is the counterpoint to the Northern-Style Sweet Corn Bread on page 100. As described in more detail on that page, typically, Americans in the Northeastern states like their corn bread thicker and sweeter, and made with flour; Southerners like it thinner and made without sugar or flour. Though, for reasons stated with that earlier recipe, Southern-style corn bread recipes have included flour for many decades now. This bread is delicious with many of the soups in Beans, Soups, and Vegetables (page 23).

1 large egg, lightly beaten
1 cup whole milk
1/2 cup unsalted butter, melted

2 cups Corn Bread Mix (page 94)

1 Heavily butter an 8-inch x 8-inch square baking pan.
2 Combine egg with milk and butter.
3 Add corn bread mix to egg/milk mix. Stir gently until just combined, then pour into prepared pan.
4 Bake at 400° for 20 minutes or until golden brown. To test for doneness, put a knife in the middle. If it comes out clean, the corn bread is done.

Southwestern Fry Bread

Total time: 30 minutes   Yields a lot

Every culture has some version of quick fried bread. This version is one of many favorite versions in the American Southwest. You can serve it as a hot dessert with honey, powdered sugar, jam, or whipped cream and chocolate syrup, or as a main dish; for example, as the base of a tostada covered with beans and salsa.

3 cups all-purpose flour
2 tablespoon dry milk
3 teaspoons baking powder
2 teaspoons salt

1½ tablespoons lard
1 cup water
oil or lard for frying

1 Combine flour, milk, baking powder, and salt in a large bowl.
2 Cut in lard.
3 Add water slowly until dough forms a ball.
4 Knead dough lightly. Dough should be silky.
5 Pinch off small pieces to make approximately two-inch balls. Flatten each ball between the palms of your hand until it is about ½ inch thick. (Or roll with a floured rolling pin.)
6 Heat oil in a large frying pan or Dutch oven, making sure oil is at least 1 inch deep and very hot, about 350°. (This bread is usually cooked in a large pot of oil.)
7 Carefully slip flattened dough into hot oil, taking care not to spatter yourself.
8 Let dough puff up and rise to the top of the oil (a few minutes at most). Cook until a light golden color, turning once. Remove from oil and drain on paper towels. Serve hot.

Whole Wheat Bread

Total time: 4 hours   Yields one 9-inch loaf

I loved my bread machine when I had it in the 1990s, but had trouble finding good recipes for it. Eventually I found *Bread Machine Magic,* by Linda Rehberg and Lois Conway (St. Martin's Griffin, 1992). This recipe comes from that book. Unfortunately, the recipe didn't work as given in the book, but I kept `modifying it until it did work. This recipe makes a fine-textured loaf, firm enough for sandwiches, that is tasty enough to eat warm with butter only. Some people prefer to have their bread machine to do the mixing, rising, and kneading, then they bake the loaf in the oven.

1¼ cups lukewarm water   1 cup bread flour
1 scant teaspoon salt   ¼ cup instant potato flakes
2 tablespoons granulated sugar 2 teaspoons active dry yeast
2 cups whole wheat flour

1   Place water, salt, sugar, whole wheat flour, bread flour, and potato flakes in bread machine in the order listed.
2   Make a small hole in the top of the dry ingredients and put yeast in hole.
3   Select your bread machine's equivalents of Light Crust setting and White Bread cycle.
4   Run the machine as directed by the manufacturer.

Breakfasts

For the experienced cook who wants something spectacular or unusual, or for the beginning cook who wants to know how it's done, breakfast recipes can be useful. This chapter contains some of my long-time favorites, including how to make a Dutch baby, how to cook bacon perfectly every time, plus a few of my very own recipes. For more recipes, browse the other chapters for recipes suitable for breakfast.

Bacon

Total time: 20 minutes   Yields 1 pound cooked bacon

The simplest way to cook bacon without having to watch it like a hawk (or risk having it blacken while you do other things) is to bake it in the oven. I came up with this method in the 1980s and told (and continue to tell) everyone who was interested. Back then, people were skeptical of the method; now, it's promoted by big-time cooking sites as the best way to cook bacon. You must have a reasonably full baking pan of bacon for this to work right. If you only bake a few strips, they dry out and get too crisp. If your bacon is particularly fatty, drain the bacon grease half-way through. Save the grease—it's fabulous for many recipes, using in a cast-iron skillet, or for popping corn.

   1 pound bacon

1   Place strips of bacon in a single layer in a large baking sheet that has sides. The strips can touch, but try not to overlap them.
2   Bake at 350° for about 15 to 18 minutes, or until done the way you prefer. If you like it limp, bake for 15 minutes. If you like it crispy, bake it for 18 minutes. If your bacon is particularly fatty, drain off the grease halfway through.
3   Remove from oven. Carefully drain grease into a container and save it for later cooking needs. Drain bacon on paper towels a few minutes before serving.

Buckwheat Pancakes

Total time: 20 minutes   Yields 12 small pancakes

My mother used to make thin, delicious sourdough buckwheat pancakes, the size of an American dollar coin, using sourdough starter from the jar of starter that she always had fermenting on the kitchen counter. Alas, I never got her recipe. This gluten-free version, which I adapted from America's Test Kitchen's excellent *The How Can It Be Gluten Free Cookbook* (America's Test Kitchen, 2014), makes fat, delicious pancakes. Buckwheat is not wheat, nor even a grain. It's an herb, first cultivated in Southeast Asia about 8,000 years ago. Therefore, this recipe is gluten-free. If you don't need to avoid gluten, you can substitute all-purpose flour for the gluten-free flour. You can keep the cooked pancakes in the refrigerator for a few days (or freeze them for about three months). Serve with apricot jam, or with butter and maple syrup.

¾ cup gluten-free flour
¾ cup buckwheat flour
1 teaspoon baking powder
1 cup buttermilk or whole milk
2 large eggs, lightly beaten

2 tablespoons unsalted butter, melted and slightly cooled
1 tablespoon honey
Cooking oil or butter for skillet

1 Combine flour, buckwheat, and baking powder. Stir and set aside.
2 In a separate bowl, combine buttermilk, eggs, butter, and honey.
3 Stir wet mixture into dry until everything is wet. You don't need to be thorough about it—lumps are fine. The batter will be quite thick; for thinner pancakes, add more buttermilk.
4 Heat cooking oil or butter into a cast iron skillet on high for a few minutes, then switch to medium-high.
5 Carefully ladle batter into skillet (a few tablespoons of batter per pancake) and cook until bubbles form on surface and bottoms brown. Flip once and cook on the other side a few minutes longer, until the other side is also brown and pancakes are cooked through.
6 Remove pancakes from skillet and serve immediately, or keep warm in the oven until ready to serve.
7 The batter doesn't keep, so continue cooking batter until it's gone.

Cinnamon Toast

Total time: 30 minutes   Yields 2 slices

Cinnamon toast is a fast, excellent, sweet breakfast snack (though you can make it any time of the day). You can use any kind of bread; however, whole wheat bread makes an unusually delicious version of this recipe. Figure one to two pieces of toast per person. The instructions are for two slices, but you can multiply the recipe as you wish. You can also make this by spreading the bread with butter before toasting, topping with sugar, cinnamon, and cream, then cooking in the oven for about five minutes.

2 slices bread
1 tablespoon butter (salted or unsalted)

2 tablespoons brown sugar
1 teaspoon ground cinnamon
2 teaspoons cream (optional)

1   Toast the bread.
2   Spread liberally with butter.
3   Cover one side of each slice with brown sugar; top with cinnamon.
4   Optional: pour about a teaspoon of cream on each slice.
5   Place under broiler for about 30 seconds to a minute. Watch carefully so the slices don't burn.
6   Serve immediately.

Dutch Baby

Total time: 20 minutes   Yields one 13- x 9-inch puff

A Dutch baby is like an American popover. It's sometimes called a Dutch puff, a German pancake, or a Bismarck. It looks like a large Yorkshire pudding, but is sweet and thick, not savory and thin. The recipe may have originated with the Pennsylvania Dutch, who are descendants of German-speaking Amish and Mennonite groups who came from Germany and Switzerland. In German, the word for the German language is Deutsche. To many other Americans, that sounded like Dutch; . That explains the "Dutch" part; I haven't yet found why these are called a baby, though. Serve immediately dusted with powdered sugar or with toppings of your choice—jam, fruit and whipped cream, maple syrup, and so on.

8 tablespoons butter (salted or unsalted)
6 large eggs, beaten well
1 cup whole milk
1 cup all-purpose flour

½ cup granulated sugar
1 teaspoon vanilla extract
2 teaspoons ground cinnamon (optional)

1 Preheat oven to 425°.
2 Slice butter into 8 squares and place in a 13- x 9-inch pan. Put pan in the oven so the butter can start melting.
3 Combine eggs, milk, flour, sugar, vanilla, and cinnamon if you're including it. Mix well. There will be many small lumps, but this is okay.
4 Once butter has melted, pour batter into pan.
5 Bake 10 to 15 minutes. The Dutch baby puffs up and curls around the edges. When it's golden brown, remove from the oven.

French Toast

Total time: 30 minutes   Yields 4 servings

The "French" in French toast is from Joseph French, who claimed to have invented it in 1724. However, according to The Breakfast Shoppe, once again, like so many fine dishes, the Romans were making it long before. As with any popular dish, French toast has many aliases: German toast, eggy bread, French-fried bread, Poor Knights of Windsor, Spanish toast, nun's toast, and *pain perdu* ("lost bread" in French). As with Cinnamon Toast (page 118), you can use any kind of bread to make French toast; however, whole wheat bread makes a heartily delicious and satisfying breakfast. Try sourdough bread as well. This recipe is great when camping or river rafting. You can adjust the amounts according to your needs. Serve with butter, jam, maple syrup, fruit preserves, or powdered sugar.

4 large eggs, beaten   **1** teaspoon ground nutmeg
1 cup whole milk   **8** slices bread
2 teaspoons ground cinnamon

1 Combine eggs, milk, cinnamon, and nutmeg. Beat well.
2 Soak each piece of bread in the egg/milk mixture and place immediately in a hot, lightly buttered frying pan or griddle. If you are using whole wheat bread, soak a little longer to let the inside become a little more soaked; that makes the final product tenderer. As you dip the slices, stir the egg mixture frequently to keep the cinnamon mixed in. Otherwise, you'll get some slices with too much cinnamon and some with not enough.
3 Cook each slice on the first side about 2 minutes; flip and cook the second side 2 more minutes or until eggs are cooked and a light golden brown.

Fried Egg Sandwiches

Total time: 10 minutes   Yields 4 sandwiches

This is my global take on an American favorite. My daughter likes the uniquely different taste of my fried egg sandwiches. So I'm including this recipe in my cookbook so she can make them if I'm not around. You can fry eggs **sunny side up** (eggs cooked without flipping; served while yolks are still runny), **over easy** (flipped; runny yolks), **over medium** (flipped, yolk mostly cooked but still slightly runny), or **over hard** (flipped; yolk cooked all the way through). For my garam masala recipe, see page 294.

8 slices bread
mayonnaise
butter for frying eggs

8 large eggs
⅛ teaspoon celery seed
⅛ teaspoon garam masala

1   Spread mayonnaise on each slice of bread to desired thickness.
2   In a well-seasoned cast iron skillet, melt butter on high heat.
3   Crack eggs into skillet and fry to desired degree of doneness.
4   Flip eggs (if not cooking sunny side up). Sprinkle lightly with celery seed and garam masala. If you don't flip the eggs (for example, if you're cooking them sunny side up), sprinkle eggs after they have cooked a bit.
5   When eggs are done, put two on a slice of bread and top with another slice.

Pancake and Waffle Mix

Total time: 15 minutes

Yields about eight 3½ inch pancakes
per cup of mix

My family loves pancakes and waffles, but I don't like to buy store-bought mixes. On the other hand, it takes time to mix pancakes or waffles from scratch every time. The solution? My own homemade pancake mix. This mix stores well and gives the satisfaction of knowing you are saving lots of money while providing your family with better food. You can use many combinations of flour; I encourage you to experiment. Our favorite: 2 cups all-purpose flour, 2 cups whole wheat flour, and 2 cups buckwheat flour. Fresh buttermilk is the key to tender, delicious pancakes and waffles. You'll need sourdough starter for the sourdough versions. If you just want to make the pancakes or waffles without making the mix, substitute 1 cup flour, 2 teaspoons baking powder, and 1 tablespoon granulated sugar for the 1 cup of mix in the instructions for making the pancakes and waffles. For an extra treat, slice bananas into, or add blueberries to the batter.

Ingredients for Pancake Mix

6 cups flour (see headnotes for types of flour to use)

2 tablespoons baking powder
¼ cup granulated sugar

1   Mix all ingredients together very well and store in an airtight container in a cool, dry place.

To Make Pancakes

1 cup pancake mix
1 cup whole milk or buttermilk
1 large egg, beaten

2 tablespoons cooking oil or butter (salted or unsalted), melted

1   Combine pancake mix, milk, egg and oil. Stir until dry ingredients are wet. Lumps are okay.
2   Cook as you would any pancakes.

To Make Sourdough Pancakes

1 cup pancake mix
½ teaspoon baking soda
½ teaspoon salt
½ cup sourdough starter
1 cup whole milk or buttermilk

1 large egg, beaten
1 tablespoon vegetable oil or butter (salted or unsalted), melted

1   Combine pancake mix, baking soda, and salt.

2 In a separate bowl, combine sourdough starter, milk, egg, and oil.
3 Combine dry and wet ingredients until dry ingredients are wet.
4 Cook as you would any pancakes.

To Make Waffles

1 cup pancake mix
1 cup whole milk or buttermilk
2 large eggs, beaten

2 tablespoons oil or butter
   (salted or unsalted), melted

1 Combine mix, milk, eggs, and oil.
2 For a 6-inch waffle iron, pour ¼ cup batter onto griddle and cook according to manufacturer's instructions.

For Particularly Fluffy Waffles

1 cup pancake mix
1 cup whole milk or buttermilk
2 large eggs, separated

2 tablespoons oil or butter,
   (salted or unsalted), melted

1 Bring egg yolks and whites to room temperature.
2 Combine egg yolks, milk, oil, and pancake mix.
3 Beat egg whites until they are stiff but not dry, then fold into batter.
4 For a 6-inch waffle iron, pour ¼ cup batter onto griddle and cook according to manufacturer's instructions.

Budget Pancake Syrup

My mother made this often when my brothers and I were kids. Serve when hot, or store in refrigerator for up to a week.

2 cups packed brown sugar
1 cup water

½ cup butter (optional)

1 Combine sugar and water until sugar dissolves.
2 Add butter.
3 Heat until hot, but not boiling.

Pumpkin Pancakes

Total time: 30 minutes   Yields fifteen 3-inch pancakes

A local pancake house offers light, delicious pumpkin pancakes in the fall and winter only. After Christmas, I used to have to wait a full year until I could taste them again. I finally came up with a recipe that duplicates the restaurant's so closely that I can't tell the difference when tasting them. Serve sprinkled with powdered sugar or cinnamon sugar or topped with whipped cream sprinkled with cinnamon sugar. You can also make waffles with this batter.

½ cup pumpkin purée
1½ cups buttermilk or whole
   milk
3 large eggs, well beaten
2 tablespoons unsalted butter,
   melted and slightly cooled

1½ cups all-purpose flour
2 teaspoons baking powder
½ teaspoon salt
¼ teaspoon nutmeg

1 Combine pumpkin, buttermilk, eggs, and butter. Stir until well mixed.
2 In a separate bowl, combine flour, baking powder, salt, and nutmeg.
3 Add dry ingredients to wet. Stir until thoroughly mixed.
4 For each pancake, pour ¼ cup batter onto a hot, buttered griddle or iron skillet. Cook until golden on each side. If making waffles, follow the waffle maker's directions.

Scrambled Eggs

Total time: 10 minutes

Yields 1 serving

There are two complimentary techniques for making moist, tender scrambled eggs that don't stick to the pan. The first is to cook them in a properly seasoned cast iron skillet. The second is to use milk, not water, for the liquid. Some people prefer a drier, tougher texture to their scrambled eggs; in that case, use water instead of milk. (Water guarantees tough eggs.) You can use this recipe whether you like your eggs scrambled hard or scrambled soft. Most people are familiar with eggs scrambled hard—that's the default way of cooking them, and is what you get if you don't say anything when ordering scrambled eggs in a restaurant. Eggs scrambled soft (my favorite) are less cooked, so the eggs are softer, moister, and in larger chunks. For a hearty morning meal, you can cut up leftover steak and baked potatoes, chop some fresh green onions, fry the meat, potatoes, and onions with lots of butter in a skillet, then scramble your eggs around them.

3 large eggs, well beaten
1½ tablespoons whole milk or half-and-half or cream

1 tablespoon butter (salted or unsalted) for cooking eggs

1 Melt butter in a cast iron skillet over high heat.
2 Combine eggs and milk and beat well.
3 Pour egg mixture into skillet. Let eggs sit without stirring for a few seconds, then stir and reduce heat to medium. For scrambled soft eggs, use a spatula to gently move the eggs around, flipping edges as needed, but not too much.
4 Continue to cook eggs over medium heat. Stir just enough to cook the eggs without turning them into tiny pieces.

Shrimp Omelettes

Total time: 15 minutes   Yields 1 omelette

This savory seafood omelette (again, one of my improvisations) cooks quickly, so it's essential that you have all ingredients prepared before you start cooking.

2 large eggs, well beaten
1½ tablespoons whole milk or half-and-half or cream
1 tablespoon butter (salted or unsalted)
1½ tablespoons tiny precooked shrimp, rinsed and patted dry

2 teaspoons green onions, finely chopped
1 tablespoon fresh cilantro, chopped
1½ tablespoons grated Monterey Jack cheese

1 Combine eggs and milk and beat well.
2 Heat a six-inch frying pan over high heat, then melt butter in pan.
3 Quickly pour egg mixture in pan and lift and rotate pan so bottom is covered. If the temperature is right, the egg mixture will make a sizzling sound when it hits the pan.
4 Immediately put shrimp on one half of the egg circle. Cook a few minutes. If there's too much liquid egg mixture in the middle, use a spatula to lift edges all around to let egg mixture run under.
5 When eggs are nearly cooked (about one to two minutes), sprinkle green onions, cilantro, and cheese over the shrimp half of circle.
6 Cook for another minute, then fold the plain half of the egg circle over the filled half, making a half circle.
7 Cook for 30 seconds more, then carefully flip and cook for another 30 seconds on the other side.
8 Serve immediately.

Sourdough Pancakes

Total time: 30 minutes   Yields about 24 medium pancakes

I f you're making sourdough bread, you have sourdough starter on hand. If you're not making sourdough bread, I encourage you to give it a whirl (see page 107). Once you get your sourdough starter going, you'll have sourdough starter for miles. Use some of it to make bread, yes, but try sourdough pancakes, too. I never got my mother's sourdough buckwheat pancakes recipe, but this one, adapted slightly from TastesofLizzyT.com, is delicious in its own right. My daughter never cared for pancakes until I made these sourdough pancakes for her. You can also make sourdough waffles with this recipe. When making sourdough pancakes or waffles, cook all the batter; the batter doesn't keep. Serve pancakes warm, buttered, with maple syrup or jam. You can freeze extra pancakes for later.

2 cups all-purpose flour
4 teaspoons baking powder
1 teaspoon baking soda
2 tablespoons granulated sugar
1 teaspoon salt
1 cup sourdough starter

1½ cups whole milk
2 large eggs, beaten
2 tablespoons vegetable oil
butter for cooking
butter, maple syrup, and jam
   for topping

1 Combine flour, baking powder, baking soda, sugar, and salt. Mix well. This recipe uses a lot of baking powder and you don't want pockets in the batter.
2 Add sourdough starter, milk, eggs, and oil. Mix until just barely combined. Lumps are okay.
3 Heat a griddle or cast iron skillet until hot, and melt some butter on the griddle. For each pancake, ladle about ¼ cup batter onto the griddle. Cook until bubbles form on top.
4 Flip each pancake once and cook a few more minutes or until light brown on the bottom. Never flip repeatedly. The TV shows that show people flipping their pancakes over and over have misled generations of cooks into making tough, dry pancakes.

Spicy Kielbasa

Total time: 1 hour   Yields about 25 to 30 2-inch patties

Kielbasa is a spicy yet delicate pork sausage. This is my own version. Normally, kielbasa recipes call for stuffing the results into casings, but I just form it into small round patties. (Some people call sausage patties "country style.") Since home-made sausage is made from younger and tenderer meat than commercial sausage, you'll notice a tremendous difference in flavor and texture. You can cook and eat this sausage immediately, refrigerate (keeps a few days), or freeze. This recipe calls for chile powder from New Mexico chiles, but you can experiment. What's the difference between chiles and chili powder? Chili powder is a blend of the dried powders of chile peppers, plus (often) other ingredients, like oregano, cumin, and paprika.

3 pounds pork shoulder
1 cup chopped onion
1½ tablespoons kosher salt
1 tablespoon coarsely ground black pepper
1 tablespoon red pepper flakes, crushed
1 teaspoon paprika

1 teaspoon New Mexico chile powder
½ teaspoon fine Himalayan pink salt
¼ teaspoon whole-leaf dried tarragon
¼ teaspoon cumin seed
⅛ teaspoon ground cinnamon
1⁄16 teaspoon ground cloves

1 Put the pork and onion through a ⅝-inch meat grinder plate. (Or have your butcher grind it for you.)
2 Mix meat with kosher salt and pepper.
3 In a small, dry skillet, toast pepper flakes, paprika, chile powder, and Himalayan salt over medium heat for 2 to 3 minutes.
4 Add pepper flake mixture to meat mixture.
5 Add tarragon, cumin, cinnamon, and cloves to meat mixture.
6 Knead the meat mixture thoroughly (about 10 minutes). Form into small patties.
7 To cook: fry or broil about 20 to 25 minutes.

Desserts

You can find many of my favorite dessert recipes in *Delectable Desserts*, the first volume in this cookbook series. But not all my favorites. Why? It's a question of quantity. I have multiple versions of some recipes—for example, I have many brownie recipes, each different, each equally delicious. Did I really need to include so many brownie recipes in *Delectable Desserts*? No matter how delicious each of them are? Maybe. But I decided the answer was "no."

But I still want to share those recipes, and I knew I'd include a desserts chapter in this volume of the *Delicious Connections* series. In this chapter, you'll find most of those favorites, including, yes, more delicious brownie recipes. With two exceptions, you won't find duplicates of any recipes from *Delectable Desserts*. After all, don't you feel a little taken advantage of when you buy a new cookbook and find that half the recipes were in the author's previous cookbook? I do, and I don't want to do that to my loyal readers/bakers.

The two exceptions are my perfect pie crust recipe (the savory version; see Perfect Savory Pie Crust on page 103). and a frosting recipe. In *Delectable Desserts*, I included many delicious frosting recipes (plus useful information about types of frostings) and I refer you to that cookbook for those recipes. But several recipes in this chapter are best with frosting, so I include one basic, versatile buttercream frosting from *Delectable Desserts* that you can dress up or down as you please.

Apricot Bars

Total time: 1 hour 10 minutes   Yields one 11- x 7-inch pan

F rances Buran shared this delicious classic recipe when we were working together at Borland in the late 1980s. (Frances is also responsible for sharing the original
version of my Steamed Bread Pudding recipe, which you can find in *Delectable Desserts*.) Although this recipe calls for apricot jam, you can use any jam you like, such as
blackberry, raspberry, strawberry, and so on. Use more or less jam as desired.

1½ cups all-purpose flour   ½ cup packed brown sugar
1½ cups rolled oats   ¾ cup unsalted butter
1 teaspoon baking powder   ¾ cup to 1½ cups apricot jam
¼ teaspoon salt

1   Combine flour, oats, baking powder, salt, and sugar.
2   Cut in butter until crumbly.
3   Put ⅔ of the crumb mix in an 11- x 7-inch pan.
4   Spread bottom crust with jam; top with remaining crumb mix.
5   Bake at 375° for about 35 minutes.
6   Remove from oven and cool 30 minutes.
7   Cut into bar-shaped sections (2-inch squares or 2-inch x 3-inch
    rectangles) and serve in pan, or remove bars to a plate.

Baked Egg Custard

Total time: 2 hours   Yields 10 servings

This classic custard makes an excellent low-fat, high-protein dessert, especially if you use skim milk. You can bake it in ramekins or one large dish; use six eggs if you are use one large dish. I've been making this recipe for so many decades, I've forgotten where I got it. It's possible it came from an old cookbook, or it might have been my mother's recipe.

1 quart skim milk or 1 pint
   whole milk and 1 pint cream
   or 1 quart half-and-half
5 large eggs (or 10 egg yolks)
⅔ cup granulated sugar

¼ teaspoon salt
½ teaspoon ground cinnamon
1 teaspoon vanilla extract
Freshly grated nutmeg

1 Preheat oven to 325°.
2 Butter 10 custard cups or one 13- x 9-inch pan.
3 Scald milk by bringing it to just under the boiling point (when bubbles start to form around the edges—180°). Set aside.
4 Beat eggs lightly with sugar, salt, cinnamon, and vanilla. Gradually stir in hot milk.
5 Pour custard into prepared custard cups or pan.
6 Sprinkle with nutmeg to taste, then set cups or pan in a larger shallow pan. Pour warm water into the outer pan (not into the custard!) to the depth of 1 inch.
7 Bake for about 1 hour or until a knife inserted midway between rim and outer edge comes out clean (like testing a pumpkin pie).
8 Remove from oven and remove custard from water bath. Cool to room temperature (about 30 minutes) and serve, or refrigerate 1 hour and serve chilled.

Baklava

Total time: Yields one 13- x 9-inch panful

Baklava is a Middle Eastern delight with ancient origins. Though the name we use today is from Ottoman Turkish, the Greeks and the Turks both claim it as their invention. In 160 BC in his *De agri cultura*, Cato the Elder, an ancient Roman statesman, scholar, orator, soldier, and author, presents what could well be the earliest extant recipe for baklava. If you've never tasted well-made baklava, it'll be a revelation. Properly made baklava has many alternating layers of phyllo (a very thin dough) and filling, and is far superior to anything you can buy at any bakery or restaurant. Yes, that's a bold statement, but I love baklava so much I sample it everywhere I go. Even in Middle Eastern restaurants and bakeries where I've been offered "the best baklava ever," it's always been disappointingly dry, with too many layers of dry phyllo and not enough layers of filling. I understand why I haven't found a good commercial baklava—making it the way I was taught takes more time, and maybe no commercial baker wants to bother. But baklava made right is many layers of deliciousness. This recipe is adapted from Eva Zane's excellent *Greek Cooking for the Gods* (101 Productions, 1970). For another favorite recipe, see Brandy Pecan Fig Baklava on page 135. Making baklava is easier if you have someone helping you—one person to create the layers, the other to carefully peel off the phyllo sheets and hand them to you and keep them covered with a dampened tea towel in between. If the instructions look complicated, take heart. I shared this recipe with a Facebook connection who had never made baklava. She said the instructions were perfect and the outcome flawless.

Baklava

1½ pounds almonds, coarsely chopped
1 pound walnuts, coarsely chopped
⅔ cup granulated sugar
2 teaspoons ground cinnamon

1 teaspoon ground allspice
1 pound unsalted butter, melted, plus ¼ cup for the pan
1 pound phyllo dough (14- x 9-inch sheets), thawed

Syrup

2 cups honey
2 cups water
2 cups granulated sugar

2 three-inch sticks cinnamon
5 whole cloves
1 teaspoon fresh orange zest

1 Heavily butter a 13- x 9-inch baking pan with the ¼ cup butter.
2 Wet a spotlessly clean cotton tea towel and wring it out well until it's only very slightly damp.

3 Combine almonds, walnuts, sugar, ground cinnamon, and allspice.

4 Remove phyllo from its container and spread the slightly dampened tea towel over the stack. (To keep phyllo from drying out.)

5 You need to do the next steps quickly. If you have help, have your helper hand you sheets while you layer and baste. Lay a sheet of phyllo in the buttered pan, with some of the sheet going up the sides. Baste sheet with melted butter. You don't need a lot of butter on each layer, but do your best to get full coverage.

6 Repeat until you have 12 sheets of buttered phyllo in the pan's bottom. Baste top layer. Keep phyllo sheets covered with dampened tea towel whenever you aren't removing a sheet from the stack.

7 Spread a thin layer of nut filling on top of the first 12 phyllo layers. It's okay to spread filling thinly—cumulatively, the filling will have a presence. Top with a phyllo sheet. Baste sheet with butter.

8 Spread another thin layer of filling. Top with a phyllo sheet. Baste sheet with butter.

9 Repeat step 8 until you've used up all filling.

10 For the final layers, spread a sheet of phyllo on the last layer of filling and baste with butter. Repeat with layers of phyllo until you're nearing the top of the pan or you've run out of phyllo, whichever comes first.

11 Cut baklava into even diamond shapes. The easiest way is to cut diagonal lines in one direction, then cut diagonal lines crossing the first set of lines. You should have about 28 diamonds (though the number depends on the size of your triangles).

12 Bake at 350° until golden brown (1 to 1½ hours).

13 While the baklava bakes, make the syrup. Combine honey, water, sugar, cinnamon sticks, whole cloves, and orange zest in a saucepan. Bring to a boil and simmer for 10 minutes.

14 Remove syrup from heat and set aside to cool.

15 When baklava is done baking, remove from oven. Strain syrup to remove cinnamon and cloves, and immediately pour syrup evenly over the top of the hot baklava.

16 Cool several hours before eating.

Bananas Foster

Total time: 10 minutes   Yields 2 servings

I used to buy a fried bananas dessert in a Malaysian restaurant in Tucson in the early 1980s. The proprietress coyly refused to share her recipe, saying it was a rare Malaysian specialty. She said she didn't want to share the recipe because she was afraid I'd stop coming to the restaurant. Then she closed her restaurant, making the point moot. In vain, I searched restaurants and cookbooks for something like her fried bananas recipe. At last, in July 1999, on my way to a white-water rafting trip on the Salmon River, I stopped at a small, casually elegant restaurant in Idaho called Danskin Station (alas, now closed), where they served the same dessert I'd often enjoyed in Tucson. The server told me it's a common recipe called Bananas Foster. She shared Danskin Station's version, which I've adapted to my family's tastes. I've since learned that in the early 1950s, Owen Brennan, owner of Brennan's Restaurant in New Orleans (it's still there), asked his chef Paul Blange to invent a banana dessert. To meet that challenge, Chef Blange invented Bananas Foster. (Name after Owen's friend, Richard Foster.) Sometimes people light the sauce on fire right before serving.

2 firm bananas, cut into bite-sized chunks
⅓ cup dark rum
2 tablespoons triple sec
¼ cup salted butter
¼ cup heavy cream
⅔ cup packed brown sugar
2 bowls vanilla ice cream

1 Combine bananas, rum, and triple sec. Set aside.
2 Melt butter in a large skillet over low heat. (Don't use high heat for this recipe.)
3 Stir in heavy cream and brown sugar and stir until the sugar dissolves.
4 Bring to a simmer. Stir constantly 2 to 4 minutes more until mixture is thickened and deep golden brown.
5 Stir in bananas and some of the soaking alcohol and cook until the bananas are tender.
6 If you want to ignite the sauce, pour ¼ cup rum over the bananas in the skillet and carefully set it alight. When the flames die, serve as described in the next step.
7 Divide the sauce over the two bowls of ice cream and serve immediately.

Brandy Pecan Fig Baklava

Total time: 2 hours   Yields one 13- x 9-inch panful

T his recipe, adapted from a Maker's Mark recipe, is one of our two favorite baklava recipes; the other (page 132) is plainer but still delicious; see that recipe for tips on making baklava. You can use the honey-maple syrup on pancakes or waffles.

Baklava

1½ cups dried figs, finely chopped
5 tablespoons brandy
3 cups pecans, lightly toasted and finely chopped
1 teaspoon ground cinnamon
¼ cup granulated sugar

¼ cup honey
1½ cups unsalted butter, melted, plus ¼ cup for the pan
1 pound phyllo dough (14- x 9-inch sheets), thawed

Honey-Maple Syrup

¼ cup sugar
¼ cup honey

¾ cup maple syrup
½ cup water

1 Butter a 13- x 9-inch baking pan very well with the ¼ cup butter.
2 Wet a spotlessly clean cotton tea towel and wring it out well until it's only very slightly damp.
3 Combine figs and brandy in a medium mixing bowl. Let stand until figs have soaked up most of the brandy.
4 Add pecans, cinnamon, ¼ cup sugar, and ¼ cup honey to figs.
5 Remove phyllo from its container and spread a slightly dampened tea towel over it. (To keep phyllo from drying out.)
6 You need to do the next steps quickly. If you have help, have your helper hand you sheets while you layer and baste. Lay a sheet of phyllo in the buttered pan, with some of the sheet going up the sides. Baste sheet with melted butter. You don't need a lot of butter on each layer, but do your best to get full coverage.
7 Repeat until you have 12 sheets in the pan's bottom. Baste top layer. Keep phyllo sheets covered with the dampened tea towel whenever you aren't removing a sheet from the stack.
8 Spread a thin layer of fig mixture on top of the first 12 phyllo layers. It's okay to spread filling very thinly—cumulatively, the filling will have a presence. Top with a phyllo sheet. Baste sheet with butter.
9 Spread another thin layer of filling. Top with a phyllo sheet. Baste sheet with butter.

10 Repeat step 9 until you've used up filling.

11 For the final layers, spread a sheet of phyllo on the last fig layer and baste with butter. Repeat with just layers of phyllo until you're nearing the top of the pan or you've run out of phyllo, whichever comes first.

12 Cut baklava into even diamond shapes. The easiest way is to cut diagonal lines in one direction, then cut diagonal lines crossing the first set of lines. You should have about 28 diamonds.

13 Bake at 350° until golden brown (1 to 1½ hours).

14 While baklava bakes, make topping. In a small saucepan, combine ¼ cup sugar and ¼ cup honey with maple syrup and water. Bring to a boil, then reduce heat to medium and simmer 5 minutes. Set aside to cool.

15 When baklava is done baking, remove from the oven and immediately pour the syrup evenly over the top.

16 Cool several hours before eating.

Brownie Madness

Total time: 45 minutes   Yields 1 panful of brownies

My friend Chris invented this recipe when he was a young teen. He was alone in the kitchen and threw together whatever he could find in the cupboards. His recipe uses premade mixes, which I normally don't use, but his story and recipe are both charming and fun. I love imagining a 13-year-old boy going wild in the kitchen and coming up with such an inventive and all-inclusive recipe.

- **1** box of your favorite brownie mix
- **1** packet chocolate instant breakfast mix
- **1** heaping tablespoon of Dutch process cocoa
- **1** packet chocolate pudding mix
- Milk or chocolate milk (see instructions for quantity)
- **1** egg in addition to what the box calls for

- **¼** cup chocolate syrup
- **1** tablespoon honey
- However much oil or melted butter the box calls for
- **2** cups shredded coconut (toasted or not, your choice)
- **1** cup raisins
- **1** cup sliced almonds
- **1** cup toasted pecans
- **1** cup semisweet chocolate chips or dark chocolate chunks

1   Pour brownie mix into a medium mixing bowl.
2   Stir in breakfast mix, cocoa, and pudding mix, and mix well.
3   Substitute milk for the amount of water the box calls for, then add 1¾ cups more to adjust for the additional dry ingredients.
4   Bake according to the box directions.

Chocolate Buttermilk Cake

Total time: 50 minutes   Yields one 13- x 9-inch cake

This classic recipe makes a deliciously chocolate-y and moist cake. Because this recipe uses buttermilk, you can use either natural or Dutch process cocoa. The rule of thumb for cocoa in cakes: Use the naturally acidic natural cocoa in recipes calling for baking soda; use the more neutral Dutch process cocoa for recipes calling for baking powder. Use either type of cocoa in recipes using acidic ingredients like buttermilk or sour cream. For a fuller explanation, see *Delectable Desserts*.) A tip for making light cakes: never use an electric mixer; always beat batter by hand. You can frost the cake or dust it lightly with powdered sugar.

2 cups all-purpose flour	¼ cup cocoa
2 cups granulated sugar	½ cup buttermilk
1 teaspoon baking soda	2 large eggs
1 cup unsalted butter	1 teaspoon vanilla extract
1 cup water	

1 Preheat oven to 375°. Grease and flour a 13- x 9-inch pan.
2 Mix flour, sugar, and baking soda; set aside.
3 In a large saucepan, combine butter, water, and cocoa. Bring to a boil, then remove from heat.
4 Add flour mixture, buttermilk, eggs, and vanilla to chocolate mixture. Beat until well mixed.
5 Pour batter into pan. Bake for 20 to 30 minutes or until cake tests done.
6 Cool in pan. You can then either remove the cake from the pan or leave it there.

Chocolate Chip Brownie Cookies

Total time: 1 hour   Yields 3 dozen

This recipe was a happy mistake in my kitchen. It was supposed to be chocolate chip cookies, but a printout of one of my brownie recipes was also on the kitchen counter, and at some point, the cooking process jumped from the cookie recipe to the brownie recipe. At first I thought I'd have to throw out the batter and start over, but in the spirit of experimentation (and being loath to waste food), I baked the batter as cookies, and the results were perfect.

12 ounces (2 cups) chocolate chips
1 cup unsalted butter, softened
3/4 cup granulated sugar
3/4 cup packed dark brown sugar

2¼ cups all-purpose flour
1 teaspoon baking soda
½ teaspoon salt
2 eggs, lightly beaten
1 cup chopped walnuts

1 Preheat oven to 350°.
2 In a double boiler, combine 1 cup chocolate chips with butter and sugars. Melt chocolate over simmering water, stirring often. Use a wooden spoon to stir.
3 Remove from heat.
4 Combine flour, baking soda, and salt in a medium mixing bowl.
5 Add half the flour mixture to chocolate mixture. Mix well.
6 Add eggs. Mix well.
7 Add remaining flour mixture. Mix well. The batter will be quite stiff. Set aside to cool.
8 When the batter is cool, fold in the remaining chocolate chips and the walnuts.
9 Shape into 1-inch balls and place on an ungreased cookie sheet.
10 Bake for 10 to 12 minutes. When the tops begin to crack,the cookies are done. Remove from oven and place cookies on a wire cooling rack.

Chocolate Chip Coconut Bars

Total time: Yields one 12- x 8-inch panful

Billie (I don't remember her last name after all these decades), a co-worker in the early 1980s, shared her recipe for these bars, which she brought to a potluck one day. Billie was savvy and kind, and perhaps those are the most important things to remember about her.

2 cups all-purpose flour
1 tablespoon baking powder
½ teaspoon salt
2 tablespoons butter
2¼ cups packed brown sugar

4 large eggs, lightly beaten
1 teaspoon vanilla extract
12 ounces (2 cups) semisweet
   chocolate chips
1½ cups shredded coconut

1   Combine flour, baking powder, and salt, then cut in butter until well combined.
2   Stir in sugar and mix well.
3   Add eggs and vanilla and mix well.
4   Add chocolate chips and coconut. The mix will look dry, but that's okay.
5   Spread in a 12- x 8-inch baking pan.
6   Bake at 350° for 30 minutes. Check after 15 minutes and cover with foil if needed to prevent sides from over-browning.
7   Remove from oven, cut, and cool.

Chocolate Mousse

Total time: 1½ hours   Yields 8 to 10 servings

C hocolate mousse is possibly my favorite dessert, at least when it's in front of me. But in years of testing many recipes, I'd never found a recipe that produced what I consider a good chocolate mousse. (Light and fluffy, but with a definite dark chocolate presence.) It turns out the problem came down to ingredients. I was avoiding all recipes that called for gelatin and was trying to get good results from recipes that called for eggs. Those all failed big time. When I decided to try recipes that relied on gelatin, I found Alton Brown's almost-perfect recipe on FoodNetwork.com. I ditched the coffee and rum the original recipe called for, and rewrote the instructions for ease. Gelatins can vary in effectiveness; I use Knox brand. You only need the tiniest amount. After chilling, let mousse stand at room temperature 20 to 30 minutes.

1¾ cups heavy cream
1 teaspoon granulated gelatin

12 ounces (2 cups) semisweet chocolate chips
4 tablespoons unsalted butter

1   Chill mixing bowl and whisk.
2   Sprinkle gelatin over ¼ cup of the cream in a tiny saucepan. Let stand 10 minutes (to bloom). The gelatin will wrinkle the top of the cream. Don't be alarmed.
3   Using a double boiler, melt chocolate chips and butter, stirring constantly. Remove from heat and scrape chocolate into a cool, medium mixing bowl. Set aside to cool. Don't cool completely, or the chocolate will harden too much.
4   After 10 minutes, carefully warm gelatin and cream over low heat for a few minutes. Do not scald! Just get it barely hot.
5   Stir gelatin mixture into cooled chocolate. Stir until chocolate is smooth. Set aside.
6   In chilled mixing bowl, whip remaining 1½ cups cream to medium peaks, about 3 minutes on high. Don't overwhip.
7   Stir about a fourth of the whipped cream into chocolate. This is to make the chocolate less dense so the remaining whipped cream can do its mousse magic.
8   Fold in remaining whipped cream in two to four batches. It's okay to have visible streaks of whipped cream at the end.
9   Distribute mousse into small serving bowls or glasses and chill 1 hour or until set. Alternatively, cover mixing bowl with plastic wrap and chill the entire batch in one bowl. The mousse gets much firmer as it sits, though, so serving it out of one bowl can be challenging.

Chocolate Pancakes

Total time: 1 hour   Yields about 12 pancakes

The chocolate pancakes offered at our local pancake house don't have nearly enough chocolate or chocolate chips for dedicated chocolate lovers like me. My friend AJ came up with a version of this recipe as a gift for me in the mid-1990s, and we've been indulging ourselves ever since. I streamlined and simplified his recipe, though the essential ingredient— chocolate, and lots of it—remains the same. You can substitute sour milk or buttermilk for the fresh milk; if you do, omit the baking powder and substitute 1 teaspoon baking soda. Melt the butter in the frying pan you'll be cooking the pancakes in.

1 cup unsalted butter, melted
6 tablespoons cocoa
2 tablespoons granulated sugar
2 cups whole milk (you may need more)
1½ cups all-purpose flour

2 teaspoons baking powder
12 ounces (2 cups) chocolate chips (mini morsels work great)
2 cups whipped cream
1 cup powdered sugar

1 Place melted butter in a medium bowl.
2 Add cocoa and sugar to butter, with enough milk to make it creamy.
3 In a separate bowl, combine flour and baking powder and stir well.
4 Add flour mixture to wet ingredients.
5 Add remaining milk to make the entire mixture quite liquid.
6 Ladle batter on a hot buttered griddle or skillet to make 2-inch circles. Cook until delicately browned; turn and brown on other side. It'll be hard to see the browning since the pancakes are chocolate.
7 Serve with lots of chocolate chips and butter underneath the pancakes, between each pancake, and on top of each stack of pancakes. Top it all with whipped cream or powdered sugar.

Chocolate Sauerkraut Cake

Total time: 50 minutes   Yields one 13- x 9-inch cake

People's mouths pucker when they hear that I make this cake with sauerkraut. But they change their minds if they're brave enough to try a taste of this moist, rich, flavorful cake. Most of the sauerkraut is alchemically transformed in the cooking process. The coconut flavoring leaves the impression that the few remaining strands of sauerkraut are coconut. Some day I may try this recipe with my homemade kimchi.

1 cup packed brown sugar
1 cup granulated sugar
2/3 cup unsalted butter, softened
2 teaspoons baking soda
1/2 cup hot water
2/3 cup sauerkraut
1/2 teaspoon coconut flavoring

1 teaspoon vanilla extract
2 large eggs, lightly beaten
2 1/2 cups all-purpose flour
1/2 cup cocoa (natural or Dutch process)
1/4 teaspoon salt
1 cup cold water

1 Grease a 13- x 9-inch baking pan.
2 Cream together brown sugar, granulated sugar, and butter.
3 In a separate bowl, dissolve baking soda in hot water.
4 Add sauerkraut, coconut flavoring, vanilla extract, eggs, flour, cocoa, salt, hot water with the baking soda in it, and cold water.
5 Pour batter into prepared baking pan and bake at 350 degrees for 25 to 35 minutes or until cake tests done.
6 Remove from oven and set aside to cool.

Clotted Cream

Total time: 1 day   Yields 1½ cups

C lotted cream is heavy cream transformed into a thick, delicious spread, traditionally used on scones in the British Isles. "Clotted" may sound horrible, but
it's so delicious. If you're on the fence, give it a try. The worst that can happen is you'll
waste a quart of cream. (So maybe try this recipe with just 2 cups cream.) This recipe
makes clotted cream that's close to the clotted cream my daughter and I often enjoyed when traveling in Cornwall and Devonshire in 1999. When I returned to the US, I
tried many methods to make clotted cream, but the results were always a spectacular
waste of perfectly good cream. The jarred stuff I found in specialty shops was a trav-
esty. Eventually, someone came up with a process using an electric pressure cooker,
shared the recipe on the internet, and suddenly everyone was making clotted cream.
My daughter perfected the process and can now make flawless clotted cream every
time. **Important**! Your pressure cooker *must* have a yogurt setting. Refrigerated, the
clotted cream keeps for two to three days.

> **1** quart (4 cups) heavy cream,
>   *not* ultra-pasteurized
>   (regular pasteurization is
>   okay)

1 Pour heavy cream into your pressure cooker's removable pot.
2 Put lid on. Venting or sealing doesn't matter since you aren't using
   the pressure cooker function.
3 Set yogurt setting to boil.
4 The pressure cooker should beep when the cream comes to a boil.
   When it does, switch over to the keep warm setting and let cream
   sit in the pressure cooker on that setting for 10 hours.
5 Remove pot from pressure cooker and cover pot with a clean cloth
   towel or a lid.
6 Set pot on a counter to cool to room temperature (2 to 3 hours). The
   cream may have a light crust on top, but don't worry if it doesn't.
   Have faith. Resist the urge to poke at the cream.
7 Once cream is at room temperature, put pot in refrigerator, still
   covered, for another ten hours.
8 After ten hours, remove pot from refrigerator. Carefully scrape off
   thickened top and store in a container with a lid. That's the clotted
   cream part. There will be some thin liquid underneath the thickened
   top—save that for making biscuits, scones, scrambled eggs, or any
   cooked item that normally uses milk, half-and-half, or cream.

Company Brownies

Total time: 45 minutes   Yields one 13- x 9-inch pan

This King Arthur Flour recipe makes the perfect brownie. The texture is fudgy, but not too fudgy, and, made correctly, the top is delicately crisp, shiny, and slightly rumpled. I call this recipe "Company Brownies" because the results are intensely rich—one small brownie is enough to satisfy all but the most inveterate chocolate lover, and the brownies don't keep well. So you need guests to share them with to help consume them before they go stale. If you make these and don't have company, enjoy them while hot, then use the remainder to make a truly decadent steamed bread pudding using the recipe from my *Delectable Desserts* cookbook.

4 large eggs, lightly beaten
1¼ cups Dutch process cocoa
1 teaspoon salt
1 teaspoon baking powder
1 tablespoon vanilla extract

1 cup unsalted butter
2¼ cups granulated sugar
1½ cups all-purpose flour
12 ounces (2 cups) chocolate chips

1 Preheat oven to 350°. Grease a 13- x 9-inch baking pan.

2 Beat eggs with cocoa, salt, baking powder, and vanilla until smooth (about 1 minute). Use a fork, not a whisk. The batter at this point is quit thick and will clog your whisk.

3 Melt butter in a 10-inch skillet over medium heat.

4 Gradually stir sugar into butter, giving the sugar time to incorporate with the butter before adding more. Continue to heat until mixture is hot (about 110°F to 120°F), but not bubbling; it'll get shiny as you stir it. You're heating the mixture to this point to dissolve more of the sugar. That helps produce the shiny crust on your brownies.

5 Add hot butter/sugar mixture to egg/cocoa mixture. Stir until smooth.

6 Stir in flour and chocolate chips, and stir until smooth. The batter will be stiff.

7 Spoon batter into prepared baking pan. Spread batter until it's evenly spread and fills the corners.

8 Bake 28 to 32 minutes, until a toothpick inserted into the center comes out clean, or with just a few moist crumbs clinging to it. The brownies should be set on the edges, and the center should look moist, but not uncooked.

9 Remove from oven and cool pan on a wire rack.

Crispy Cookies

Total time: 45 minutes   Yields about 3½ dozen

In 2020, my cousin Marcia shared her mom's (my aunt Gayle) recipe. Marcia said my aunt "would make these cookies whenever we took a driving vacation since they held up very well. Everyone seems to like them." Whether I ever tasted them growing up (in the 1950s and 60s), I don't remember, though my siblings and I often visited our aunt and uncle, so probably. Inexplicably (because of COVID-19, I'm assuming), crispy rice cereal was sold out at my local grocery store for months, so I couldn't test the recipe. I finally turned to ordering from my trusty Target. You can add chocolate chips or chopped nuts in addition to or instead of the cranberries. The cookies are soft when warm and crispy when cool. Cool completely before storing.

2 cups all-purpose flour
1 teaspoon baking soda
½ teaspoon baking powder
½ teaspoon salt
½ cup unsalted butter, softened
1 cup packed light brown sugar
1 cup granulated sugar

2 large eggs, lightly beaten
1 teaspoon vanilla extract
2 cups crispy rice cereal
2 cups oats
1 cup unsweetened shredded coconut
1 cup dried cranberries

1   Preheat oven to 350°.
2   Prepare a baking sheet by lining it.
3   Mix flour, baking soda, baking powder, and salt. Set aside.
4   Cream butter and shortening with brown and granulated sugars until well blended.
5   Stir eggs and vanilla into butter/sugar mix.
6   Add flour mix to butter/sugar mix.
7   Add crispy rice cereal, oats, coconut, and cranberries to batter. Mix until just blended.
8   Drop by tablespoons onto prepared baking sheet.
9   Bake 8 to 12 minutes.
10 Remove from oven and cool cookies on wire racks.

Date Bars

Total time: 50 minutes   Yields about 35 1½-inch square bars

I love the intense date, orange juice, brown sugar, and oat flavors in this bar. And it's so simple! You cook down the dates with orange juice and sugar until you have a thick paste, then you layer that paste between two layers of oatmeal crust. Because dates are naturally sweet, you need little added sugar, so don't pack the brown sugar either for the filling or the crust. Soften the butter until it's almost melted. I adapted this recipe from allrecipes.com. That recipe's filling was delicious, but the crust was not to my taste. I changed amounts and instructions to suit my ideal date bar scenario. These bars keep and ship well. If shipping them, wrap each bar individually with plastic wrap, then put about eight each in Ziploc bags. Pad the bags well in the shipping box.

Date Filling

1 pound pitted dates, coarsely chopped
¼ cup brown sugar

⅔ cup orange juice
zest of 1 orange
2 teaspoons vanilla extract

Oatmeal Crust

1½ cups rolled oats
¾ cup all-purpose flour
⅓ cup brown sugar

¾ teaspoon baking soda
¼ teaspoon salt
1 cup unsalted butter, softened

1   Preheat oven to 350°. Lightly grease an 11- x 7-inch baking pan.
2   Combine dates, ¼ cup brown sugar, orange juice, and orange zest in a medium saucepan. Cook over low heat, stirring occasionally, until dates have softened, absorbed the liquid, and mixture is a sticky paste, about 10 minutes. Remove from heat.
3   Stir in vanilla extract.
4   While dates are cooking, in a medium mixing bowl, combine oats, flour, ⅓ cup brown sugar, baking soda, and salt.
5   Work butter into crust mix. You want the mix to be moist, not dry.
6   Lightly press ½ of the crust mix into bottom of prepared pan.
7   Bake bottom crust 10 to 15 minutes or until golden brown.
8   Remove crust from oven and immediately spread date mixture evenly over crust. You may need to use a spatula or your hands.
9   Pat remaining crust mix evenly over top of date mixture.
10 Bake until top is golden brown, 20 to 25 minutes.
11 Remove from oven and cool on a wire rack or in freezer (about 1 hour). Once cooled, slice into bars.

Duntemann's Pumpkin Pie

Total time: 1 hour 20 minutes   Yields one 9-inch pie

Jeff and Carol Duntemann kindly shared their tasty pumpkin pie recipe with me in the later 1980s. Before then, I'd never found a pumpkin pie recipe I liked. Maybe it's the half-and-half in this recipe rather than the more usual condensed milk. When serving, bury each slice in whipped cream. For a nice touch, sprinkle grated nutmeg and ground cinnamon lightly over the whipped cream.

2 eggs, lightly beaten
1 can (16 ounces) pumpkin purée
3/4 cup granulated sugar
1/2 teaspoon salt

1 teaspoon ground cinnamon
1/2 teaspoon ground ginger
1/4 teaspoon ground cloves
1 cup half-and-half
1 unbaked 9-inch pie shell

1 Preheat oven to 425°.
2 Blending well after each addition, combine eggs, pumpkin, sugar, salt, cinnamon, ginger, cloves, and half and half.
3 Pour batter into unbaked pie shell.
4 Bake 15 minutes at 425°.
5 Reduce heat to 350° and bake another 45 minutes, or until a knife inserted in the center of the pie comes out clean.
6 Remove from oven. Cool completely before serving.

Flourless Chocolate Cake

Total time: 1 hour   Yields one 8-inch single-layer cake

Because my daughter must avoid gluten, I was happy to find this gluten-free recipe, which I've adapted, on the King Arthur Flour website. (My changes: more sugar, more eggs, more cocoa, no salt, no espresso powder). It's *intensely* chocolate. A small slice goes a long way. Serve warm, with vanilla ice cream, or chilled later.

Cake

6 ounces bittersweet chocolate, roughly chopped, or 1 cup bittersweet chocolate chips

½ cup unsalted butter

1 cup granulated sugar

¾ cup Dutch process cocoa powder

4 large eggs, lightly beaten

Ganache

½ cup heavy cream

1 cup semisweet chocolate chips

1   Preheat oven to 350°. Grease an 8-inch round cake pan very well.
2   Heat bittersweet chocolate and butter together. (I use a double boiler.) Stir occasionally until chocolate and butter are completely melted. Remove from heat.
3   Combine sugar and cocoa. Add to melted chocolate and stir until combined.
4   Add eggs to chocolate mixture and mix well.
5   Pour batter into prepared pan. Bake until just set in the middle and a thin crust forms, 25 to 30 minutes. To test for doneness, insert a butter knife halfway between the center and the sides of the cake. It should come out clean. (Or bake until 200° in the center.)
6   Remove from oven, then cool cake in pan 5 minutes. Remove from pan. Invert onto a plate, then invert again if you wish.
7   While the cake cools, make ganache.

- Place chocolate chips in a heatproof bowl.
- Heat heavy cream in a small saucepan until fine bubbles form on the edges, just a few minutes.
- Pour cream over chocolate chips. Let sit 5 minutes, then stir until silky and glossy.

8   Pour ganache over the completely cooled cake and smooth. Give it time to set (several hours at room temperature).

Koláčky

Total time: 30 minutes   Yields about 1½ dozen 2-inch cookies

Koláčky (koh-LAH-chee) are slightly sweet Eastern European cookies made with cream cheese or sometimes sour cream. I first tasted them in high school in the 1970s when a friend (whose parents were from Poland) brought some of her mother's cookies to school. I asked for the recipe and her mother gladly shared it, typed neatly on an index card. I thought I'd lost the card, but found it again while selecting recipes for this cookbook. These cookies are great with tea or coffee.

1½ cups all-purpose flour
½ teaspoon baking powder
1 tablespoon granulated sugar
8 ounces cream cheese,
  softened

½ cup butter, softened
1 large egg yolk
1 tablespoon whole milk
½ cup jam, any flavor you like

1   Prepare a baking sheet by lining it.
2   Combine flour, baking powder, and sugar. Set aside.
3   In a separate bowl, cream together cream cheese and butter.
4   Add egg yolk and milk to cream cheese and butter. Mix well.
5   Stir flour mix into cream cheese mix. Stir until you have a smooth, silky, somewhat wet dough.
6   Pull dough from bowl and form a ball with your hands. Pat ball into a flattened circle on a floured surface.
7   Roll dough out to about ¼ inch thickness. Cut with a 2-inch biscuit cutter. Alternatively, when you are shaping the dough, form into desired shapes and sizes by hand.
8   Lay cookies on prepared baking sheet. Press a thumb into center of each cookie.
9   Fill each thumb print with ½ to 1 teaspoon jam. Some people cut out squares, fill with jam, then fold the opposite corners over the jam.
10 Bake at 400° for 8 to 10 minutes. Watch carefully; the jam may run off the cookies. While baking, the cookies puff up to about double but stay pale; don't let them brown.

Lemon Caraway Cakes

Total time: 30 minutes   Yields about 2 dozen

Although the recipe's name says "cakes," these are cookies. The recipe, which dates to the late 1970s, was in my collection of recipes on index cards I'd carefully stored and hauled around with me through many, many moves. Researching this recipe for this cookbook, I found that something like it dates back more than 200 years. (See "Desart Cakes" by Alyssa Connell, *Cooking in the Archives*, November 20, 2014. "Desart" isn't a typo—it's just an old spelling.) I don't remember the origin of this recipe, though the whole wheat pastry flour is a clue, as I was experimenting with making sweets using whole wheat flour in the late 1970s. These cookies are great with tea.

½ cup unsalted butter, softened

⅔ cup honey

1 lemon, zested and juiced

2 large eggs, lightly beaten

2¼ cups whole wheat pastry flour or all-purpose flour

1 tablespoon caraway seed

2 teaspoons ground allspice

1 pinch salt

1 Prepare a baking sheet by lining or greasing it.
2 Cream butter until fluffy.
3 Add honey to butter and mix well.
4 Add lemon zest and juice to butter/honey mixture.
5 Mix in eggs, flour, caraway, allspice, and salt. Stir until mixed
6 Drop by teaspoonfuls onto prepared baking sheet and flatten slightly.
7 Bake at 350° for 10 to 12 minutes or until golden brown.

Lemon Crisps

Total time: 4 hours   Yields 7 dozen 2-inch cookies

This recipe makes a thin, flat cookie delicately flavored with lemon. I'm not a lemon fan and I love these cookies. The lemon zest must be fresh, not dried.

3 cups all-purpose flour
1 teaspoon baking powder
½ teaspoon baking soda
½ teaspoon salt
1 cup butter, softened
1¼ cups granulated sugar, plus extra to sprinkle on top

2 large eggs
½ teaspoon lemon extract
½ teaspoon vanilla extract
zest of one large lemon (1 to 2 tablespoons)
2 cups rolled oats, uncooked
½ cup sour cream

1 Prepare baking sheets by lining with parchment paper or silicone mats.
2 Combine flour, baking powder, baking soda and salt. Set aside.
3 Cream butter and sugar together.
4 Add eggs, lemon extract, vanilla extract, and lemon zest to butter and sugar mixture. Beat well.
5 Add flour mixture to butter and sugar mixture. Stir well.
6 Alternately add oats and sour cream to batter, blending well after each addition.
7 Cover dough and chill 3 hours.
8 Roll dough out on a lightly floured board to a thickness of ¼ inch. Cut with a floured 2- or 3-inch round cookie cutter.
9 Place cookies about 2 inches apart on prepared baking sheets.
10 Lightly sprinkle each cookie with granulated sugar if you want.
11 Bake at 375° for 10 to 12 minutes or until the cookies are just starting to brown on the edges. Remove from oven and place cookies on a wire rack immediately (so they don't keep cooking on the bottom).

Mascarpone Custard

Total time: 10 minutes plus 1 hour   Yields 6 servings
chilling time

When my daughter and I attended *Othello*, performed by the Royal Shake-speare Company in Stratford-upon-Avon in 1999, we enjoyed a dinner included with our tickets. The dessert, which they called *fiori della notte* (in Italian, "flowers of the night"), was so fantastic, we ordered seconds. It was a soft, delicious, not-too-sweet custard with a pool of slightly thickened chocolate sauce in one corner. The wait staff couldn't divulge the recipe, of course, but they hinted that mascarpone was involved. Mascarpone is essentially Italian cream cheese, though it's softer and a tiny bit sweeter than American cream cheese. Over the years, I tried to duplicate the recipe, but never came close. Until, that is, I was inspired to search online for mascarpone custard. I found (and tried) many recipes online; many were bogus, as is often the case with online recipes. The one I found on TheRealItalianFood.com, which I've adapted for this recipe, was not only *not* bogus, it was fantastic. In this recipe, I've done my best to replicate the *fiori della notte*, but you can also leave out the chocolate and serve the custard with fresh fruit, or use just the custard in tiramisu.

Mascarpone Custard

2 large eggs, separated
6 tablespoons granulated
    sugar

2 teaspoons vanilla extract
16 ounces mascarpone

Chocolate Sauce

¾ cup semisweet dark
    chocolate

3 tablespoons cream
1 teaspoon butter

1 Beat egg yolks with sugar until well blended, about 3 minutes. Use a fork, not a whisk or stand mixer.
2 Add vanilla and beat a few seconds.
3 Add mascarpone. Beat until creamy and smooth, about 5 minutes.
4 Whip egg whites until they stand in stiff peaks.
5 Fold egg whites into the mascarpone mix.
6 Pour custard into individual serving dishes (ramekins or large martini glasses). Chill 30 minutes.
7 Make chocolate sauce by melting chocolate with cream and butter. Stir until smooth.
8 Pour a few teaspoons chocolate sauce onto each dish of custard.
9 Chill another 30 minutes, then serve.

Marshmallow Brownies

Total time: 1 hour   Yields one 13- x 9-inch pan

These brownies have a wonderfully rich fudgy bottom layer, a middle layer of marshmallows, and a frosting top. You make the recipe in three stages: first, you mix and bake the batter, then you add the marshmallows, then you spread frosting over everything. You can use either natural or Dutch process cocoa in this recipe. For a variation, spread 1 cup peanut butter on the middle layer and cover with the mini marshmallows before baking the second time, and skip the frosting.

Bottom Layer

4 ounces unsweetened chocolate	1 cup all-purpose flour
2 cups unsalted butter	1/8 teaspoon salt
2 cups granulated sugar, divided equally	4 large eggs, lightly beaten
	1 cup chopped walnuts

Middle Layer

3 cups mini marshmallows

Top Layer (Frosting)

9 tablespoons cocoa	1 teaspoon vanilla extract
1/2 cup buttermilk	4 cups powdered sugar

1 Lightly butter a 13- x 9-inch baking pan.
2 Place chocolate and 1 cup butter in a medium saucepan or a double boiler. Melt over low heat, stirring often. Remove from heat when butter is melted.
3 In a separate bowl, combine granulated sugar, flour, and salt.
4 Add flour mixture to chocolate mixture.
5 Add eggs and nuts.
6 Pour batter into prepared baking pan. Bake at 350° for 25 to 30 minutes, or until a clean wooden toothpick inserted in center comes out clean.
7 While batter is baking, make frosting. Combine cocoa, buttermilk, and 1 cup butter in a medium saucepan (you can use the same one you used to melt the chocolate). Cook over low heat, stirring often, until butter is melted and everything is well blended. Remove from heat.
8 Transfer cocoa/buttermilk mixture to a large mixing bowl. Add vanilla extract.

9 Slowly blend in powdered sugar until frosting is smooth. Set aside until you take brownie base out of the oven.

10 When you remove brownie base from the oven, quickly cover surface with marshmallows.

11 Gently pour and spread frosting over marshmallows until you've completely covered the marshmallows. (This step is tricky, because whatever tool you're using to spread the frosting will pull the marshmallows around with the frosting.)

12 Set aside until cool enough to eat.

Mom's Vanilla Ice Cream

Total time: 3 hours   Yields 2 quarts

This was my mother Jean's own custard-based vanilla ice cream recipe. She used to make it for the Fourth of July, and my brothers and I would take turns turning the crank, starting with me (the youngest) turning while it was easy, and ending with my oldest brother Norm turning as the ice cream hardened. Because my mother never wrote down her recipe, I watched her make the custard one time and recorded quantities, ingredients, and instructions. You can prepare the custard a day in advance. These instructions are for making ice cream with an old-fashioned, crank-style ice cream maker, though you can use a modern ice cream maker.

6 large or extra large eggs	2½ pints heavy cream
1 scant cup granulated sugar	1 quart half-and-half
3 cups whole milk	lots of ice cubes
2 teaspoons vanilla extract	rock salt

1   Beat eggs with a fork until pale.
2   Add sugar and milk to eggs, then cook over medium heat, stirring constantly, until mixture coats a spoon.
3   Stir in vanilla.
4   Cool custard in pan, then refrigerate until it is time to make ice cream.
5   When ready to make ice cream, pour custard into your ice cream maker's freezer can.
6   Add whipping cream and half-and-half. Mix well. Be sure to leave room for the mixture to expand!
7   Put paddle into freezer can and place lid on top. Place freezer can into your ice cream maker.
8   Pack your ice cream maker with ice and rock salt according to the manufacturer's directions, then start cranking (or turn the motor on). Crank or run your machine until the motor starts to run more slowly or until crank is hard to turn.
9   Stop. Carefully lift the lid and remove paddle, then cover the opening of the can with plastic wrap or foil. Replace lid.
10 Put into the freezer or back into the ice cream maker with plenty of ice and rock salt and chill until it is of eating consistency.

Moo-Less Chocolate Pie

Total time: 3 hours

Yields one 9-inch pie

Made from tofu, this vegan pie (Alton Brown's recipe) is surprisingly delicious. It doesn't keep well, so make it when you have enough company to consume it all in one evening. If you're wondering about the chocolate wafer cookies, that's a cook's generic term for Nabisco's Famous chocolate wafer cookies. They come in a narrow, yellow, cardboard box with a clear cellophane wrapping. Most grocery stores carry them. Nutritionally, they're not great, but they're the only game in town unless you make your own.

Chocolate Wafer Crust

6½ ounces chocolate wafer cookies, crushed to a fine crumb

1 tablespoon granulated sugar
3 ounces unsalted butter, melted

Filling

12 ounces (2 cups) semisweet chocolate chips
⅓ cup coffee liqueur

1 teaspoon vanilla extract
1 pound silken tofu, drained
1 tablespoon honey

1 Combine crushed cookies and sugar and mix well.
2 Stir in melted butter.
3 Make crust by pressing crushed cookie mix into a 9-inch pie pan, covering bottom and sides.
4 Bake crust at 350° until crust appears dry, 18 to 20 minutes. Remove from oven and cool completely, about 1 hour.
5 Melt chocolate chips with liqueur and vanilla, stirring often. Use a double boiler if you have one; otherwise, watch carefully so you don't burn the chocolate.
6 Mix together tofu, chocolate mixture, and honey. Stir until smooth. (A food processor or stand mixer will help with this step.) Pour filling into cooled crust and refrigerate 2 hours or until filling is firm.

Orange Coffee Cake

Total time: 45 minutes   Yields two 8-inch loaf pans

nother recipe I've had for so long that I don't remember where I first got it. This coffee cake recipe is delicious with hot black tea or coffee.

Cake

4 cups all-purpose flour
4 teaspoons baking powder
1½ teaspoons baking soda
2 teaspoons salt
2 large eggs

1 cup granulated sugar
2 tablespoons fresh orange
   zest
1½ cups orange juice
1 cup unsalted butter, melted

Topping

¼ cup unsalted butter, melted
⅛ cup all-purpose flour

⅛ cup packed brown sugar
1 teaspoon ground cinnamon

1   Prepare two 8- or 9-inch loaf pans, or one 13- x 9-inch baking pan, by greasing them well.
2   Make cake first. Combine flour, baking powder, baking soda, and salt. Mix well.
3   Add eggs, sugar, orange zest, orange juice, and the 1 cup melted butter. Stir well.
4   Pour into prepared pans.
5   Combine the ¼ cup flour, brown sugar, and cinnamon.
6   Pour the ¼ cup melted butter evenly over the tops of the batter, then sprinkle with flour/brown sugar/cinnamon mix.
7   Bake at 400° for 25 minutes.

Peanut Butter Stars

Total time: 1 hour   Yields 40 cookies

K elly Tyler, with whom I worked at Borland in the late 1980s, shared her recipe for these delicious cookies she'd sometimes bring to potlucks.

1¾ cups all-purpose flour
½ teaspoon salt
1 teaspoon baking soda
½ cup unsalted butter
½ cup creamy peanut butter
½ cup packed brown sugar
½ cup granulated sugar

1 large egg
1 teaspoon vanilla extract
2 tablespoons milk
40 Hershey's Kisses, unwrapped (plus extras, in case you run out through snacking shrinkage)

1 Preheat oven to 350°.
2 In a medium mixing bowl, combine flour, salt, and baking soda.
3 In a separate bowl, cream together butter, peanut butter, brown sugar, and granulated sugar.
4 Add egg, vanilla extract, and milk to peanut butter mix.
5 Add flour mix to peanut butter mix. Stir well.
6 Roll batter into 1-inch balls and place on ungreased baking sheets (silicone baking sheet liners are useful).
7 Bake 5 to 8 minutes.
8 Remove from oven.
9 Gently press one Hershey's Kiss into top of each cookie.
10 Return baking sheet to oven and bake for 3 more minutes.
11 Remove from oven and cool cookies on wire cooling racks.

Persimmon Pudding and Brandied Hard Sauce

Total time: 2 hours

Yields one 2-quart pudding and 1¼ cups hard sauce

I n the British Isles, "pudding" means broadly any kind of dessert, not just a custard as we think of it in the US. Louise Nicholson shared this recipe, which was her (Irish) mother Kathy's, for a classic steamed persimmon pudding. It's a delectable way to enjoy persimmons. It's best served warm, but you can steam it well in advance and serve cold or reheated. To store, wrap the pudding with a spotlessly clean cotton towel and store in the refrigerator for a few days or place in an air-tight container and freeze for a few months. To reheat, bring pudding to room temperature (if frozen) and warm in oven at 300° for 10 minutes. You'll need a steamed pudding mold for this recipe. A "steamer kettle" can be anything that holds a fair amount of water, such as a canning kettle. Store hard sauce in an airtight container and refrigerate for up to two weeks.

Pudding

1 cup persimmon pulp (from 2 to 3 peeled ripe persimmons)

2 teaspoons baking soda

½ cup unsalted butter, softened, or ½ cup light cooking oil

1½ cups granulated sugar

2 large eggs

1 teaspoon lemon juice

½ teaspoon vanilla extract

2 tablespoons brandy or milk

1 cup all-purpose flour

1 teaspoon ground cinnamon

¼ teaspoon salt

1 cup raisins or currants

½ cup chopped pecans

Hard Sauce

½ cup unsalted butter, softened

1 cup powdered sugar

3 tablespoons brandy

Making the Pudding

1 Thoroughly grease a 2-quart steamed pudding mold and its lid.
2 Stir baking soda into persimmon pulp; set aside.
3 Cream butter and sugar together until fluffy.
4 Beat eggs, lemon juice, vanilla, brandy, and persimmon pulp/baking soda mix into butter/sugar mix.
5 In a separate bowl, combine flour with cinnamon and salt. Add to creamed mixture; stir well.

6 Stir in raisins and nuts.

7 Spoon mixture into prepared mold and fasten lid.

8 Place mold on a rack 1 inch above boiling water in a steamer kettle; cover. Boiling water should come up to but not touch bottom of mold.

9 Steam 1½ hours, adding more boiling water if needed. Keep water boiling gently while pudding cooks. If you need to add water during cooking, use boiling water so the steam cooking proceeds uninterrupted.

10 Remove from oven. Cool 30 minutes. Unmold.

Making the Brandied Hard Sauce

1 Beat ½ cup butter until smooth.

2 Slowly add powdered sugar and the 3 tablespoons brandy. Beat until thoroughly blended.

3 Cover and chill until needed. Serve with slices of steamed pudding.

Pound Cake

Total time: 1 hour 20 minutes   Yields 1 loaf

I adapted this recipe from Rose Levy Beranbaum's Perfect Pound Cake recipe in book, *The Cake Bible* (William Morrow and Company, Inc., 1988). I highly recommend her book. Her recipes are perfect, so there was very little I wanted to change. And she explains the science behind making cakes, which the science nerd in me appreciates. I make this cake in a tea loaf pan, though you can also bake it in an 8-inch by 4-inch (4-cup) loaf pan. To make a substitute for cake flour: start with 1 cup all-purpose flour, leveled. Remove 2 tablespoons flour. Stir in 2 tablespoons cornstarch or arrowroot. Et voilà! You have 1 cup cake flour.

3 tablespoons whole milk,
   room temperature
3 large eggs, lightly beaten
1½ teaspoons vanilla extract
1½ cups cake flour

¾ cup granulated sugar
¼ teaspoon baking powder
¼ teaspoon salt
1½ cups unsalted butter,
   softened

1   Preheat oven to 350° and grease a tea loaf pan (12 inches by 4 inches by 2½ inches). Line the pan's bottom with parchment paper.
2   Combine milk, eggs, and vanilla. Set aside.
3   In a separate bowl, combine flour, sugar, baking powder, and salt.
4   Add butter and half the milk/egg mix to flour mixture.
5   Stir until moistened, then beat 1 minute.
6   Gradually add remaining milk/egg mixture to batter in two batches, beating well after each addition.
7   Pour batter into prepared pan. Smooth surface and fill the corners.
8   Bake 55 to 65 minutes or until cake tests done. Watch for the last 15 minutes to avoid overbaking. If it starts to brown but doesn't test as done, tent with aluminum foil until done.
9   Remove from oven and cool 10 minutes on a wire rack, then remove from pan and cool more.

Pumpkin Pudding

Total time: 20 minutes plus chilling time

Yields about 2½ cups

Most pumpkin pies have soggy, doughy, tasteless crusts. But I generally love the filling. One Thanksgiving, I found this delicious recipe for custard-style pumpkin pudding on CincyShopper.com. I've rewritten this recipe in a way that makes sense to me. You *can* make a pumpkin pudding by just making pumpkin pie filling and not using a pie crust, but this recipe is lighter and more delicate. Serve plain or with whipped cream.

1¾ cups whole milk
1 large egg, lightly beaten
½ cup pumpkin purée
1 teaspoon vanilla extract
1 teaspoon ground cinnamon

¼ teaspoon freshly grated nutmeg
6 tablespoons granulated sugar
2 tablespoons cornstarch

1 Combine milk and egg and set aside.
2 Combine pumpkin purée, vanilla, cinnamon, and nutmeg. Mix very well, then set aside.
3 Combine sugar and cornstarch in a medium saucepan.
4 Turn heat to medium and slowly add milk/egg mixture, stirring constantly.
5 Bring to a boil and cook for 1 minute, continuing to stir constantly.
6 Turn heat to low and gradually stir in pumpkin mixture, blending well.
7 Cook 3 to 4 minutes more or until heated thoroughly, still stirring constantly.
8 Remove from heat and put into either one large bowl or individual serving containers, such as ramekins. Chill thoroughly.

Strawberry Compote

Total time: 15 minutes   Yields 2 cups

I t's tempting to pronounce this as kom POH, without the ending "t," but it's properly pronounced kom POAT. But however you pronounce it, it's delicious served over moist slices of pound cake (page 162), light-as-clouds angel food cake, or flaky slices of shortcake (my shortcake recipe is in *Delectable Desserts*). Top with whipped cream for extra lusciousness. You can make this compote with any berries (raspberries, black berries, blueberries, and so on), or some combination, and put it on anything you want. Vary the amount of sugar according to how tart the berries are.

2 cups strawberries, sliced in halves and quarters
1/3 cup brown or granulated sugar

1 tablespoon unsalted butter
1/4 cup water
1 tablespoon lemon juice

1   Put strawberries, sugar, butter, water, and lemon juice in a saucepan.
2   Heat, stirring occasionally, until hot. Be careful not to mash the berries while cooking; you want about half left as whole pieces.
3   When it's hot enough, mash about half strawberries, then serve.

Whole Wheat Oatmeal Cookies

Total time: 30 minutes   Yields

Yet another recipe from my friend AJ. This recipe dates to when I was experimenting with replacing sugar with honey and white all-purpose flour with whole wheat flour. Sometimes the substitutions worked, sometimes they didn't. This one worked. I don't remember this recipe's circumstances, but AJ must have thrown himself willingly into the experimentation—for scientific purposes, of course.

11 tablespoons unsalted butter, softened
½ cup light honey
2 large eggs, lightly beaten
1¾ cups whole wheat flour
⅛ teaspoon salt

½ teaspoon baking soda
1 tablespoon vanilla extract
3 tablespoons whole milk
½ cup rolled oats
½ cup semisweet chocolate chips

1 Prepare a baking sheet by lining it.
2 Cream butter and honey together.
3 Stir in eggs.
4 In a separate bowl, combine flour, salt, and baking soda.
5 Stir flour mix into butter mixture.
6 Add vanilla and milk.
7 Stir in oats.
8 Add chocolate chips.
9 Drop by tablespoonfuls onto prepared baking sheet.
10 Bake at 350° for 12 minutes or until the edges are golden.

Meat, Fish, & Cheese Dishes

This chapter's recipes can be the central part of a meal. You can have most of these recipes ready in a short amount of time, giving you the satisfaction of eating a fine meal without spending a lot of time in the kitchen.

Several of these dishes are one-pot meals; that is, you throw everything into one pot, and that's your entire meal. One-pot meals are great when you're in a hurry; they're also excellent for potlucks. Of course, as with any meal, you can serve salads, vegetables, soups, bread, or other dishes to complement any of these recipes.

As an interesting approach, I've included a few recipes that are in pairs—both are similar, but one is more complicated and one much simpler. For example, I've included two chicken pot pie recipes, two recipes for lasagna, and two recipes for rosemary chicken.

The recipes in this chapter all include meat or cheese (or both), so none are vegan, though a few are lacto-ovo vegetarian. For recipes that don't include meat, but that you can use as a main dish, see Beans, Soups, and Vegetables chapter on page 23.

Cooking Dry Pasta
● ●

Once upon a time, the method for cooking dry pasta was to fill a pot with water, add salt and sometimes a bit of oil, then boil the water, add the dry pasta, and continue boiling until the pasta was done. This method works, but the following method works just as well, is lower in salt and fat, and saves energy.

1　Fill a large stock pot and bring the water to boil. You can add salt to the water, but there's no need; whatever toppings you put on the pasta won't need that extra salt. Some people add oil to prevent boiling over; again, that isn't needed in this method.

2　Add the pasta.

3　Bring water to a boil again. Boil for two minutes.

4　Turn off heat, cover, and let pasta sit for eight to twelve minutes or until done to your preference. Stir now and then so the pasta cooks thoroughly and doesn't stick to itself. (I let a pound of pasta sit for 14 minutes.)

5　Drain and use according to the recipe.

Reheating Leftovers

Here's my rule of thumb for reheating leftovers: Whatever it is you're reheating, reheat it using the same method you used to cook it. If you baked something in the oven, reheat it in the oven. If you cooked it on the stovetop, reheat it in a pot on the stovetop. Whichever way you reheat the food, you might need to add a bit of water if the ingredients absorbed most of the moisture. If a recipe can be prepared either way, you can reheat it either way. Many recipes call for baking something in the oven that could also be cooked on the stovetop (such as beef stew); those dishes can be reheated on the stovetop. You can, of course, use a microwave oven instead of either, but I prefer the taste and texture of food reheated in the oven or on the stovetop.

Amazing Chicken Salad

Total time: 20 minutes   Yields 3 cups

This chicken salad (another of my originals) tastes best when made with all organic ingredients and chicken breasts. You could also use cooked turkey or canned chicken, though I like it best made with cooked chicken. You can serve this as a sandwich, as a salad on a bed of lettuce, or as is.

1 cup finely chopped celery
1 shallot, diced
1 small carrot, diced
3/4 cup fresh parsley, chopped
3/4 cup fresh cilantro, chopped
1/2 teaspoon dry mustard
1/2 teaspoon celery seed
2 cups chopped cooked
   chicken
1/3 cup mayonnaise
1 dill pickle, diced
1 avocado, sliced, for garnish

1   Combine chopped celery, shallot, carrot, parsley, cilantro, mustard, celery seed, cooked chicken, mayonnaise, and pickle.
2   Serve with slices of avocado.

Baked Macaroni and Cheese

Total time: 45 minutes   Yields 6 servings

T his easy, old-fashioned recipe is how my mother made macaroni and cheese. Instead of precooking noodles and making a cheese sauce, you put uncooked noodles, cheese, and milk into a casserole dish and bake it. The noodles cook in the milk while baking. Unless you manage to submerge every noodle, this dish will have crispy bits of noodle sticking up from the top; I particularly like those bits. Use real cheese, not pasteurized, processed cheese foods. Some good choices are cheddar (especially sharp cheddar), Monterey Jack, and Colby.

1 pound elbow macaroni,   **2** cups whole milk
     uncooked   **2** to 3 tablespoons salted butter
1 pound cheese, grated

1   Prepare a 12-inch round, 3-inch deep casserole dish by buttering it well. (You can use a different size and shape; just be sure the ingredients will fit.)
2   Pour elbow macaroni into casserole dish.
3   Thoroughly mix in cheese; reserve ¼ cup cheese for the top.
4   Pour in milk. Some noodles may peek out from the top, but try to cover most of them.
5   Dot suface with butter, then sprinkle with reserved cheese.
6   Bake at 350° for 30 minutes or until golden brown on top. The noodles should be cooked and tender; if not, cover and cook until they are.

Barbecue Meat Loaf

Total time: 1 hour   Yields one 12- x 4-inch loaf

In my experience (and maybe in yours), meatloaf has been a dry, tasteless waste of perfectly good ingredients. I'd tried a few recipes over the years and had given up finding anything I liked. That is, until my friend Bryan introduced me to a recipe he'd found on ColdWeatherComfort.com. While trying the recipe (and, as always, adapting it to my tastes), I used the bread I had on hand, which happened to be Bread Machine Potato Bread (page 90). Using that bread, I discovered that the bread you use in your meatloaf makes a huge difference in the texture, flavor, and moistness. Once again, quality ingredients make a better meal.

$1\frac{1}{2}$ pounds lean ground beef
$\frac{3}{4}$ cup fresh bread crumbs
   (potato bread is fantastic)
$\frac{1}{2}$ cup minced yellow onion
1 large egg, lightly beaten

2 teaspoons oregano
1 teaspoon dried thyme
$\frac{1}{2}$ cup plus ¼ cup barbecue
   sauce

1 Thoroughly grease a 12- x 4-inch tea loaf pan. (If you wish, you can use a 9- x 5-inch loaf pan: it has the same capacity.)
2 Mix together until well combined: meat, bread crumbs, onion, egg, oregano, and thyme. The traditional way to mix meatloaf ingredients is to use your hands. That way, you can really get in there to mix the ingredients.
3 Add the ½ cup barbecue sauce. Mix well.
4 Put meatloaf into prepared pan, leveling out the top and filling the corners.
5 Bake at 350° for 45 minutes or until internal temperature is 160°. Test the temperature at the ends and in the middle of the loaf.
6 15 minutes before the loaf is done, baste loaf with the remaining ¼ cup barbecue sauce.

Batter-Fried Fish

Total time: Yields about 4 pieces

I'm sure you've heard about adding beer to fired fish batter. It works; through the magic of chemistry, the batter is lighter and tenderer (because it has less gluten). But you can't just buy one cup of beer, and I'm not much of a beer drinker; leftover beer just goes to waste. So I was pleased to discover you can also use carbonated water. I adapted the Daring Gourmet's British Fish and Chips recipe (leaving out the chips) to make a version that involves no beer. I recommend frying in a cast iron Dutch oven. I also recommend the ThermoWorks ChefAlarm thermometer; you'll find many uses for it in the kitchen. Serve this fish with lemon wedges and the fantastic Best-Ever Tartar Sauce (page 291) on the side.

1 cup all-purpose flour, plus more for dredging the fish
1 teaspoon baking powder
1/2 teaspoon salt
1¼ cups seltzer water

2 pounds fresh cod, haddock, halibut, or other firm-fleshed white fish, cut into 4-inch pieces
oil for frying

1 Spread paper or cloth towels on a flat surface, then put a gridded wire cooling rack on the towels.
2 Combine flour, baking powder, and salt in a large bowl. (Prepare batter just before you need it so you don't lose the carbonation.)
3 Whisk in carbonated water until batter is smooth.
4 Spread about ¼ cup flour in a large plate or shallow bowl.
5 Rinse fish if needed. Blot fish dry.
6 Heat oil to 365°.
7 Dredge each piece of fish in flour, then dip fish into batter. Coat all sides with batter. When you're done dipping, hold fish briefly over bowl so excess batter can drip off. You want the fish pieces coated with batter, but not too thickly, and without bare spots.
8 Carefully slide fish into oil. It's better to fry just a few pieces at a time. The temperature drops each time you add fish, so as you fry, watch the temperature. Too low and the batter will be greasy and the fish undercooked; too high and the batter will burn. The internal temperature should be a minimum of 145°.
9 If using a deep fat fryer, fry fish 5 to 8 minutes or until golden brown. If using a cast iron skillet or Dutch oven, fry 2 to 3 minutes on each side or until golden brown (3 to 5 minutes total).
10 Remove fish from oil. Place fish on cooling rack until ready to serve.

Beef and Noodles

Total time: 30 minutes   Yields 4 servings

My friend Morgan Harrington shared this recipe, which comes from the Fast Metabolism Diet website. It's fast, savory, and deeply satisfying. As a bonus, it's gluten free and sugar free. I use TInkyada brand brown rice noodles—they're the best rice noodles I've ever used. They're tasty and they don't get gummy or weird when cooked. Target carries them. You can get brown rice flour many places; I buy mine from VitaCost.com.

1 pound ground beef
1 medium yellow onion, coarsely chopped
4 garlic cloves, minced
1 teaspoon dried oregano
1 teaspoon salt

¼ teaspoon coarsely ground black pepper
¼ cup brown rice flour
4 cups chicken broth
8 ounces brown rice noodles, uncooked

1 In a large, deep skillet with a lid, brown beef until no red shows on the beef, about 5 minutes.
2 Stir in onion and garlic and cook about 1 minute.
3 Sprinkle with oregano, salt, and pepper and give a quick stir.
4 Add rice flour and stir until everything is coated.
5 Pour in chicken broth.
6 Add noodles and push them into broth with your wooden spoon. If there isn't enough fluid to cover the noodles, add more water or broth.
7 Bring to a boil, then reduce heat to a simmer.
8 Cover with a lid and continue to simmer 8 to 10 minutes or until noodles are done to your preferred amount of tenderness.

Beef Lasagna

Total time: 1 hour   Yields 8 servings

One of the nicest features of this recipe is that you don't have to pre-cook the lasagna noodles; this simplifies preparation time considerably. The recipe is quite flexible and forgiving. You can vary the ingredients in this recipe; for example, leave out the meat; use ricotta instead of cottage cheese; eliminate the cheddar and use more mozzarella.

1 pound ground beef
1 teaspoon Italian seasonings
2 garlic cloves, coarsely chopped
2 quarts spaghetti sauce
2 teaspoons fennel seed
1 (one-pound) box lasagna noodles

1 quart cottage cheese or ricotta
1 pound cheddar cheese, grated or thinly sliced
1 pound mozzarella cheese, grated or thinly sliced
½ cup grated Parmesan cheese

1 In a large skillet, cook meat with Italian seasonings and garlic. If you are using extra lean ground meat, you shouldn't need to drain the meat; otherwise, drain the fat.
2 Add spaghetti sauce and heat. For better flavor, you can cook for 15 to 20 minutes, but that isn't necessary.
3 Spread ½ cup of meat sauce in a 13- x 9-inch pan.
4 Place one layer of lasagna noodles on top of sauce in bottom of pan; add a fairly thick layer of cottage cheese, then a thinner layer of cheddar and mozzarella, then a thick layer of sauce. You aren't trying to cover each layer completely with any one ingredient, as the ingredients will melt and spread when baking. Repeat. End with a layer of noodles and then a final layer of sauce.
5 Sprinkle top with Parmesan cheese.
6 Cover and bake at 350° for 40 minutes or until bubbly on top. Uncover for the last 10 minutes of cooking.
7 You can serve immediately, although it will be sloppy. If you have the restraint, let stand 30 minutes. The lasagna gets firmer as it stands. Store leftovers (if any) in the refrigerator. The next day, the lasagna will be nicely firm and easy to cut.

Breaded Pork Chops

Total time: 30 minutes   Yields 6 thin chops

T his tasty way to cook moist, flavorful pork chops came from my friend AJ. You can use the breading in this recipe on catfish, chicken, and other meats as well.

4 dashes sesame oil, plus more
  for frying
4 dashes hot pepper sauce
1½ teaspoons tamari
⅛ cup buttermilk
½ cup all-purpose flour
1 tablespoon cornmeal

⅛ teaspoon black pepper
1 tablespoon powdered garlic
¼ teaspoon lemon pepper
  seasoning
6 thinly-sliced boneless pork
  chops

1 Combine the four dashes sesame oil, hot pepper sauce, tamari, and buttermilk.
2 In a separate bowl, combine flour, cornmeal, pepper, garlic, and lemon pepper.
3 Coat chops in liquid mixture, then dredge in flour mixture.
4 Fry in hot sesame oil for 6 minutes on each side.

Cajun Lamb Chops

Total time: 1¾ hours   Yields 4 to 6 servings

Spicy and flavorful, this is another of AJ's original recipes. The list of ingredients is long, yes, but you combine most of them to make the marinade. You can use any barbecue sauce you want, or AJ's Barbecue Sauce (page 289). Likewise, you can use any Cajun spice blend, or my blend (page 292). I specify Lea & Perrins Original Worcestershire Sauce because it's gluten free, but only if you buy it in the US.

6 garlic cloves, diced
4 tablespoons Cajun spice blend
2 teaspoons cayenne
1 tablespoon paprika
¼ teaspoon onion powder
1 teaspoon black pepper
2 teaspoons chili powder
1 tablespoon sesame seeds
1 teaspoon celery seed
½ cup apple cider vinegar

½ cup water
1 tablespoon barbecue sauce
2 tablespoons lemon juice (or the juice from one lemon)
4 squirts habanera sauce
¼ cup Lea & Perrins Original Worcestershire Sauce
3 tablespoons olive oil
3 pounds rack of lamb, cut into chops

1 Make the marinade by combining garlic, Cajun spice, cayenne, paprika, onion powder, pepper, chili powder, sesame seeds, celery seed, vinegar, water, barbecue sauce, lemon juice, habanera sauce, Worcestershire sauce, and oil. Mix well.
2 Coat lamb chops in marinade and marinate 45 minutes. (You can marinate them longer, including overnight, if you like.)
3 Broil lamb chops 15 minutes on each side, or barbecue over the grill for a truly exquisite flavor.

Chicken Baked with Rice

Total time: 1 hour 10 minutes   Yields 8 servings

This extraordinarily easy recipe, which I learned from my mother when I was a child, has a full, rich flavor. For maximum flavor and economy, buy a whole chicken and have your butcher cut it up for you. Serve with fresh sourdough bread and butter and a simple salad. A Dutch oven is endlessly useful and worth buying if you don't already have one.

1 whole chicken, cut up
2 cups brown rice
4 cups water or chicken broth

1 pound fresh mushrooms, sliced
2 yellow onions, chopped
1 clove garlic, minced

1   Combine chicken pieces, rice, water, mushrooms, onions, and garlic in a 5-quart Dutch oven or casserole dish.
2   Cover pot and bake at 350° for about 1 hour or until rice and chicken are tender.

Chicken Curry

Total time: 1 hour   Yields six servings

This fantastic chicken curry is another of my friend AJ's inventions. If you want to make this gluten free, omit the Better Than Bouillon. You can use any mild curry powder, or you can make my Madras-Style Curry Powder (page 303). Dry garlic chutney (also known as *vada pav* chutney, because it's often served with *vada pav*, a popular Mumbai street food) is made with fresh garlic, dry coconut, peanuts, and Kashmiri chili powder. You can usually find it in a specialty food shop.

½ cup unsalted butter
1 yellow onion, diced
2 tablespoons garlic purée
2 tablespoons ginger purée
½ cup coarsely chopped
    tomato
3 tablespoons Madras-style
    curry powder
4 tablespoons dry garlic
    chutney

¼ cup plus 2 cups water
3 pounds boneless, skinless
    chicken, cut into bite-sized
    pieces
2 tablespoons Better Than
    Bouillon brand chicken
    bouillon paste, undiluted
3 medium-sized Yukon gold
    potatoes, cubed (no need to
    peel)

1   Sauté onions in butter on high heat until onions just start to caramelize.
2   Add garlic purée, ginger purée, tomato, curry powder, garlic chutney, and the ¼ cup water. Blend well, continuing to heat.
3   Add chicken and brown on all sides.
4   Add bouillon paste, the 2 cups water, and potatoes. Bring to a simmer, then cover and continue to cook until everything is tender, about 45 minutes.

Chicken Chile Casserole

Total time: 40 minutes   Yields a 2-quart casserole

Everyone in the Southwestern United States has their own version of this recipe. This is mine. It's perfect for taking to a potluck or picnic, as it tastes good even when cold, and freezes and reheats well. My version doesn't have the more usual tortillas or tortilla chips, which get unpalatable if you freeze the dish. During the pandemic, when basics were hard to find, I replaced the canned soup with a homemade version: I cooked some celery, onions, and carrots in three cups of chicken stock until the veggies were tender. While the veggies were cooking, I made a roux with butter and flour, then stirred the broth into the roux until thickened.

4 cups cheddar cheese, grated (about 8 ounces)
1 can condensed cream of mushroom soup (undiluted)
1 can condensed cream of chicken soup (undiluted)
1 can (4 ounces) green chopped chiles

1 can (4 ounces) sliced black olives
1 cup sour cream
1 small yellow or white onion, diced
3 cups leftover chicken or turkey, cut into bite-sized pieces

1   Combine 3¾ cup cheese (reserve the remaining ¼ cup), mushroom soup, chicken soup, chiles, olives, sour cream, and onion.
2   Layer the soup mix and chicken in a 2-quart casserole dish in the following order: soup/cheese mixture, chicken, mixture, chicken, until everything is used up, starting and ending with the soup/cheese mixture.
3   Sprinkle reserved ¼ cup cheese on top.
4   Cover and bake at 350° until edges are bubbling and cheese is melted on top (about 20 minutes).

Chicken Karaage

Total time: 1 hour   Yields about 20 pieces

Breaded with potato flour instead of wheat flour, this Japanese version of fried chicken is a popular street food in Japan. It's tender and incredibly delicious. (Karaage, pronounced kah RAAH gay, stretching out the middle *ah* sound, is a Japanese frying technique.) I first saw this recipe in Adam Liaw's video (AdamLiaw.com). The chicken is usually cooked with the skin on, but you can use skinless chicken, or (small) thighs still with their bones and skin. (If you do, adjust frying times.) You can also use this recipe to fry other meats (pork, beef, other poultry). Tamari is a type of soy sauce, and is typically gluten-free (check the label if avoiding gluten). The potato flour is essential. Although potato flour and potato starch aren't quite the same thing, you can substitute potato starch. Sake is traditional in the marinade, but I like it better without. (If you want to try it, add 2 tablespoons sake to the marinade.) Serve with lemon wedges (for squeezing over the karaage), Japanese mayonnaise sprinkled with shichimi togarashi (a Japanese red pepper blend) for dipping the pieces, and nori (seaweed) flakes for sprinkling over everything. I've listed a substitute for Japanese mayonnaise after the instructions. There really isn't a substitute for shichimi toragashi, though you can combine a teaspoon of cayenne pepper and a dash of powdered ginger and use that.

1 pound boneless chicken
1/4 cup tamari or soy sauce
1 teaspoon roasted sesame oil
1 tablespoon grated fresh
    ginger or 1 teaspoon
    ground ginger
1/2 teaspoon garlic powder or
    minced fresh garlic

3/4 cup potato flour
2 quarts sunflower or other
    frying oil
1 lemon, cut into wedges
1/2 cup Japanese mayonnaise
shichimi togarashi
nori flakes

1 Cut chicken into 2-inch pieces.
2 In a medium bowl, combine tamari, sesame oil, ginger, and garlic.
3 Add chicken pieces to marinade and coat well. Cover bowl and refrigerate 10 to 30 minutes. (No more than 30 minutes though; in this case, a longer marinating time isn't better.)
4 Place potato flour in a large bowl.
5 Drain chicken well and discard marinade. Don't be tempted to save the marinade for later; it's been touched by raw meat and is no longer food safe.
6 Dredge chicken pieces in potato flour. You can do this one piece

at a time or just dump all the chicken pieces into potato flour and dredge. After dredging, place chicken pieces in a clean bowl. The chicken should be lightly coated. Set aside for 5 minutes.

7 While chicken rests, heat oil to 360°. You can fry in a deep skillet, though it's more convenient to use a cast iron Dutch oven (my favorite) or a deep fat fryer with a basket you can lift out.

8 Add chicken to oil in small batches. As is true for all frying, don't overcrowd the frying vessel or the oil temperature will drop too much. Use two utensils for handling the chicken: one to place uncooked chicken into the oil, and a second to fish it out. I use tongs to put pieces in oil and a flat stainless steel slotted strainer to fish them out. **For food safety, never touch cooked chicken with the uncooked chicken utensil**. For each batch,

- Fry each piece 2 to 3 minutes, then remove each piece to a rack (or lift it out of the oil if using a deep fat fryer), and rest for 30 seconds.
- Return chicken to oil and fry for another minute, and then set pieces on rack again (or on a plate covered with a paper towel) while you fry the next batch. You want a crispy, golden brown crust. For food safety, the chicken's interior *must* be 165°.
- Serve once you've fried all the chicken pieces.

Important! For food safety, you *must* discard the marinade and the dredging flour. They've been contaminated with raw chicken.

Substitute for Japanese Mayonnaise

Japanese mayonnaise is a touch sweeter and eggier than American-style mayonnaise. If you can find it, Sir Kensington's Classic Vegan Mayo comes close. Or you can buy Japanese mayonnaise, make your own, or use this substitute, which comes close. Rice vinegar is sweeter than apple cider vinegar, but you can substitute apple cider vinegar. You can also substitute mirin or seasoned rice vinegar.

2 tablespoons rice vinegar   1 cup American-style
1 teaspoon granulated sugar   mayonnaise

1 Dissolve sugar in vinegar.
2 Combine mayonnaise and sugar/vinegar mix. Mix until well-blended.
3 Refrigerate in an airtight container for up to 3 days.

Chicken or Turkey Pot Pie 1

Total time: 1 hour   Yields two 9-inch deep dish pies

I love chicken pot pie, but unfortunately, most of the frozen ones on the market are either too expensive for what you get, or have questionable ingredients, or have too much crust and not enough filling, or all three. My version is 100% delicious, with perfect proportion. Instead of making your own gravy, you can use leftover gravy (say, from roasting a chicken of turkey). I've included a streamlined version of this recipe immediately after this recipe—see the head notes for that recipe for bouillon alternatives.

Filling

2 tablespoons butter (salted or unsalted)
6 medium carrots, sliced
4 stalks celery, sliced
2 large onions, coarsely chopped
2 teaspoons Italian seasonings

4 cups cooked chicken or turkey, cut into 1-inch cubes
1 (16-ounce) package frozen mixed vegetables (for example, carrots, corn, green beans, and peas)
1 cup frozen pearl onions

Gravy

3 cups water
3 cubes (3 teaspoons) chicken bouillon

2 tablespoons butter (salted or unsalted)
2 tablespoons all-purpose flour

Crust

Two single 9-inch pie crusts

1 Preheat oven to 400°.
2 Melt the 2 tablespoons butter in a large, deep sauté pan.
3 Stir in carrots, celery, onions, and Italian seasonings. Cook 10 minutes, stirring frequently.
4 While carrots, celery, and onions cook, start making gravy: bring the 3 cups water to a boil in a medium pot and add bouillon.
5 In a small sauté pan, melt 2 tablespoons butter, then stir in flour. Mix well and cook until very lightly browned. (You're making a light roux.)

6 Slowly pour bouillon into roux, stirring as you add, until well-mixed. Cook until slightly thickened (about 5 minutes).

7 Add chicken, frozen vegetables, frozen onions, and gravy to carrot/ celery/onion mix. Cook over medium heat until it is bubbling merrily.

8 Divide mixture evenly between two 9-inch deep-dish pie pans, then cover each pie with a crust. Tuck edges of crust inside pie pan, cut vents in crust, and bake for 20 to 30 minutes or until crust is a lovely golden brown.

Chicken or Turkey Pot Pie 2

Total time: 40 minutes   Yields two 9-inch deep dish pies

This recipe is the streamlined version of the previous recipe. It strips the ingredients to the essentials: carrots, celery, and onions. In cooking, this trio is called mirepoix and is known as the holy trinity of French cooking. I consider it essential for many non-French dishes as well. Because you don't precook the mirepoix as you do in the previous recipe, this chicken pot pie's veggies have a bit more crunch. For the gravy, if you want to use Better Than Bouillon brand chicken bouillon (which I recommend), use two teaspoons paste instead of 3 cubes of bouillon. If you have homemade chicken stock, use three cups of stock instead of the water and bouillon.

Filling

6 medium carrots, sliced
4 stalks celery, sliced
2 large onions, diced

4 cups cooked chicken or
   turkey, cut into 1-inch cubes
2 teaspoons Italian seasonings

Gravy

3 cups water
3 cubes (3 teaspoons) chicken
   bouillon

2 tablespoons butter (salted or
   unsalted)
2 tablespoons all-purpose flour

Crust

Two single 9-inch pie crusts

1 Preheat oven to 400°.
2 Fill two 9-inch deep-dish pie pans with carrots, celery, onions, and chicken. Sprinkle with Italian seasonings.
3 In a medium saucepan, bring water to a boil. Add bouillon.
4 In a small sauté pan, melt butter, then stir in flour. Mix well and cook until very lightly browned. (You're making a light roux.)
5 Slowly pour bouillon into roux, stirring as you add, until well-mixed. Cook until slightly thickened (about 5 minutes).
6 Divide gravy into two equal portions. Pour one portion each over ingredients in filled pie pans.
7 Cover each pie with a crust. Tuck edges of crust inside pie pan. Cut vents in crust. Bake 15 minutes. Reduce heat to 350° and bake another 15 minutes or until crust is a lovely golden brown.

Chicken, Rice, and Celery Sauté

Total time: 30 minutes   Yields 4 to 6 servings

I invented this one-pot recipe when I had some leftover roast chicken, celery, onions, leftover rice, and plenty of fresh organic lemons from my garden. You can also use leftover turkey. The flavors are so wonderful it doesn't need seasonings.

1/4 cup butter (salted or
    unsalted)
2 cups diced yellow onion
1 1/2 cups sliced celery
Juice of 5 lemons

2 cups leftover chicken,
    chopped into bite-sized
    pieces
2 cups cooked brown rice

1   Melt butter in a 12-inch skillet or sauté pan.
2   Add onions and stir until slightly translucent, 3 to 5 minutes.
3   Add celery and stir until celery barely starts to soften (about 3-5 minutes).
4   Stir in lemon juice.
5   Add chicken. Stir and cook 5 more minutes.
6   Add rice and stir until everything is thoroughly mixed and chicken is heated through (about 5 minutes).

Chicken Tenders

Total time: 30 minutes   Yields 6 servings

This, my own recipe, makes incredibly tender chicken "fingers." The butter is essential to the flavor in this recipe. If you need to, you can substitute a blend of avocado oil and butter. (Though remember that recent research shows that we need to consume some "good" saturated fats, such as butter.)

2 pounds boneless, skinless chicken, cut into 1-inch by 3-inch strips
2 cups buttermilk

2 cups seasoned flour (page 312)
1 cup salted butter

1   Melt ½ cup butter in a large frying pan on high heat.
2   Place 1 cup buttermilk in a small, shallow dish, such as a 9-inch glass or ceramic (not metal) pie pan.
3   Place 1 cup seasoned flour mixture in another small, shallow dish. (Alternatively, you can place it in a heavy duty "zip" type food storage bag or in a lunch-sack sized brown paper bag.)
4   Dip individual chicken pieces in buttermilk, then dredge in flour. (Or, instead of dredging after dipping in buttermilk, place several chicken pieces at a time in the bag of flour, then close and shake.) As you dip and dredge, you may need to add more buttermilk or flour to the containers.
5   When butter is melted, carefully place coated chicken pieces in butter and fry until completely cooked through, with no pink. (To a minimum of 165° interior temperature.) Turn each piece once. As needed, add more butter.
6   If chicken does not all fit in the pan at once, cook a batch, then remove cooked chicken, melt more butter, and add more pieces to the pan. **For food safety reasons,** don't place uncooked chicken in the pan with pieces that are almost done.

Chili Verde

Total time: 2 hours   Yields 8 servings

This classic Southwestern favorite is another of those recipes that, like Chicken Chile Casserole (page 179), has many variations. This is my version, made many times. I love this recipe served over brown rice, though you could also serve it with Spanish rice and whole or refried beans topped with grated cheddar or Monterey Jack cheese.

2 pounds fresh tomatillos
2 tablespoons olive oil
2 pounds pork loin or chicken, cut into cubes
1 small onion, diced
1 clove garlic, diced
1/2 teaspoon cumin seed
1/4 cup fresh cilantro, chopped

4 ounces green chiles, diced, or one 4-ounce can diced green chiles
1 teaspoon jalapeño pepper, diced
1 teaspoon salt
1 cup water (as needed)

1   Peel tomatillos. Place in a pot with enough water to cover. Bring to a boil. Boil 10 minutes. Drain and purée. Set aside.
2   Heat oil in deep 12-inch skillet. Add meat, onion, and garlic. Brown 3 to 5 minutes, or until there's no pink on the outside of the meat.
3   Add tomatillos, cumin, cilantro, green chiles, jalapeño, and salt to meat/onion/garlic mix. Usually the tomatillos are liquid enough to make the recipe watery (which you want); if not, add 1 cup water.
4   Bring to a boil, then reduce heat to a simmer.
5   Cover skillet and simmer for one hour. The chili verde is ready to eat after 30 minutes, but it likely won't be tender, so keep cooking until you can easily cut the meat with a fork. (About 1 hour more.) Alternatively, you can bake the chili verde in a covered Dutch oven at 350° for 1 hour.

Coconut Chicken

Total time: 2 hours   Yields 6 to 8 servings

O ne night after a lively tabletop gaming session, my friends and I were all hungry, but didn't know what we wanted. I suggested Chicken Baked with Rice (page 177), but that didn't appeal. Then I started suggesting alterations to that recipe to make it more appealing (based on what I had on hand), and everyone else joined in on the fun. This is the delicious result of our collaborative brainstorming.

3 cups short-grain brown rice
2 (14-ounce) cans coconut milk
4 cups water
1½ cups finely chopped red
   and green bell peppers
½ cup chopped red onion

¼ cup chopped fresh cilantro
6 half-breasts of chicken, bone
   in
6 chicken thighs, bone in
2 cups cubed fresh pineapple

1 In a large roasting pan, combine rice and coconut milk. Stir until thoroughly mixed (the grains of rice should be coated).
2 Add water, bell peppers, onion, and cilantro. Stir well.
3 Place chicken pieces in pan, wiggling them to the bottom. As much as possible, cover chicken with rice.
4 Scatter pineapple on top.
5 Cover pan with aluminum foil. Bake at 350° for 45 minutes.
6 Uncover and bake an additional 30 to 40 minutes.

Coq au Vin à la Jean

Total time: 1 hour   Yields 4 servings

" Coq au Vin" means chicken (the "coq"—more specifically, rooster) cooked with wine (the "vin" part). In the 1960s and 1970s, my mother, Jean, often made this French-inspired dish. She probably learned it from Julia Child's cooking show, *The French Chef*, which aired from 1963 to 1973. I'd always assumed my mother's recipe was authentic. Until, that is, I started researching this recipe. I discovered that my mother had taken great liberties with the traditional Coq au Vin. Whole carrots and potatoes are usual, but she never used them. Sometimes she'd throw in two cups of rice and increase the fluids accordingly. And she used much less wine than they do in France—where the French use an entire large bottle of red wine, she used only one cup of whatever wine she had on hand—usually white, because that's what she drank. Coq au Vin is traditionally made with red wine, burgundy preferably, which the French will assure you isn't true burgundy unless it comes from the Burgundy region. (In which case, you capitalize the word: Burgundy from Burgundy is Burgundy, not burgundy. Burgundy from anywhere else is burgundy or, from the French perspective, red wine.) As always when cooking with wine, whatever you use and wherever it comes from, the wine doesn't have to be expensive, but it must be excellent and fit for drinking.

4 tablespoons butter   **1** cup chicken stock
1 whole chicken, cut up   **1** cup good wine
2 yellow onions, coarsely
   chopped

1   Melt butter in a large skillet.
2   Add chicken pieces to butter and brown lightly on all sides.
3   Add onions and brown slightly, 1 to 3 minutes.
4   Place chicken and onions in a 4-quart pot or casserole dish or Dutch oven. Whatever you use must have a cover.
5   Add chicken stock, water, and wine. You can add more wine if you like, but it isn't necessary for my mother's recipe.
6   Cover pot and bake at 350° for 45 to 60 minutes.
7   When it's done cooking, the chicken should be tender and the fluids should be thickened. If the fluid hasn't thickened, you can serve it anyway, or lift out the chicken and make a gravy with the liquid. (Note: if you use red wine, the chicken will be a deep, rich purple.)

Cornish-Style Pasties

Total time: 4.5 hours   Yields 6 pasties

A Cornish pasty is a sturdy meat pie held together by a thick shortcrust pastry. By Cornish law, unless you make this recipe in Cornwall using locally sourced ingredients, you can't call these Cornish pasties; at least, not if you're selling them. (The "a" in pasty is a short "a" that rhymes with cat, not a long "a" that rhymes with bake.) I adapted this recipe, which is the traditional, legally defined Cornish pasty, from the Cornish Pasty Association's recipe. This recipe still meets the legal definition, but I made the instructions clearer and more explicit. Also, a shortcrust pastry has about twice as much flour as fat by weight and less water than, say, pie crust dough. Because proportions are essential to making a good shortcrust, I added American cups and tablespoons to the shortcrust ingredients, but also kept the grams and milliliters of the original recipe. I've made this recipe with all American butter, all European-style butter, and a combination of American butter and lard. I prefer the shortcrust made with all European-style butter, but all three variations are delicious. Depending on how much you fill each pasty, you may have leftover filling. You can easily make more dough to use it up. To reheat a pasty, wrap edges with aluminum foil and heat at 350° for about 35 to 30 minutes.

Shortcrust

- **4** cups (500 grams) bread flour
- **1** cup plus 1 tablespoon (245 grams) butter or lard or a combination
- **1** teaspoon salt
- ¾ cup (175 milliliters) cold water

Filling

- **1** pound beef skirt steak, cut into bite-sized pieces
- **2** cups diced waxy potatoes (red, yellow, or purple)
- ½ cup diced rutabaga (swede or Cornish turnip)
- ½ small yellow onion, diced
- salt and pepper to taste
- **1** egg, lightly beaten (for brushing crust)

1   Combine salt and flour.
2   Cut butter into ½-inch cubes, then cut butter into flour/salt mixture until flour mixture resembles fine cornmeal. I recommend using a food processor for this step.

3   Stir in water.

4   Using your hands, knead dough until it's silky and elastic, about 5 minutes. Dough is dry and stringy at first, but will come together. Don't be tempted to add more water! That makes dough tough.

5   Cover dough with plastic wrap and refrigerate 3 hours or overnight. Don't skip this step; chilling is essential for handling the dough.

6   After dough has chilled, combine beef, potatoes, rutabaga, and onion. (Or do this step after you roll out the dough.)

7   Divide dough into six equal portions (a scale is useful here). Roll each portion out into circles about 8 inches across.

8   Lay each rolled-out portion on a clean surface. Spread filling on half the circle, leaving enough edge (about 1 inch) to crimp pasty closed.

9   Sprinkle filling with salt and pepper.

10 Wet inside edges of rolled-out pasty. Fold empty half over filling to make the shape of a capital D. Crimp edges together like you would crimp edges of a pie. Seal well to avoid leakage.

11 Cut a small slit (about ½ inch) in top of pasty.

12 Set pasty on a lined baking sheet.

13 Fill and crimp remaining pasties.

14 Brush each pasty with beaten egg.

15 Convection bake at 325° for about 45 minutes. (Or 350° in a non-convection oven for about 55 minutes.) The tops will be a glossy golden color when done.

16 Remove from oven and let cool slightly, then devour.

Cumin Sweet Potato Pork Pot

Total time: 2 hours   Yields 4 to 6 servings

This is my own recipe, invented out of curiosity and a desire to use up some of the many sweet potatoes I had on hand, purchased in a sudden rush of enthusiasm for sweet potatoes. The spices add an interesting, vaguely Moroccan flavor, and the pork comes out falling-apart tender.

¼ cup avocado oil
2 medium yellow onions, coarsely chopped
3 cups cubed sweet potatoes
1 teaspoon cumin seed
1 teaspoon ground cinnamon

2 pounds top loin boneless pork roast, cut into 2-inch cubes
4 cups chicken stock
2 cups water

1   Preheat oven to 350°. This step is not optional.
2   Put oil in an 8-quart Dutch oven and heat until oil is shimmering.
3   Add onions and stir until barely translucent, about 3 minutes.
4   Add sweet potatoes, cumin, and cinnamon. Stir well and cook 3 minutes.
5   Add meat and brown each piece on all sides, until no pink shows.
6   Add chicken stock and water. Bring to a boil.
7   Place aluminum foil over top of Dutch oven and fold down to form a good seal. Place lid firmly on top of foil, making sure it's seated.
8   Bake 1½ hours.

Dawn's Steak Stew

Total time: 3½ to 4 hours   Yields 6 servings

My friend Dawn came up with this delicious recipe. It is everything a beef stew should be: richly flavorful with chunks of beef that are so tender they almost dissolve in your mouth. If you choose a gluten-free vegetable bouillon, or leave it out entirely, this recipe is gluten free. On making this recipe, Dawn notes, "I basically steam the meat in olive oil, onions, and garlic first, instead of the pan browning process." She adds that this stew is "best served the next day or after a few hours of finishing." The red wine must be a dark red wine, like a merlot.

3½ pounds stew steak, cubed
5 cups water
1 cup olive oil
3 garlic cloves, chopped
2 yellow onions, diced
1 shallot, coarsely chopped
½ teaspoon ground pepper
½ teaspoon oregano
½ teaspoon thyme
½ teaspoon basil
1 to 2 sprigs fresh rosemary
½ teaspoon paprika
½ teaspoon ground cloves
½ teaspoon ground cumin
½ teaspoon Chinese 5 Spice

2 cubes (2 teaspoons) vegetable bouillon
2 tablespoons brown sugar
1½ cups red wine
1½ cups heavy cream or half-and-half
4 large russet potatoes, cubed
2 tomatoes, chopped, or 1 can (6 ounces) tomato paste
2 large carrots, sliced
3 stalks celery, chopped
2 to 4 tablespoons all-purpose flour
2 tablespoons unsalted butter

1   In a medium saucepan, bring water to a boil. Lower heat and keep water simmering.
2   While heating water, pour olive oil into a 12-quart stock pot. The oil should cover bottom of pot to a depth of ⅛ to ¼ inch.
3   Heat oil on medium until hot. Reduce heat to medium-low and add onions, garlic, and shallot. Give a quick stir.
4   Layer stew steak in a single packed layer on top of onion mix.
5   Sprinkle spices over meat and cover stock pot. Leaving heat on medium-low, steam meat until brown (not seared) on undersides, then turn meat and steam until brown on the other side. Once meat is brown, stir regularly to prevent the meat from sticking.
6   While meat is cooking, in a small bowl, dissolve bouillon cubes in 1 cup of the simmering water. Stir in brown sugar, then pour bouillon/sugar/water mix over meat once it's brown on all sides.

7   Add another cup of simmering water to stock pot so that the water just covers the meat and onions. Stir and simmer stew a few minutes.

8   Add red wine and heavy cream. Give a quick stir.

9   Add potatoes, tomatoes, carrots, and celery. Add 3 more cups simmering water, or just enough to cover all ingredients.

10 Keeping heat on low, simmer for 1½ hours, stirring occasionally.

11 When stew has been cooking for 1½ hours, melt butter in a frying pan and blend with flour. Stir into stew.

12 Simmer stew for another 30 minutes to an hour, or until meat is tender.

Enchiladas

Total time: 1 hour   Yields 18 to 20 enchiladas

These enchiladas are surprisingly delicious for such a simple list of ingredients. You can make these ahead of time up to the point where they are ready to put in the oven, then wrap them well and freeze for a quick meal later. You can also make a vegetarian version of these by leaving out the meat. Years ago, I experimented with substituting some ricotta for some of the cottage cheese, but found the results unsatisfactory. On the other hand, I experimented with a variety of cheeses and found them all to be tasty. You can use any enchilada sauce; try my Red Enchilada Sauce (page 311). Serve with sour cream, guacamole, and chopped lettuce or mesclun (a mix of baby salad greens, sometimes with other greens).

1 pound cheddar cheese, grated, or ½ pound each cheddar and Monterey Jack
16 ounces cottage cheese
1 small can (4 ounces) sliced black olives

1 small can (4 ounces) diced green chiles
1 to 2 cups coarsely chopped, cooked chicken, turkey, or beef
20 ten-inch flour tortillas

1 Prepare three 13- x 9-inch baking pans by oiling heavily or spraying liberally with cooking spray.
2 Combine cheddar cheese, cottage cheese, olives, and chiles.
3 Stir in meat and mix well.
4 Scoop a small amount of mixture (a few tablespoons) and spread out along edge of a tortilla.
5 Roll tortilla tightly into a tube and place in one of the prepared pans, seam side down.
6 Repeat steps 4 and 5 until you have used up all filling.
7 Cover enchiladas in each pan liberally with enchilada sauce.
8 At this point you can freeze one or more pans of enchiladas. Or you can cook them now: cover each pan with aluminum foil, making sure the foil doesn't touch the enchiladas, then bake at 350° for 20 to 25 minutes. If cooking from frozen, bake 30 to 35 minutes.

Fettuccine Alfredo

Total time: 30 minutes   Yields about 1½ quarts sauce

Over the years, I've experimented with making my own Alfredo sauce (without the benefit of a recipe; I was just reasoning it out). I always started by making a béchamel sauce (a roux-based white sauce) and adding cheese, and it was never quite right. Finally Google showed me many nearly identical recipes for Alfredo sauce, and the light dawned. For Alfredo sauce, unlike béchamel, you don't use a roux. This recipe makes about twice as much Alfredo sauce as you'll need for 1 pound of pasta, giving you extra sauce for those who want to drown their noodles. Or use the extra sauce for dipping bread. Refrigerate sauce for a few days to make another meal. For a new meal, heat leftover turkey or chicken with freshly made noodles and leftover sauce. The sauce thickens when chilled, but reheats nicely. **Always reheat on the stovetop, not in the oven or microwave**. I use Tinkyada brand brown rice fettuccine noodles, which makes this meal gluten-free. When serving, I grate black pepper over each serving. This recipe works best with freshly grated Parmesan cheese in fine strands, not the powdery bottled stuff.

1 pound fettuccine noodles
½ cup unsalted butter (no substitute)
2 large garlic cloves, minced

4 cups heavy cream
1½ cups plus ¼ cup finely grated Parmesan cheese

1   Heat water for pasta. When pasta water boils, stir in fettuccine noodles, boil 2 minutes, turn off heat and let sit, stirring occasionally, until noodles are done to your taste. Drain and set aside.
2   While the noodle water heats, make Alfredo sauce. Melt butter in a 3-quart saucepan over medium-low heat.
3   Stir minced garlic into melted butter and sauté until fragrant, about 2 minutes. Don't brown the garlic or butter.
4   Stir in ½ cup cream until incorporated.
5   Stir in remaining cream, increase heat to medium, and bring to a simmer. Continue to simmer, stirring frequently, for about 10 minutes. The sauce should be just starting to thicken.
6   Sprinkle the 1½ cups Parmesan over cream and stir in. Continue to stir until Parmesan is completely melted and sauce thickens more (about another 10 minutes). It will seem like it's taking forever, but eventually the sauce *will* thicken. Be patient. It won't be super thick, but should coat a spoon.
7   Combine drained noodles with about half the Alfredo sauce. Sprinkle each serving with some of the remaining ¼ cup Parmesan.

Fried Chicken

Total time: 45 minutes   Yields 4 to 6 servings

Y ou can find all manner of fried chicken recipes online, each author swearing their's is the best. And I'm sure they all are! Here's my recipe, which I'll only commit to saying it's pretty darn tasty. Peanut oil is traditional for frying chicken. But if nut allergies are an issue, you can use another cooking oil with a high smoke point, such as avocado oil. Use organic peanut oil—non-organic peanuts are in the Environmental Working Group's dirty dozen list, which means they test as having pesticides, carcinogens, and molds. Your butcher should know that "cut up for frying" means cutting each breast half in half, which gives you four breast pieces, two wings (if you want to fry them), two thighs, and two drumsticks per chicken. Save the backs (and wings, if you don't want to fry them) for soup or stock.

2 cups peanut oil
1½ cups all-purpose flour
1 tablespoon Italian seasonings
1 tablespoon garlic powder
1 tablespoon paprika
½ teaspoon salt

1 teaspoon ground black
   pepper
¼ teaspoon cayenne
2 cups buttermilk
1 to 2 whole chickens, cut up
   for frying

1 Pour peanut oil into in a deep frying pan or cast iron skillet to a depth of ½ inch.
2 Combine flour with Italian seasonings, garlic powder, paprika, salt, pepper, and cayenne.
3 Pour 1 cup buttermilk into a medium-sized bowl.
4 Put ¾ cup of flour mixture into a different medium-sized bowl.
5 Dip each chicken piece in buttermilk, then dredge in flour mixture. As you dip and dredge, add more buttermilk or flour to the respective bowls as needed. (To prevent waste, only add as much as you need. **For food safety reasons**, once the buttermilk or flour has been exposed to raw meat, you *must* discard it when done.)
6 Rest chicken ten minutes and start heating the oil.
7 Once oil reaches 350°, use tongs to carefully lower chicken pieces, skin side down, into oil. Fry 10 to 15 minutes on each side (to 165° interior temperature). Fry in batches to keep oil hot. If you add too much chicken at a time, the oil temperature drops too much. Be careful of spattering oil.
8 Drain chicken on a wire cooling rack (*not* on paper towels). Set rack over a large baking sheet to catch drips.

Fish with Lemon and Almonds

Total time: 15 minutes   Yields 6 servings

My mother used to cook filet of sole this way. The technique is simple and the results are delicious. You can use filets of Pacific Red Snapper, tilapia, catfish, or any other similar fish. The recipe calls for two filets per person, but because filets vary greatly in size, you may need to adjust quantities. The fish cooks quickly (just a few minutes on each side), so have all ingredients on hand and all side dishes prepared (or almost done) before you start cooking the fish. I like to serve the fish on a bed of brown rice with a side of steamed vegetables.

½ cup unsalted butter	**1** cup cornmeal (fine to coarse)
12 filets of Dover sole	**½** cup sliced almonds
1 cup buttermilk	**½** cup lemon juice

1   Melt butter in a large, deep sauté pan.
2   Dredge each filet in buttermilk, then coat thickly with cornmeal. I find it helpful to pour some buttermilk into a small, flat dish that has sides, and then some cornmeal into another, similar dish. If you don't have any buttermilk, you can just dredge the fish directly in the cornmeal.
3   Drop filets into melted butter and fry until fish is lightly browned on one side.
4   Gently flip filets and start frying on the other side. While you are frying on the second side, sprinkle fish liberally with some lemon juice, and toss on some sliced almonds. You will need to use your judgment and divide the lemon juice and almonds so you have enough for each panful of fish. Also, adjust the amount of lemon juice and almonds to your taste. (Although you *can* sprinkle the lemon juice on both sides, if you do it when you first start frying the fish, you may wash off the cornmeal.)
5   The filets are done when the fish is white and flaky. Remove from pan and serve immediately.

Hamburger Patties

Total time: 20 minutes   Yields 4 patties

This is my own simple, delicious way to make hamburger patties. My daughter isn't normally fond of hamburgers and she loves these. Serve them plain with a salad, fries, or potato chips on the side, or on burger buns loaded with dill pickles, lettuce, sliced tomatoes, and condiments (mustard, ketchup, and mayonnaise), or both. You can use a different cooking oil, but the sesame oil adds a wonderful flavor. Ancho chile powder is made from dried poblano chiles, a mild chile pepper originating in the state of Pueblo, Mexico.

1 tablespoon Italian seasonings
1 teaspoon garlic powder
1 tablespoon ancho chile
   powder

1 pound ground beef, no more
   than 80% lean
¼ cup diced yellow onion
2 tablespoons sesame oil

1 Rub Italian seasonings vigorously between your (clean!) palms until it's powdery.
2 Combine Italian seasonings, garlic powder, and chile powder.
3 Add seasoning mix to beef and mix evenly.
4 Combine onion with seasoned beef.
5 Form 3- to 4-inch flattened patties. You should be able to get 44 patties, each about 4 ounces. Make sure patties are evenly thick from center to edges.
6 Heat sesame oil in a 10-inch cast iron skillet until shimmering, then put patties in skillet.
7 Fry on one side of each pattie until nicely browned. Flip and fry the other side until done. Only flip once; resist the urge to keep flipping. And don't press patties with your spatula—that squeezes the juice out of the meat, making the patties drier. To test for doneness, use a probe thermometer. For food safety, the internal temperature should be a minimum of 160°.

Heidi's Crustless Quiche

Total time: 1 hour 20 minutes   Yields one 8-inch deep-dish quiche

My friend Heidi O'Claire invented this quiche recipe. It's crustless, gluten free, and fairly low fat. Plus super simple! And it's an excellent way to use up extra eggs. She says the Fage brand yogurt is essential because it's so thick, so either use that brand, or try another brand of Greek-style yogurt, or make your own. I list some possibilities for veggie or meat additions in the list of ingredients, but encourage you to experiment with ingredients that go well in a quiche. Or maybe some ingredients that conventional wisdom says *don't* go well. Experimentation can bring you to great finds. Don't mind the occasional failure—that's how we all become better cooks.

12 large eggs, well beaten
1 cup Fage plain yogurt
1 cup low-fat cottage cheese
Optional: 1 to 2 cups fresh vegetables (broccoli, bell peppers, grated carrots, cauliflower, spinach, summer squash)

Optional: 2 fully cooked sausages, sliced, or several slices of bacon or 1 cup chopped, cooked chicken or turkey, or any other meat ingredients that go well in a quiche

1   Prepare a 2½ quart casserole dish by greasing very well.
2   Combine eggs, yogurt, and cottage cheese.
3   Stir in any other ingredients you want that will fit.
4   Bake at 375° for 1 hour. Start watching it around 45 minutes; if it's browning too quickly, lightly cover with aluminum foil for the rest of the cooking time. The quiche is done when the center is no longer liquid.

Honey Ginger Glazed Chicken

Total time: 30 minutes   Yields 2 servings

Delicious, fast, flexible, and economical, this recipe has all manner of good things going for it. It takes about 30 minutes from start to finish, and most of that time is in the prep; the chicken and glaze cook in minutes. You can multiply the quantities to serve more people. I adapted this from a recipe on the Lord Byron's Kitchen website. Serve over steamed brown rice with a side of Sunomono (page 275).

Glaze (Makes about 1 cup)

1 tablespoon tamari
1 tablespoon rice wine vinegar
⅓ cup honey
⅛ teaspoon salt
⅛ teaspoon ground black
    pepper
1 tablespoon cornstarch

zest from 1 lemon or lime
juice from 1 lemon or lime
    (about ⅓ cup)
5 large garlic cloves, minced
    (about 2½ tablespoons)
3 tablespoons fresh ginger, half
    grated and half minced

Chicken

1 pound boneless, skinless
    chicken breasts, cut into
    bite-sized pieces
3 tablespoons sesame oil

1 cup cauliflower florets, fresh
    or frozen
1 teaspoon sesame seeds, for
    garnish (optional)

1 Make the glaze by combining tamari, vinegar, honey, salt, pepper, and cornstarch, mixing well to make a creamy fluid. Stir in lemon zest, lemon juice, garlic, and ginger. Set aside.
2 Heat sesame oil in a 12-inch skillet. When oil is shimmering, add chicken and sauté over high heat until no pink remains visible (about 160° interior), about 5-7 minutes. Chicken should reach 165° once you've cooked it in the glaze.
3 Remove chicken from skillet and set aside.
4 Pour glaze into skillet. Stir until thickened—about 3 minutes.
5 Add chicken to glaze. Keep heat on high. Stir chicken to coat with glaze. Add cauliflower and stir to coat. Keep stirring until glaze caramelizes (turns a dark brown); about 3 minutes.
6 Remove chicken. Garnish with sesame seeds. Serve immediately.

Hoppin' John

Total time: 4 hours   Yields 8 servings

Eating Hoppin' John (made with black-eyed peas or, in some states, Sea Island red peas) on New Year's Day is said to ensure financial success in the coming year. Regardless of whether this is true, it's a delicious and thrifty custom. If you leave out the meat, this is a perfectly acceptable vegan recipe.

2 tablespoons avocado oil

2 pounds boneless pork shoulder or boneless country-style pork ribs, cut into 2-inch cubes (you can also substitute thinly sliced strips of turkey or a smoke ham hock)

2 cups fresh or frozen black-eyed peas

2½ quarts water

2 yellow or white onions, coarsely chopped

4 carrots, cut into 1-inch segments

3 stalks celery, cut into ¼-inch segments

2 bay leaves

2 garlic cloves, diced

½ teaspoon cayenne

½ teaspoon black pepper

1   Preheat oven to 350°. Preheating isn't optional.
2   Heat oil in a 3- to 5-quart Dutch oven until oil shimmers.
3   Lightly brown meat on all sides in oil.
4   Add black-eyed peas, water, onions, carrots, celery, bay leaves, garlic, cayenne, and black pepper.
5   Bring to a boil.
6   Put a square of aluminum foil over top of Dutch oven. Place lid on aluminum foil. Bake for 1 to 1½ hours or until pork is tender.

Jamaican Lamb Curry

Total time: 2 hours, plus overnight   Yields 8 servings

The West Indies are home to a delicious melange of flavors and cooking techniques. This recipe, adapted from Melissa Clark's recipe (New York Times, October 16, 2015), gets much of its flavor from the combination of the Jamaican curry powder (recipe on page 301) and the green marinade. Ms. Clark adapted her recipe from a recipe shared by chef Martin Maginley of the Round Hill resort in Montego Bay, Jamaica. Instead of or in addition to the lamb, you can use goat, pork, or beef. Serve with rice; optionally, cook the rice with 2 tablespoons coconut oil or with coconut milk substituted for half the rice's cooking water.

3 pounds boneless lamb, cut into 2-inch chunks
2 tablespoons Jamaican curry powder (page 301)
2 teaspoons Himalayan salt
1 teaspoon ground ginger
1 teaspoon ground black pepper
1 large onion, coarsely chopped
4 green onions, coarsely chopped

6 garlic cloves, diced
¼ inch coarsely chopped fresh ginger (no need to peel)
4 whole allspice berries
4 sprigs fresh thyme
6 tablespoons avocado oil
2 cups diced potatoes
1 cup diced carrots
Lime wedges and fresh cilantro for garnish

1   Combine 1 tablespoon of curry powder with salt, ground ginger, and black pepper.
2   Put lamb in a large bowl and coat with salt/spice mixture.
3   Combine onion, green onions, garlic, ginger, allspice, thyme, and 2 tablespoons of oil. Purée.
4   Coat lamb with wet mixture, then cover bowl and refrigerate for a minimum of 2 hours and up to 8 hours. The longer, the better.
5   Heat 2 tablespoons oil in a 6-quart Dutch oven over medium-high heat. Stir in 1 tablespoon curry powder and heat one minute. Then, working in batches (to prevent overcrowding the pot), brown meat on all sides. As needed, add more oil a little at a time (adding it a little at a time helps avoid cooling the oil). As you brown each batch, transfer browned meat to a bowl or plate.
6   Once all meat is browned, put it all back into the Dutch oven, pouring any juices back in as well. Add water to barely cover. Bring to a simmer, then cover and simmer 45 minutes.

7 Stir in potatoes and carrots. Simmer some more until vegetables and meat are tender (about 45 minutes more).

8 Serve over rice with lime wedges and fresh cilantro (or parsley for your cilantro-loathing friends). Encourage your guests to squeeze the lime over their servings before they dive in.

Jamaican-Style Turkey Breasts

Total time: 1 hour   Yields about 4 servings

You're in the kitchen and think you have nothing to cook. You find some boneless turkey breasts in the refrigerator and, in the cupboard, some cumin seed and a jar of Jamaican curry powder (page 301). Your daughter gathers fresh limes from your Bearss lime tree. You cut up some yellow squash and get it steaming along with a pot of black rice. And this is the kind of meal you come up with. Simple, fast, delicious.

⅓ cup olive oil
2 pounds boneless turkey
   breasts
juice of 2 limes

½ cup Jamaican curry powder
   (page 301)
⅛ teaspoon cumin seed

1   Pour olive oil into bottom of a 13- x 9-inch baking pan.
2   Lay turkey pieces in oil (in one layer) and turn each piece so all sides are coated.
3   Pour lime juice over turkey.
4   Sprinkle ¼ cup curry powder on turkey, then flip turkey pieces and sprinkle remaining ¼ cup on the other side.
5   Sprinkle lightly with cumin seed.
6   Bake at 350° for 45 minutes or until turkey is done.

Lamb Curry

Total time: 4 hours   Yields 6 to 8 servings

Lamb is one of those polarizing meats—some people can't stand it, while others love it. I find it delicious when properly cooked. Although the ingredient list for this recipe (my own) is long, you just throw everything together and cook until the lamb is tender. My Madras-style curry powder recipe is on page 303, though you can use any other mild Madras-style curry powder. Serve over brown rice, with chutney on the side.

3 pounds boneless lamb shoulder, trimmed of excess fat and cut into 1-inch cubes

1 tablespoon Madras-style curry powder

2 cups plain yogurt

1/4 cup unsalted butter

3 medium yellow onions, thinly sliced

2 garlic cloves, crushed

10 thin slices fresh ginger

1 green chile pepper, sliced thinly (including seeds)

2 three-inch sticks cinnamon

6 whole cloves

1 tablespoon cumin seed

1 tablespoon coriander seed

2 tablespoons ground cardamom

2 teaspoon ground turmeric

1/2 teaspoon cayenne

1 (6-ounce) can tomato paste

2 cups water

1½ teaspoons salt

1   Place lamb in a large bowl. Sprinkle with curry powder and toss to mix.

2   Stir in yogurt and let stand at room temperature for one hour. (Or prepare the lamb a day ahead and refrigerate overnight after adding curry powder and yogurt.)

3   Melt butter in a large, heavy kettle over moderate heat.

4   Add onions and garlic to butter and sauté, stirring, 12 to 15 minutes until golden brown.

5   Add ginger, chile pepper, cinnamon, cloves, cumin, coriander, cardamom, cayenne, and turmeric. Heat, stirring, 2 to 3 minutes.

6   Stir in meat/yogurt mixture, tomato paste, water, and salt.

7   Cover, then simmer slowly 1½ to 2 hours or until lamb is tender, stirring now and then.

Lamb Rogan Josh

Total time: 1½ to 2 hours   Yields 4 to 6 servings

The Mughals were Muslims who ruled most of India and Pakistan in the 16th and 17th centuries. They picked up rogan josh from the Persians and in turn brought the recipe to Kashmir, where it became a signature Kashmiri dish. Adapted from *Best-Ever: 500 Simply Delicious Recipes* (Bay Books, 2007), this savory recipe is also made with beef or goat. Traditional rogan josh takes its characteristic red color from dried Kashmiri chile peppers and from alkanet, an herb in the borage family. This recipe uses the more widely available paprika. My garam masala recipe is on page 294. If you don't have whole spices, you can use ground spices. Serve garnished with almonds and cilantro.

1 tablespoon ghee or avocado oil

2 large yellow onions, coarsely chopped

½ cup plain yogurt

1 tablespoon paprika

1 teaspoon chili powder

1 tablespoon coriander seed

2 teaspoons cumin seed

1 teaspoon hulled green cardamom

½ teaspoon whole cloves

1 teaspoon ground turmeric

4 garlic cloves, coarsely chopped

1 tablespoon finely chopped fresh ginger

1 bay leaf

1 (14.5-ounce) can whole stewed or diced tomatoes

2½ pounds boneless leg of lamb or lamb shoulder roast, cut into 1-inch cubes (or 4½ pounds lamb blade chops, de-boned and cut into cubes)

1 teaspoon garam masala

¼ cup slivered almonds

½ cup fresh cilantro, chopped

1 Heat ghee in a large saucepan with deep sides.

2 Add onion and cook 5 minutes or until soft.

3 Stir in yogurt, paprika, chili powder, coriander, cumin, cardamom, cloves, turmeric, garlic, ginger, bay leaf, and tomatoes. Bring to a simmer and simmer for 5 minutes.

4 Add lamb and stir until coated.

5 Cover and cook over low heat, stirring occasionally, for 1 to 1½ hours, or until lamb is tender.

6 Uncover and simmer until liquid thickens.

7 While lamb is cooking, toast almonds in a dry skillet over medium heat for 3 to 4 minutes, lightly stirring, until golden brown. Remove from pan immediately. Be careful not to burn almonds.

8 Add garam masala to curry. Mix well, then serve.

Lamb Stew

Total time: 3 hours   Yields 8 servings

This is my own recipe. I like to serve it ladled over a fragrant bowl of brown rice. For a more subtly complex flavor, substitute 2 cups of seasoned flour (page 312) for the first five ingredients. To make this gluten-free, substitute brown rice flour for the all-purpose flour.

2 cups all-purpose flour
2 tablespoons Italian
   seasonings
1 tablespoon garlic granules
½ teaspoon freshly ground
   black pepper
½ teaspoon cayenne
2½ pounds boneless lamb
   shoulder roast, cut into 1½-
   inch cubes (or 4½ pounds
   lamb blade chops, de-
   boned and cut into cubes)

4 tablespoons avocado oil or
   olive oil
2 large yellow onions, coarsely
   chopped
4 garlic cloves, coarsely
   chopped
2¼ cups chicken broth or
   water
2 bay leaves

1 Combine flour, Italian seasonings, garlic, pepper, and cayenne in a gallon-sized Ziploc bag. Close bag and shake well to combine.
2 Put several pieces of lamb into Ziploc bag and shake to coat. Take pieces out and set aside in a bowl. Repeat until all lamb pieces are coated and in a bowl. Discard Ziploc bag and flour mix.
3 Heat oil in a heavy-bottomed stock pot or 6-quart Dutch oven until shimmering.
4 Add lamb pieces to pot and brown, turning to brown on all sides. Some flour will fall off, but that's okay.
5 Remove browned lamb and set aside in a bowl.
6 Add more oil to pot and add onions and garlic. Cook, stirring and scraping bottom the whole time, until onions are translucent.
7 Add lamb back to the and add chicken broth. Bring to a simmer.
8 Add bay leaves and cover pot. Simmer until lamb is tender, about 1½ hours. You can also cook it in the oven for the same length of time.

Lamb Tagine

Total time: 2 hours   Yields 6 to 8 serving

A tagine is both a style of food dish and the pot it's cooked in. A Berber and Moroccan food, tagines are richly flavorful, slow-cooked meals of meat or meat and vegetables. Often, the meat is cooked with dried fruit(s). I adapted this recipe from the second edition of *The New Best Recipe* (America's Test Kitchen, 2004). It takes a lot of time, but most of that is cooking time, and the results are deeply satisfying. To make this gluten-free, substitute cornstarch or arrowroot for the flour. Serve with organic brown rice and garnish with fresh cilantro.

2½ pounds boneless lamb shoulder roast, cut into stew-sized cubes, or 4½ pounds lamb blade chops, de-boned and cut into cubes
3 tablespoons avocado oil
2 large yellow onions, coarsely chopped
4 garlic cloves, coarsely chopped
3 tablespoons all-purpose flour
1 teaspoon cumin seed

1 teaspoon ground cinnamon
1 teaspoon ground ginger
½ teaspoon coriander seed
½ teaspoon cayenne
2 cups chicken broth
1 (14.5-ounce) can diced tomatoes
2 bay leaves
1 cup dried apricots, roughly chopped
¼ cup fresh cilantro, coarsely chopped

1   Preheat oven to 300°.
2   Heat 1 tablespoon oil in a large Dutch oven over medium-high heat until oil is shimmering but not smoking.
3   You may need to repeat this step a few times, depending on how much meat you have: Add meat to Dutch oven so pieces barely touch. Brown meat 2 to 3 minutes. Turn each piece and continue browning, another 2 to 3 minutes. When one batch of meat is done, transfer it to a bowl. Add more oil and brown another batch. Keep doing this until all meat is browned and removed from Dutch oven.
4   Reduce heat to medium. Add 1 tablespoon oil to Dutch oven. Stir in onion, garlic, and ¼ teaspoon salt until coated. Cook, stirring vigorously, scraping bottom of pot to loosen the tasty brown bits, until onion is soft (about 5 minutes).
5   Add flour, cumin, cinnamon, ginger, coriander, and cayenne. Stir until onions and garlic are coated (about 1 minute).

6 Gradually add broth, scraping sides and bottom of pot.

7 Stir until flour dissolves and liquid is thick.

8 Stir in tomatoes, bay leaves, and apricots. Bring to a simmer.

9 Add lamb and any accumulated juices in bowl.

10 Cover top of Dutch oven with a sheet of aluminum foil. Put lid on over foil, making sure the lid is seated well. (The foil helps seal the pot so liquids won't evaporate in the oven.)

11 Cook 1½ hours or until lamb is tender.

Magyar Chicken Paprikash

Total time: 1½ hours   Yields 4 servings

'**I**'ve been making this simple, savory recipe for so many decades, I don't remember who first shared it with me. The Magyar peoples have a rich history; today, "Magyar" is used to refer to Hungarians as a whole, though technically it means a specific ethnic group. *Paprikash* is a Hungarian word for a meat-based stew with lots of paprika. Be careful not to go overboard with the paprika. One young house guest making this dish from my recipe for the first time thought, "Some paprika is delicious; surely more will be even better, yes?" and he dumped a cup of paprika into the dish. The answer was "no." What was supposed to be a medium-thick sauce turned into inedible paprika cement. I was annoyed at the waste, but now I chuckle over it, and I can't fault experimentation in the kitchen—some of my best recipes come from experimenting. It was a good reminder that one important cooking skill is understanding proportions and knowing your ingredients. Sometimes you just need to cook enough to gain that expert's intuition. Serve over large flat noodles, rice, or mashed potatoes.

½ cup salted butter
1 chicken, cut up (boneless, skinless chicken also works)
2 cups diced onion

1½ cups red wine
3 tablespoons paprika
1 cup sour cream

1 Melt butter in a large skillet, then add chicken pieces and brown on all sides.
2 Add onions and cook 3 to 5 minutes.
3 Add wine.
4 Sprinkle chicken with paprika, then spoon some of the wine/onion sauce over the top of each piece of chicken.
5 Cover and bake at 350° degree for 45 minutes to 1 hour. (The longer you cook it, the tenderer the chicken.)
6 Remove from oven and transfer chicken from skillet to a serving dish.
7 Stir sour cream into what remains in the skillet. Stir until well mixed. Pour sour cream mix over chicken and serve.

Mango Ginger Beef Curry

Total time: 7 to 25 hours   Yields 2 servings

My friend Bryan created this recipe. For more servings, increase ingredients, keeping the same proportions. If you want to tone the brightness down, add ½ tablespoon tomato paste to the yogurt mix. If you don't have access to Penzey's, you can make your own curry powder using my Madras-style curry powder recipe (page 303), or use your favorite curry powder. You can also use my garam masala recipe on page 294. Serve over brown rice or noodles.

1 pound beef, cubed
½ mango, puréed, or ¾ cup mango pulp
2 tablespoons plus ½ teaspoon ginger (ground or fresh—if using fresh, dice it)
2 tablespoons plus ½ teaspoon Penzey's sweet curry powder
1 tablespoon Penzey's hot curry powder

½ cup yogurt (in-pot, unstrained, whole-milk Indian-style yogurt)
2 small potatoes, cut into 1-inch cubes
1 clove garlic, minced
3 tablespoons oil or ghee
Salt to taste
½ teaspoon garam masala

1 Place beef in a Ziploc bag with enough mango purée to cover. Add ½ teaspoon ginger and ½ teaspoon sweet curry powder. Squish bag with your fingers until spices are mixed in and beef is thoroughly coated.
2 Put Ziploc bag of beef in refrigerator to marinate 6 to 24 hours.
3 Combine remaining mango purée with yogurt, the remaining 2 tablespoons sweet curry powder, and hot curry powder. Refrigerate while you're marinating the beef.
4 When beef has marinated, heat oil in a medium skillet. Add potatoes and cook for five minutes, then add fresh garlic and the remaining 2 tablespoons ginger.
5 Cook 3 to 4 minutes or until the potatoes soften a bit.
6 Add beef and marinade. Cook a few minutes.
7 Add yogurt/mango mix and cook 5 more minutes. The beef should be done. The sauce thickens as it cooks.
8 Turn off the heat and stir in garam masala.

Mom's Pot Roast

Total time: 4½ hours   Yields 1 roast

My mother's pot roast "recipe" was really more a style of cooking. Like all her recipes, I had to watch her cook to get the instructions. Her pot roast was tender, but dry. I cooked pot roast her way for years—no, decades—before I found out pot roast is supposed to be moist and have a lovely, rich gravy. I've come to the conclusion that expediency was her catchphrase; as a working single mother of four, she didn't have time to get fancy. I now prefer the pot roast recipe on page 218, but I'm including this recipe here as a historical document and for my siblings if they want it.

3½ pounds boneless chuck-eye beef roast

4 to 6 medium carrots, sliced into 2-inch lengths

4 to 6 large russet potatoes, quartered

2 cups water

1 Preheat oven to 300°F.
2 Place roast in a shallow roasting pan. Arrange carrots and potatoes around it.
3 Pour water into pan.
4 Roast until tender (3 to 4 hours).

Moroccan Chicken

Total time: 50 minutes, plus optional
marinating time

Yields a variable amount

This is more a process than a recipe, derived from a *Better Homes and Gardens*. recipe. You can increase or decrease the amount of chicken (adjusting the quantities of spice, salt, and oil accordingly), or substitute beef, pork, or lamb for the chicken, or added carrots, eggplants, potatoes, dried apricots, or other compatible vegetables or fruits.

1 teaspoon Himalayan salt
3 tablespoons Moroccan spices
   (page 305)
¼ cup avocado oil

2 pounds boneless chicken,
   cubed (or beef, pork, or
   lamb)

1 Combine salt with Moroccan spices.
2 Stir salt/spice blend into oil in a medium bowl.
3 Thoroughly coat chicken with oil/spice/salt blend.
4 Optional: Marinate in refrigerator 30 minutes or overnight.
5 Place chicken in one layer in a 13- x 9-inch pan and bake at 350° for
  30 to 40 minutes or until chicken is 165° inside.

Oven-Baked Quesadillas

Total time: 1 hour   Yields 2 quesadillas

My friend Kat Macfarlane, may she rest in peace, invented this recipe the day after the October 17, 1989 Loma Prieta earthquake. We worked and lived just miles from the epicenter. Her electric power was restored much sooner than mine, but I had a car and she needed some help, which I provided. Afterward, we both sat, shaky and companionable, on the floor of her living room eating these quesadillas. Later, she gave me the recipe with this comment: "You can also add shaved beef or chicken to these, or anything else you like. Think of them as Mexican pizza, and improvise at will."

4 burrito-sized flour tortillas
1 can (15½ ounces) refried
   beans
hot pepper sauce to taste

2 cups grated cheddar or
   Monterey Jack cheese
½ cup fresh cilantro, chopped
2 tablespoons cumin seed
½ cup sour cream for topping

1 Prepare four 15-inch square pieces of aluminum foil. Place two sheets on a large baking sheet.
2 Place one flour tortilla on each square of aluminum foil.
3 Spread half the can of refried beans on a tortilla. Repeat for the other tortilla.
4 Sprinkle beans with hot pepper sauce and spread sauce evenly.
5 Sprinkle 1 cup of cheese and ¼ cup cilantro over each quesadilla.
6 Crush cumin in a mortar and sprinkle evenly over quesadillas.
7 Top each quesadilla with a second tortilla, then top with a second sheet of foil. Crimp edges of foil to form a packet. Bake at 350° until the cheese melts (about 20 minutes).
8 Remove quesadillas from foil and transfer to a plate. Cut in wedges, and top with sour cream.

Pizza

Total time: 1½ hours   Yields 2 medium pizzas

According to Franceso Salvo, "The essence of Neapolitan pizza is family sharing its passion." ("Pie is a constant," *Smithsonian*, March 2021). The same could be said for any family favorites. This delicious recipe uses my mother's pizza dough. Intriguingly, she added the dough's oil to the yeast and water. Toppings can vary wildly, and you can make this a tasty vegetarian or vegan meal.

Dough

- 1 cup warm water
- 1 package (2¼ teaspoons) active dry yeast
- 3 tablespoons olive oil

- 3 cups all-purpose flour or bread flour
- 2 tablespoons granulated sugar
- A pinch of salt

Toppings

- ½ cup olive oil or 24 ounces marinara sauce
- 2 to 3 cups grated cheese (Monterey Jack, cheddar, and mozzarella are good choices)

- 1 cup each of any topping you like; for example, olives, pepperoni, artichoke hearts, Canadian bacon, bell peppers, thinly sliced mushrooms

1 Dissolve yeast in warm water and add the 3 tablespoons olive oil.
2 In a separate bowl, combine flour, sugar, and salt.
3 Make a well in the flour and pour yeast and oil blend into well. Mix thoroughly.
4 Knead dough until it feels elastic and springy, about 5 to 10 minutes.
5 Set aside to rise 30 minutes.
6 Punch dough down and spread into well-oiled baking pan(s): a single 13- x 9-inch baking pan for a thick crust, or two 13- x 9-inch pans for a thinner crust. For the thinner crust, you'll have to stretch the dough to fit two pans, but don't worry; it will rise while baking.
7 Mold dough to pan, creating rims to hold sauce.
8 If making two pizzas, spread ¼ cup olive oil or 12 ounces marinara sauce on each pizza. If making one pizza, spread ¼ cup oil or 12 ounces marinara on dough.
9 Cover sauce thickly with grated cheeses and other toppings.
10 Bake at 350° for 20 to 25 minutes or until crust is lightly browned.

Pork Tablecloth Stainer

Total time: 3 hours   Yields a large pot of stew

I found this unusual sweet and spicy stew recipe in the 1980s in Moira Hodgson's *The Hot & Spicy Cookbook* (McGraw-Hill, 1977). This recipe originates in either Mexico or South America and is called *mancha manteles de cerda*. You can also make it with chicken or other meats. I've modified the recipe slightly so the instructions are more efficient and to use easier-to-find the ingredients.

- **2** pounds boneless pork shoulder roast, cubed
- **1** bay leaf
- **½** teaspoon oregano
- **½** teaspoon thyme
- **4** dried red chiles (mild or spicy, your choice)
- **½** pound tomatoes, chopped
- **1** medium onion, coarsely chopped
- **8** sprigs fresh cilantro
- **2** garlic cloves, coarsely chopped
- **¼** teaspoon ground cloves
- **¼** teaspoon ground cinnamon
- **2** tablespoons avocado oil
- **½** teaspoon cumin seed
- **2** sweet potatoes, cubed, then baked until fairly firm
- **2** tart apples, cored and sliced
- **2** large medium-ripe bananas, sliced
- **8** ounces green peas, fresh or frozen

1   Place pork in a large Dutch oven. Add bay leaf, oregano, and thyme. Cover with water and simmer for 1½ hours.
2   While pork is cooking, put on gloves and tear dried chiles into small pieces. Soak chiles in 1 cup boiling water for 30 minutes. Purée chiles with their soaking liquid.
3   Combine tomatoes, chile liquid, onion, cilantro, garlic, cloves, and cinnamon. Purée until smooth.
4   Heat oil in a large pot and add tomato/chile/spice mixture.
5   If the pork is done cooking, proceed. If not, wait until it's done.
6   Cook tomato/chile blend for five minutes, then stir in 1½ cups of pork cooking stock.
7   Pour tomato/chile mixture into Dutch oven. Add pork (and any liquid remaining), cumin, sweet potatoes, apples, and bananas. Simmer for 30 minutes or until pork is tender.

Pot Roast

Total time: 2½ to 4 hours   Yields 6 to 8 servings

Adapted from *The New Best Recipe*, second edition (America's Test Kitchen, 2004), this recipe makes a delicious beef stew perfect for cold nights. My mother's pot roast (page 213) is completely different but also delicious. The beef in this recipe ends up so tender that, as *The New Best Recipe*, says "the tension of a stern gaze...[is] enough to break it apart." The foil is inconvenient but indispensable; without it, the roast loses too much moisture. This recipe is best cooked in a Dutch oven.

- 2 tablespoons avocado oil or other cooking oil
- 3½ pounds boneless chuck-eye beef roast
- 1 yellow onion, coarsely chopped
- 1 carrot, sliced
- 1 celery stalk, sliced
- 4 large garlic cloves, coarsely chopped
- 2 cups chicken broth
- 1 tablespoon oregano (fresh or dried)
- 1 tablespoon thyme (fresh or dried)
- 1 bay leaf
- 1 teaspoon diced fresh ginger
- 5 small Yukon gold potatoes, quartered

1 Preheat oven to 300°F.
2 Heat oil in a 5-quart Dutch oven over medium-high heat until oil is shimmering but not smoking.
3 Brown roast in oil on all sides, about 5 to 8 minutes, reducing heat if oil starts to smoke. Transfer roast to a plate and set aside.
4 Reduce heat to medium and add onion, carrot, celery, and garlic. Cook, stirring occasionally, until onions start to brown, about 5 minutes.
5 Add chicken broth, oregano, thyme, bay leaf, and ginger, scraping bottom of pot to bring up the fond (the tasty brown bits).
6 Return roast (including any juices) to Dutch oven. Add enough water to bring liquid halfway up sides of roast.
7 Cover top of Dutch oven with aluminum foil and put lid on over foil. (The foil helps seal the Dutch oven so the liquids won't evaporate as much.)
8 Cook in oven, turning roast every 40 minutes (the foil is tricky but stick with it), until roast is tender (2 to 4 hours; the longer you cook, the more tender the roast). Halfway through cooking time, add potatoes.

Quick Sausage Korma

Total time: 45 minutes   Yields 6 servings

I created this recipe when there wasn't much in the cupboard and my friend Dawn sent over some sausages. I rummaged through cupboards, refrigerator, and freezer and put this together with things I'd found. It turned out to be quite tasty and worth preserving as a recipe. Because everything in this dish is precooked, it doesn't take long to cook this dish from start to finish.

5 six-inch pre-cooked sausages
2 tablespoons butter or oil
1 package Sukhi's Korma Curry Paste
2 cups chicken broth
2 cups water
1 (one-pound) package frozen vegetables and beans mix

1 (one-pound) package frozen green beans
1 (one-pound) package frozen peas
¼ cup heavy cream
3 cups cooked short-grain brown rice

1   Slice sausages into ¼-inch rounds and fry lightly in butter or oil in a large, deep skillet.
2   Add korma paste, chicken broth, and water. Stir well to combine, then bring to a boil.
3   Add frozen vegetables and bring to a boil again.
4   Lower heat, cover, and simmer for 15 minutes or until vegetables are hot.
5   Stir in cream and cook a few more minutes. Serve hot over brown rice.

Variations

1   Instead of serving over rice, mix cooked rice in with korma, then let sit for a few minutes.
2   Replace green beans with other frozen or fresh vegetables, such as broccoli or cauliflower.

Roast Pesto Chicken

Total time: 2 hours   Yields 1 whole chicken

I tend to like my chicken roasts plain, basted only with seasoned butter. The crisp savory flavor of the meat itself is enough for me. But this version of roast chicken is a tasty divergence. I've had this recipe since the early 1990s, and I don't remember from whom it came. The gravy is out of this world.

1 roasting chicken (6 to 7 pounds)
8 ounces pesto
3 tablespoons dry white wine
2 tablespoons all-purpose flour

2 tablespoons chicken broth
3 tablespoons heavy cream
A few leaves fresh basil for garnish

1 Preheat oven to 450°.
2 Rinse chicken with cool, fresh water and pat dry.
3 Slide hand between chicken skin and meat on breast and legs to form pockets.
4 Reserving 1 tablespoon pesto for gravy, spread remaining pesto in pockets and over outer skin of chicken.
5 Roast chicken in a large roasting pan for 15 minutes at 450°.
6 Reduce heat to 375° and roast until juices run clear when chicken is pierced in thickest part of thigh (1 hour 15 minutes). Chicken must reach an internal temperature of 165°.
7 Remove chicken to serving platter and cover with foil.
8 To make gravy, pour pan juices into a glass measuring cup. Separate fat and discard (or compost).
9 Add wine to roasting pan on stovetop and bring to boil, scraping up any browned bits.
10 Add water to pan juices to make 1 cup of fluid.
11 Transfer wine/pan juices to a small saucepan.
12 Combine flour and broth and stir until smooth.
13 Stir flour and broth into wine mixture.
14 Boil wine gravy until reduced to sauce consistency (about 5 minutes), stirring constantly. (It helps to use a hand-held mixer with one of those springy little attachments here.)
15 Mix cream and reserved pesto into wine gravy.
16 Season with salt and pepper to taste.
17 Garnish chicken with basil and serve with gravy.

Roast Turkey with Wine Gravy

Total time: Depends on turkey size and   Yields 1 whole turkey
oven, but expect it to take hours

This recipe is actually a set of recipes. It gives my method for roasting a turkey well, and roasting it in a way that gives you a good base for making an easy and delicious gravy. It also includes my own stuffing recipe (my brother Peter suggested adding artichoke hearts) and wine gravy recipe. The kind of oven you use, and whether you stuff the turkey, will affect the cooking time. If you use a convection oven, you can put a stuffed 23-pound turkey in the oven at 1:00 p.m. and have a roasted turkey coming out of the oven by or before 4 p.m. However, the same turkey will take hours longer in a normal oven. And a stuffed turkey takes longer to roast than an unstuffed one no matter what kind of oven you use. Also, the quality of the turkey affects how moist it is when done. A free range, corn-fed turkey will be moister and far tastier than a regular commercial variety. And finally, do yourself a favor and buy or borrow a real roasting pan. Don't use one of those one-use aluminum roasting pans—they are inadequate and can be quite dangerous, as they cannot support the weight of any turkey. If you choose not to stuff the turkey, or make the stuffing with gluten-free bread, and use cornstarch or arrowroot to thicken the gravy, this recipe can be gluten free.

Stuffing

1 loaf whole-grain bread
1/2 cup salted butter
1 large yellow onion, coarsely
    chopped
1/2 bunch celery, chopped

2 tablespoons poultry
    seasoning (page 308)
1 jar (12 ounces) marinated
    artichokes, cut into pieces,
    liquid reserved

Turkey

1 whole turkey

Turkey Basting Butter

1/2 cup salted butter
1 tablespoon poultry seasoning
1/8 teaspoon cayenne

1 bottle (750 ml) wine (zinfindel
    works great)

Gravy

1 to 2 cups hot water   **3** tablespoons all-purpose flour,
                                                cornstarch, or arrowroot

Making the Stuffing

1 Cut bread into ½-inch cubes and spread cubes on a large baking
   sheet. Cook in the oven at 225° until the bread is quite dry, about
   15 to 20 minutes.
2 Melt butter in a 12-inch sauté pan.
3 Add celery, onions, and poultry seasoning. Stir well and sauté lightly
   for 8 minutes or until onions are semi-translucent. Remove from
   heat.
4 Carefully fold in bread, coating pieces as evenly as possible.
5 Fold in artichoke hearts. Set stuffing aside and turn your attention
   to the turkey.

Preparing the Turkey

6 In a spotlessly clean sink, remove wrapper from turkey. Remove
   giblets and neck from inside the turkey. Chop up giblets and feed
   to the cats. Save the neck for turkey soup.
7 Rinse turkey well inside and out with fresh, cool water.
8 Place turkey, breast side up, in a roasting rack inside a roasting
   pan that is big enough for turkey without pieces sticking over the
   edge. Tuck wing tips under turkey's back. (This might take a bit of
   strength.)
9 Loosely stuff turkey's main cavity with stuffing. Sometimes I put
   stuffing into neck cavity as well if the skin allows for doing so while
   still being able to pin it shut. You may have stuffing left over; place
   it in a covered casserole dish and refrigerate. You can bake it after
   turkey comes out of the oven.

Basting the Turkey

10 Melt butter and stir in poultry seasoning.
11 Carefully pour basting mixture over the turkey, covering breast,
   wings, and legs. The basting butter should congeal onto the turkey,
   since the turkey should still be cold. That's perfect.
12 Pour one cup of wine and 2 cups of water into roasting pan.

Roasting the Turkey

13 Place roasting pan with turkey into oven. Roast at 325°. Every 30 minutes, baste turkey with liquid from bottom of roasting pan. Add more wine and water as needed to pan; you want an inch or two in depth at all times. Your goal is to have used up the bottle of wine by the time the turkey comes out of the oven, and to never let the bottom of the roasting pan get dry. Add more water than wine toward the start of the cooking; add more wine toward the end.

14 When turkey is beautifully browned, tent it with heavy duty aluminum foil and continue to roast. You don't need to keep basting at this point.

15 Every thirty minutes, check for doneness. For food safety, it should measure a minimum of 165° when testing the breast meat (without touching bone); I prefer to cook it to 180°.

16 When turkey is done, carefully remove roasting pan from oven . Remove the turkey and rack together from pan.

17 Bake extra stuffing for 30 minutes at 350°.

18 While extra stuffing is baking, remove stuffing from turkey and place in a serving dish. Let turkey rest while you make gravy.

Making the Gravy

19 You should be able to make the gravy right in the roasting pan, though if you can't, transfer the fluid from the bottom of the pan to a large saucepan.

20 Place roasting pan over two burners on stovetop. Turn heat to high. Sprinkle a few tablespoons of flour over fluids in the roasting pan. (Some people skim some of the fat first, though you need some to combine with your thickener to get a proper gravy.) Mix well. Add hot water to thin a bit if needed. Cook a few minutes or until thickened (don't worry if it seems runny; it will thicken more when it cools). Pour into a gravy serving dish.

21 Place turkey on a sturdy cutting board. Carve as desired, and enjoy your feast!

Rosemary Chicken

Total time: 1 hour   Yields 4 servings

Rosemary and chicken are a perfect pairing. And, as with many recipes, you can derive many variations, as shown in both this recipe and the next one. In this recipe, invented by my friend AJ, the rosemary is fresh and plentiful, adding an extra piquancy to the recipe. You can use any poultry seasoning you wish.

¼ cup olive oil
¼ teaspoon cayenne
½ teaspoon freshly ground
    black pepper
¼ cup chicken broth or water
1 stalk celery
¼ small white or yellow onion,
    coarsely chopped

⅛ teaspoon poultry seasoning
    (page 308)
1 one–foot sprig fresh
    rosemary
4 chicken breasts, boneless
    and skinless

1   Preheat oven to 425°.
2   Grease a 13- x 9-inch pan with olive oil and sprinkle pan with cayenne and black pepper.
3   Combine broth, celery, onion, poultry seasoning, and half the leaves from sprig of rosemary. Purée.
4   Smear half the purée on bottom of chicken pieces and place chicken in prepared pan. Spread remainder of purée on top of chicken pieces and garnish with remaining rosemary leaves.
5   Bake 15 minutes, then reduce heat to 325°.
6   Continue to bake until purée is dry on top and chicken is done; about 30 minutes or until chicken's interior reaches 165°. Watch closely to make sure you don't burn it.

Rosemary and Lemon Chicken

Total time: 1 hour   Yields 4 servings

Although the overall time for my rosemary chicken is about the same as the previous recipe, the preparation is faster and simpler. These two recipes prove that you can prepare the same main ingredients (chicken and rosemary in this case) in a thousand delicious ways. Instead of or in addition to the chicken breasts, you can use chicken thighs or a combination of breasts and thighs. You can also use turkey breasts and thighs, boneless or not. Adjust cooking times as needed; the larger, meatier turkey pieces will require more time.

2 six-inch sprigs fresh rosemary
4 breasts chicken, boneless and skinless

1 cup fresh lemon juice
¼ cup butter (salted or unsalted)

1. Grease a 13 x 9-inch pan.
2. Remove some leaves from the sprigs of rosemary and sprinkle evenly over bottom of pan.
3. Lay chicken breasts on rosemary.
4. Pour lemon juice over chicken.
5. Cut butter into small pats and place pats on the chicken.
6. Sprinkle remaining rosemary leaves over chicken.
7. Cover pan with aluminum foil.
8. Bake at 350° for 40 minutes, then remove foil and bake another 15 minutes or until chicken's interior is 165°.

Salmon or Tuna Loaf

Total time: 1 hour 10 minutes   Yields one 9-inch loaf pan

Basically meat loaf made with salmon (or tuna), this simple recipe is a family favorite, and a good way to get servings of salmon into your diet more economically. Often, people who say they don't like fish like the wholesome, slightly oily taste of salmon. You can also make this recipe using leftover cooked salmon or other firm cooked fish. As I mentioned in the recipe for Barbecue Meat Loaf recipe (page 171), the kind of bread you use makes a huge difference in flavor. Try making bread crumbs from the Bread Machine Potato Bread recipe (page 90). Serve with lemon wedges.

2 (1-pound) cans salmon or 4 (7-ounce) cans tuna
3 cups bread crumbs or coarse cracker crumbs or stuffing mix
2 large eggs, lightly beaten

1 medium yellow onion, coarsely chopped
2 stalks celery, chopped
whole milk to moisten
lemon wedges for garnish

1 Prepare a 9- x 5- x 3-inch loaf pan by greasing it well.
2 Drain salmon but reserve liquid.
3 Add enough water or chicken stock to salmon liquid to make 1½ cups.
4 Combine salmon, bread crumbs, eggs, onion, and celery. Add whole milk to moisten if needed.
5 Place in prepared pan.
6 Bake at 350° for 45 to 55 minutes.

Salmon Tuxedo

Total time: 20 minutes   Yields 4 servings

One of the best salmon pasta dishes I've ever had in my life was at the restaurant in the Adam's Mark Hotel in St. Louis in 1990. After much experimentation, I came up with this recipe, which is as close as I could come to reproducing that unforgettable experience. I call it Salmon Tuxedo because of the bow-tie pasta. For a gluten-free version, use gluten-free pasta and almond flour. This recipe is a good way to use up any leftover cooked or smoked salmon you may have. Note that, if using commercial smoked salmon, it may be too hard and dry to use as-is. In that case, soak the salmon in a little water to soften it, then drain well before using in this recipe. Because this recipe cooks very quickly, have all ingredients ready before starting.

3 tablespoons salted butter
1 tablespoon all-purpose flour or almond flour
1 tablespoon pine nuts, finely chopped
2 fresh basil leaves, minced, plus 4 whole leaves for garnish
¼ teaspoon freshly ground black pepper

½ teaspoon ground coriander
1½ cups whole milk
½ cup cream
6 ounces barbecued or smoked salmon, broken into small pieces
8 ounces bow-tie pasta, cooked and still hot

1 Melt butter in a medium saucepan over medium-low heat.
2 Add flour (or almond flour) to butter and stir, making a paste.
3 Add pine nuts, basil, pepper, and coriander.
4 Cook 1 minute.
5 Slowly stir in milk and cream and cook, stirring, until sauce is thickened, a few more minutes.
6 Stir in salmon a few tablespoons at a time. Cook another 2 to 3 minutes.
7 Serve immediately over hot pasta. Garnish with whole basil leaves.

Simple Cheese Quiche

Total time: 1 hour   Yields one 9-inch quiche

Quiche became suddenly popular in the late 1970s and early 1980s. A whole set of cultural references (today, we'd call them memes) grew up around this simple food, and unfortunately quiche became associated with yuppies (young, up-wardly mobile professionals), whose values were thought to be money and lots of it. A backlash developed, and quiche got a bad name. Quiche doesn't deserve to be relegated to history because of this backlash! It's an easy, hearty, satisfying one-dish meal prepared in less than an hour. I vary this recipe by adding sliced cooked sausages, chopped onions, cooked broccoli, and whatever else is on hand, placing those in the pie shell first, then adding the cheese next and egg/milk mixture last. Using other ingredients means less cheese. For the pie shell, try my Perfect Savory Pie Crust (page 103). This quiche is excellent served hot or cold.

1 single 9-inch pie crust
3 cups grated cheese (cheddar, Colby, and/or Monterey Jack all work well)

4 large eggs, beaten
1½ cups whole milk or cream or half-and-half or any combination of the three

1   Put pie crust in a 9-inch pie pan. Bake at 350° for 7 minutes. Remove from oven and turn oven to 400°.
2   If you're using any additional ingredients (sausage, vegetables,and so on), layer them on top of the pie crust.
3   Fill pie shell with cheese.
4   Combine eggs and milk and pour over cheese. The cheese should be barely covered.
5   Bake at 400° for 25 minutes. Reduce heat to 350° and bake another 20 minutes or until a knife inserted half-way between center and edge comes out clean.
6   Remove from oven and let cool. It will be puffed up, somewhat like a souffle, then will "fall" a bit. Serve hot. It will be juicy when hot, but will firm up as it cools.

Spaghetti with Myzithra Cheese

Total time: 25 minutes   Yields 2 servings

For this dish, I wanted to come up with my own version of a favorite dish at a spaghetti restaurant. After much experimentation. I came up with this recipe in the later 1990s. The ingredients are simple, but it took some (delicious) testing to come up with the right proportions. Myzithra cheese is an unpasteurized Greek cheese, often made from sheep's milk but also made with goat's milk or cow's milk. According to Cheese.com, myzithra has been made in Greece for thousands of years. You can get it fresh, but in this recipe I use the dry, salty, rock-hard form.

8 ounces uncooked spaghetti   4 to 8 ounces myzithra cheese,
½ cup unsalted butter   finely grated

1 Cook spaghetti as described under Cooking Dry Pasta (page 167).
2 While spaghetti is cooking, melt butter in a large frying pan. Cook butter over low heat until it is very slightly browned at the edges. Don't overcook! Remove from heat.
3 When spaghetti is ready, drain and place in a serving dish.
4 Pour browned butter over the spaghetti. Don't strain the butter; the little bits are important to the texture and flavor. Toss spaghetti noodles to coat with butter.
5 Liberally sprinkle spaghetti with 4 ounces of myzithra cheese, mixing it in well. Taste before adding more cheese to make sure you like the quantity. Add more if desired. Serve immediately with extra cheese sprinkled on top.

Spiced Cod

Total time: 30 minutes   Yields 4 servings

This recipe started out in the early 1990s as a recipe from Irma Rombauer's *Joy of Cooking* (Bobbs-Merrill Company, 1975), but the fish was too bland for my taste, so I spiced it up when researching medieval recipes. After my changes, the recipe gained an exotic, medieval flair that makes it an excellent dish for company, especially on short notice. It's important to finely chop the onion, garlic, and parsley. Serve over browned rice cooked with ½ teaspoon pounded dehulled cardamom.

4 thick cod fillets
¾ teaspoon ground black pepper
1 white onion, diced
2 garlic cloves, minced
¼ cup fresh parsley, finely chopped
1 sprig fresh thyme, stripped, stem discarded
¾ teaspoon ground coriander

½ teaspoon ground cumin
¼ teaspoon ground nutmeg
¼ teaspoon ground cayenne
⅛ teaspoon ground cinnamon
½ cup dry white wine
3 medium tomatoes, chopped, or one small can (14.5 ounces) whole tomatoes with juice

1   Rinse fish fillets and pat dry.
2   Place fish in a baking dish (approximately 8 inches square) that can be used on the stovetop.
3   Sprinkle fish with pepper, then cover fish with onion, garlic, parsley, thyme, coriander, cumin, nutmeg, cayenne, cinnamon, wine, and tomatoes.
4   Place dish on stovetop.
5   Bring to a boil, then quickly lower heat and simmer gently for 10 minutes.
6   Remove fish carefully; arrange in a hot serving dish and place in warm oven.
7   Cook sauce until it's reduced by half (8 to 10 minutes).
8   Pour reduced sauce over fish and serve immediately.

Squash Lasagna

Total time: 1 hour   Yields 12 servings

This is a larger, vegetarian version of the Beef Lasagna (page 174). See that recipe for notes on variations you can make. Refrigerate leftovers. The next day, the lasagna will be firm and easy to cut, and tastes great cold or reheated.

3 quarts spaghetti sauce
1 teaspoon Italian seasonings (page 300)
2 garlic cloves, minced, or 2 teaspoons garlic granules
2 teaspoons fennel seed
2 (one-pound) boxes lasagna noodles
2 pounds ricotta or cottage cheese

1 pound cheddar cheese, grated or thinly sliced; reserve ½ cup for the top
1 pound mozzarella cheese, grated or thinly sliced
2 pounds fresh or frozen zucchini and yellow squash, sliced

1 Combine spaghetti sauce, Italian seasonings, garlic, and fennel. For better flavor, you can optionally cook the sauce and spices 15 to 20 minutes.

2 Spread enough sauce in bottom of a 16- x 12-inch pan to thinly cover the bottom.

3 Place one layer of lasagna noodles on top of sauce in bottom of pan. Completely cover bottom with noodles; overlap noodles if you need to. Next, distribute ⅓ of the ricotta, ⅓ of the cheddar, ⅓ of the mozzarella, and ⅓ of the squash, then cover with a little less than ⅓ of the sauce. You aren't trying to cover each layer completely with cheese and squash (the ingredients will melt and spread), though you do want to cover each layer with sauce.

4 Repeat twice. You should have three layers of noodles, cheese, squash, and sauce.

5 End with a final layer of noodles and then remaining sauce. Sprinkle top with reserved ½ cup grated cheese.

6 Cover with aluminum foil. Bake at 350° for 40 minutes or until bubbly on top. Uncover for last 10 minutes of cooking.

7 Let stand 30 minutes. It gets firmer as it stands.

Stir-Fried Vegetables and Beef

Total time: 40 minutes   Yields a large amount

My tribe never liked traditional stir fry, so I experimented with different ingredients until I found a combination everyone liked. Turns out the culprit was soy sauce; once I switched to tamari and ponzu sauce, everyone was happy. (Tamari is a milder, usually gluten-free type of soy sauce. Ponzu sauce is a complex, citrusy sauce commonly used in Japan; it's also quite easy to make your own gluten-free version. For a recipe, see page 306. If you use gluten-free tamari and homemade ponzu sauce, this recipe is gluten-free.) You can make this vegan by leaving out the beef. Serve with steamed brown rice and extra ponzu sauce on the side. The leftovers keep well in the refrigerator for up to three days and are excellent cold. Vary the vegetables as you wish; for example, add thinly sliced carrots, asparagus, snow peas, fresh mushrooms, strips of sweet bell pepper, and so on. And try it with thinly sliced chicken or pork instead of beef. Yes, I use two oils in the recipe.

3 tablespoons toasted sesame oil or regular sesame oil

3 tablespoons avocado oil or other light cooking oil

8 ounces steak meat, thinly sliced (skirt steak is perfect)

2 tablespoons ponzu sauce

2 tablespoons tamari

1 cup sliced celery

1 cup coarsely chopped broccoli

1 cup coarsely chopped cauliflower

2 cups sliced leeks

2 cups coarsely chopped baby bok choy

1 can (8 ounces) sliced water chestnuts

1 can (8 ounces) bamboo shoots

1   Heat sesame and avocado oils over high heat in a deep, 12-inch sauté pan until shimmering.
2   Add meat and brown lightly on both sides.
3   Add ponzu sauce and tamari and stir once or twice.
4   Add celery, broccoli, cauliflower, leeks, bok choy, water chestnuts, and bamboo shoots. Stir well.
5   Reduce heat to medium low, cover, and steam for about 30 minutes or until celery, broccoli, and cauliflower are softened but not limp.

Stuffed Manicotti

Total time: 1 hour 30 minutes   Yields 14 stuffed manicotti

My friend Johnette shared this hearty and filling recipe in the early 1980s. I've revised it since, but the essentials are there. You can leave out the ground chuck to make this vegetarian (in which case, increase the cheeses and maybe add some spinach), and you can vary the fillings—for example, use chopped cooked chicken or seafood. I tried this with cottage cheese, but that resulted in a uniformly mushy filling.

14 manicotti noodles
2 tablespoons olive oil, plus more for the baking pan
1 yellow or white onion, diced
2 garlic cloves, diced
¾ pound ground chuck or lamb
1 cup ricotta cheese
2 large eggs, lightly beaten

½ cup Parmesan cheese, shredded
½ cup grated Monterey Jack cheese, shredded
1 tablespoon parsley (fresh or dried)
1 teaspoon oregano (fresh or dried)
1 jar (24 ounces) marinara or spaghetti sauce

1   Cook manicotti noodles for about 7 minutes. Drain and rinse with cold water, then cool until you can handle with your bare hands.
2   Prepare a 13 x 9-inch baking pan by lightly oiling it. Splash a little marinara sauce on the bottom and spread it around.
3   While manicotti cook and cool, heat 2 tablespoons olive oil in a large skillet. Add onion and stir, cooking until translucent.
4   Add garlic and stir a few times.
5   Add ground beef and cook until meat no longer shows any pink. Break meat into fairly small pieces.
6   Remove meat mixture from heat and cool a few minutes.
7   Into meat mixture, stir in ricotta, eggs, Parmesan, Monterey Jack, parsley, and oregano.
8   Holding each noodle at one end, fill manicotti with meat and cheese mixture. Fill completely; don't leave a gap in the middle. I flip the noodles and stuff from each end. Some people use a piping bag to fill the noodles.
9   Place stuffed manicotti side by side in prepared baking pan.
10 When you've stuffed and placed all the manicotti, cover with marinara sauce.
11 Bake at 350° for 40 minutes.

Tacos Doraditos

Total time: 1 hour   Yields 12 tacos (depends on tortilla size)

This recipe, shared decades ago by a former sister-in-law, is a perfect use for leftover turkey. It's a tacos dorados recipe—essentially a flour tortilla that's filled, rolled, and fried—though this recipe has more ingredients in the filling than the traditional variety. You might know this as a taquito; the name tacos dorados is more commonly used south of the US-Mexican border. Whatever you want to call them, the recipe is easy, forgiving, delicious, and filling. Even the hungriest person usually can't eat more than two of these. The tortilla is soft and just a bit crisp after frying. Serve hot with toppings.

Tacos Doraditos

1 can (4 ounces) chopped green chiles
1 can (4 ounces) sliced green olives
1 can (4 ounces) sliced ripe black olives
3 stalks celery, diced

1 tablespoon chopped fresh cilantro
1 medium onion, diced
2 cups cooked shredded turkey, chicken, or other meat
1 package large (burrito size) flour tortillas

Toppings

sour cream
guacamole
salsa

mesclun (mixed spicy greens) or chopped iceberg lettuce

1 Combine chiles, olives, celery, cilantro, and onion. Mix well.
2 Add turkey and stir until meat is well mixed in.
3 Put ¼-inch layer of oil in a 12-inch skillet. Heat until shimmering.
4 While oil heats, take a small handful of mix and spread on one edge of a tortilla. Starting on that edge, roll tortilla quite snugly. Prepare several tortillas before you start frying.
5 Place rolled tortillas in hot oil, edge down. You should be able to fit two or three at a time, depending on skillet size.
6 Cook about 1 minute on each side; 3 minutes total. While cooking, turn twice, forming a triangle. Turn as each side reaches a light golden brown. Watch carefully; these burn quickly. When each taco is done, remove and drain on towels.

Turkey or Chicken Curry

Total time: 45 minutes   Yields 6 to 8 servings

You can easily double this recipe, which is my own. Don't use leftover turkey; it won't come out right. Instead, use raw, fresh turkey. You can try other meats; my daughter prefers this made with chicken. Delicious served over brown rice. To double down on the homemade aspect, make your own garam masala (page 294) and Madras-style curry powder (page 303).

¼ cup unsalted butter or olive oil

2 medium yellow onions, diced

1 pound raw turkey or chicken, cut into bite-sized pieces

2 tablespoons Madras-style curry powder

1 teaspoon garlic powder

1 teaspoon garam masala

¼ teaspoon ground coriander

¼ teaspoon ground allspice

2 teaspoons cumin seed

½ teaspoon hulled green cardamom

¼ teaspoon hulled black cardamom or, if you are brave, one whole black cardamom (be sure not to eat it in the finished curry)

½ teaspoon ground turmeric

5 medium yellow potatoes, cubed (no need to peel)

1 can (14.5 ounces) diced tomatoes

1 Melt butter (or heat oil) in a large, deep sauté pan.
2 Add onions and sauté a few minutes until barely translucent.
3 Add spices and cook a few minutes more.
4 Add turkey and stir well. Cook until turkey shows no raw spots.
5 Add potatoes and stir until coated with the spices.
6 Add tomatoes and stir well.
7 Heat until simmering, then reduce heat to medium low and cover.
8 Simmer, stirring every 5 minutes, until potatoes are tender, about 30 minutes.

Upside-Down Pizza

Total time: 1 hour   Yields 8 servings

K ids especially enjoy this fun way to cook pizza. You could make this vegetarian by substituting Portobello mushrooms for the sausages.

Pizza Filling

1 pound sweet Italian sausage, thinly sliced
1 medium onion, sliced

14 ounces marinara sauce
1/2 cup sliced black olives
1/2 cup Jarlsberg cheese, sliced

Pizza Crust

2 large eggs, beaten
1 cup all-purpose flour
1/4 cup grated Parmesan cheese

1 cup whole milk
1 tablespoon olive oil
1/4 teaspoon salt

1. Preheat oven to 425°.
2. Sauté sausage for 5 minutes in a 10-inch cast iron skillet. Add onions and sauté 8 minutes longer or until sausage is well browned.
3. While sausage is browning, combine crust ingredients: eggs, flour, Parmesan cheese, milk, olive oil, and salt.
4. Pour off all but 1 tablespoon of fat from skillet.
5. Pour marinara sauce and olives into skillet. Bring to a boil; arrange Jarlsberg cheese on top and spread flour mixture over sausage mixture.
6. Bake, uncovered, for 30 minutes or until crust is golden brown.
7. Cut into wedges and serve from the skillet, or let stand 10 minutes and invert onto a serving platter.
8. If desired, sprinkle top of crust or pizza with additional shredded Jarlsberg.

Pickles, Ferments, and Preserves

For a few decades, it looked as though making home-made pickles and preserves was a dying art in urban and suburban America. In any group of friends and coworkers, I was often the only one who canned food. In recent years, many people have discovered how healthy, rewarding, and economical it can be to preserve one's own food. The abundance of support and recipes on the Internet has made it easier. And now, due in part to COVID, canning is popular again.

In this chapter, you'll find some family favorites that are easy to make, delicious additions to your meals. Any of these would make fine gifts for friends, co-workers, or family members as well.

Canning Safety

Before you go any further, a word of caution. If you've never canned before, this chapter is *not* the place to learn how. It's intended for people who already know how to can safely and are looking for new recipes to try. The canning recipes in this chapter are for experienced canners only. Canning is an applied science. As with any science, researchers now know a lot more about how to can safely than they did long ago. You may have grown up with unsafe canning practices and you might not even know it. Just because you survived, that doesn't mean the methods were safe. The latest thinking and research in canning is toward being more conservative in order to prevent food spoilage. Educate yourself about food safety and safe canning methods before attempting to can anything.

You must know what you're doing and follow the recipes exactly or you may end up endangering anyone who eats what you produce. Don't wing it on the ingredients or methods. Foods canned unsafely can make people sick or even kill them. The cause is botulism, from a toxin produced by the *Clostridium botulinim* bacterium. The toxin is invisible, odorless, and tasteless. Home-canned foods are responsible for over 90% of all cases of food borne botulism.

For safety, follow these three principles:

- **USE SAFE CANNING METHODS.** I cannot emphasize this enough. Learn the proper procedures and follow them. Don't listen to people who say, "Oh, I've been canning my way for years and nobody ever got sick." If a method is listed as unsafe by the National Center for Home Food Preservation or in the Ball book (both listed below), it is unsafe.
- Choose your recipes wisely. When looking at canning books online, be aware that some websites and books, even recent ones, do not teach safe canning methods.
- When in doubt, throw it out. If you think you made a mistake, throw out the food you canned. The cost of any food you throw away isn't worth the risk of getting ill.

If you're worried, that's good. I want you to be worried. If you aren't worried, you may get lax and make a fatal mistake.

For authoritative sources of safe canning methods and recipes, see

- Kingry, Judi, Lauren Devine, and Sarah Page. *Ball Complete Book of Home Preserving: 400 Delicious and Creative Recipes for Today*, ISBN 978-0778801313 (Robert Rose Inc, 2020). Any other of the recent Ball books is also good.
- The National Center for Home Food Preservation (NCHFP) website: nchfp.uga.edu.
- United States Department of Agriculture. *Complete Guide to Home Canning*, Agriculture information bulletin 539, revised 2015. Available for free download in PDF format from the NCHFP website, or for purchase from the Purdue extension site (mdc. itap.purdue.edu; product code AIG-539).

If you find a recipe online or in a book, compare it with the equivalent recipe in either the Ball book or at the NCHFP website. If the recipe in question matches one in the Ball book or on the NCHFP website, it's probably fine. If it doesn't, keep looking for a suitable recipe. Again, it's not worth risking your health and life. Be safe!

So Why Can If It's So Dangerous?

I hope I've convinced you of the necessity of learning and using safe canning methods and recipes. I may have even convinced you not to try at all, though that isn't my intention. Canning is a lot of fun, easy once you get the hang of it, and immensely satisfying. The results are so much tastier than anything store-bought, and nothing matches how satisfying it feels to use a jar of your own home-canned food.

If you're nervous, you can warm up to canning by making refrigerator pickles, jams, and chutneys. You still need to take care when making refrigerator products, but since you don't need a canner, making them is faster and you can get started right away.

Is It Jam? Jelly? A Preserve?

In the United States, we distinguish between jellies and jams, both of which are canned fruit preserves, made either from a single fruit or a mix of fruit. For an interesting read, see the free United States Department of Agriculture's (USDA) *United States Standards for Grades of Fruit Preserves (Jams)* (USDA, 1980). The differences boil down to the following:

- A jelly is a clear, firm fruit spread, usually made with fruit juice, with no pieces of fruit in it.
- A jam is a thick fruit spread made with whole or cut-up fruit, cooked so it retains a fruity texture. Jam is a bit softer and looser than jelly.

More loosely, the terms jelly, jam, and preserves are used interchangeably to mean fruit preserves. The core ingredients are fruit, pectin, an acid (such as lemon juice), and sugar.

Interestingly, in the United Kingdom, the term "jelly" is only used to refer to gelatin desserts, like those made with Jell-O. "Jam" in the UK is the same as the American jelly. If you ask for jam in either the US or UK, you should get a fruit preserve that is delicious no matter what it's called.

Refrigerator Preserves and Pickles

You can make a wide variety of foods that you store in the refrigerator—such as pickled beets, pickled cucumbers (aka pickles), and so on. I've included a few favorites in this chapter. Plus some of the canned recipes can be made as refrigerator recipes instead.

Even though you're not canning them but are instead storing them in the refrigerator for a short while, you still must follow safe practices when making refrigerator preserves and pickles. Given that, you may be as delighted and surprised as I was to find out how easy it is to make them.

Tools and Equipment

When making preserves, use non-reactive pots to cook the recipe. Non reactive means ceramic or stainless steel. Avoid Teflon, aluminum, and cast iron.

You'll also need a water bath canner (the least expensive), a steam canner (somewhat pricier), or a pressure canner (expensive), and some tongs to lift the filled jars.

To hold the results of the recipe, you'll need canning jars—specially made jars that can hold up to the canning heat and pressure without shattering. For most of these recipes, half-pint or pint jars work best, and for some, they are the only size to use. Most of these recipes only make small batches, and I recommend canning those batches in small jars. When you open the jars for use, unless you family is going to rip through the jar, you'll only want to open a small amount to the air at a time. The clock starts ticking on spoilage as soon as you open a jar.

As for sanitation, each recipe calls for "sterilized jars." According to Ball, if you're processing the jars, they only need to be clean, as do the lids (the flat things) and rings (bands), but sterilizing won't hurt anything. Just be careful with the lids—if you subject them to too much heat, you may prematurely melt the seal. And never heat canning jars in the oven—canning jar glass isn't tempered for dry heat.

You'll find a wide funnel helpful for filling the jars without much mess.

When putting on the rings, only finger-tighten them—if you tighten the rings too much, your lids will warp as the jars cool. The rings are for keeping the lids on until they seal.

When processing the jars, once the jars are cool, make sure they all sealed, label them with the contents and date, then store in a cool, dry place.

Processing Times

All processing times are for elevations from sea level to 1,000 feet. If you're at a higher altitude, you'll need to increase the processing times according to the USDA guidelines, which you can easily find online.

Apricot-Currant Chutney

Total time: 1 hour (plus overnight soaking time for dried apricots)   Yields 3 cups

This chutney recipe, which I adapted from Yamuna Devi's "Khumani Chatni" recipe in *Lord Kirshna's Cuisine: The Art of Indian Vegetarian Cooking* (Dutton - Penguin Putnam, 1987), produces a deliciously sweet, not too hot chutney, for which I won first prize at the 1995 Sonoma County Fair. You can find the Indian spice kalonji (*Nigella sativa*) at specialty shops or online. But be careful that you're buying the right seed; see the discussion of nigella on page 285.

1 pound dried apricot halves or 4 pounds fresh apricots
3 tablespoons lime juice
2 cups hot water
4 tablespoons unsalted butter or ghee
2 three-inch sticks cinnamon
1 teaspoon kalonji

1 tablespoon minced fresh ginger (no need to peel)
1⅓ cup currants or raisins
1 cup maple syrup or packed brown sugar
½ teaspoon salt
⅛ teaspoon bird's eye chile powder

Preparing the Apricots

1 If using dried apricots: cut dried apricots into quarters. Combined apricots with lime juice and the 2 cups hot water. Soak overnight. Drain before using.
2 If using fresh apricots, wash them, remove stems and seeds, and cut into quarters. Soak in lime juice and cold water (to cover) until ready to use. (The lime juice prevents browning.) Drain before using.

Making the Chutney

1 Melt butter over medium heat in a 3-quart stainless steel or enamel saucepan.
2 When butter is melted, continue to heat. Add cinnamon, kalonji, and ginger. Stir 30 seconds.
3 Drain apricots, then stir in apricots, currants, maple syrup, salt, and bird's eye chile. Increase heat to medium high and bring to a boil.
4 Reduce heat to medium low and simmer, stirring now and then, and more often in the last ten minutes, until chutney is thick and glazed. (About 30 minutes; if using dried apricots, it may take an additional 15 minutes.)
5 Serve immediately or put in sterilized half- or 1-pint jars with lids and refrigerate for up to a week. If canning, leave ½ inch headspace and process using the boiling water bath method for 10 minutes.

Apricot Nectar

Total time: 1 hour   Yields 12 cups of nectar

Ever since a doctor told me that apricot nectar is a time-tested remedy for certain mild intestinal upsets, it has been a staple in our house. But it's expensive, and most commercial varieties have high fructose corn syrup in them. So I was delighted to find a recipe for apricot nectar in the summer of 2007 (at recipegoldmine.com). This is an excellent recipe for apricots that are very soft but, of course, not yet spoiled. You're using bottled lemon juice because it has a standardized acidity. To adjust this recipe to meet your needs (if you have more or less fruit than called for), the basic proportions are one cup water to one quart fruit. These proportions make a fairly thick nectar—almost a purée; you can thin it when drinking it.

4 quarts fresh, ripe apricots, cleaned, pitted, and halved

4 cups boiling water

1 tablespoon bottled lemon juice per quart of nectar

1 cup sugar or to taste

1   Combine fruit and boiling water in a large pot. If apricots are soft enough, you will notice that a good amount of juice comes out of the apricots immediately. Stir well.

2   Simmer until fruit is soft. This shouldn't take long—perhaps 20 minutes or so on a gas range.

3   Press fruit/nectar mixture through a fine sieve, catching nectar in a clean container. This is a tedious task, and you may be tempted to whir the fruit up in a blender or food processor. Don't. The result will be too thick and more like a jam.

4   Measure sieved nectar (so that you know how many quarts of nectar you have) and put nectar in a large, clean pot.

5   Add sugar and 1 tablespoon lemon juice per quart of nectar.

6   Reheat nectar to dissolve the sugar; this should only take a few minutes, as the nectar should still be warm.

7   Pour nectar into sterilized half-pint or pint jars, leaving ¼ inch headspace. (Use *only* those sizes of canning jars.)

8   Using the boiling water bath method, process for 15 minutes.

9   When jars are cool, make sure they all sealed, label them with the contents and date, then store in a cool, dry place. For jars that didn't seal, either use nectar right away, or freeze it in ice cube trays and store cubes in the freezer.

Apricot–Pineapple Preserves

Total time: 2 hours 10 minutes   Yields about 6 cups

This unusual version of apricot-pineapple preserves uses maraschino cherries, which add color and interest.

12 ounces dried apricots, cut in halves

2 cans (13¼ ounces each) pineapple chunks, cut in halves and drained; reserve syrup

1 jar maraschino cherries, drained and cut into fourths (reserve syrup)

3 cups water

5 cups granulated sugar

2 tablespoons bottled lemon juice

1   Mix apricots, pineapple (with syrup), reserved cherry syrup (but not the cherries), and water in a 4-quart Dutch oven or stock pot. Cover and let stand 1 hour.

2   Stir in sugar.

3   Heat to boiling; boil rapidly 10 minutes.

4   Stir in lemon juice.

5   Boil, stirring occasionally, about 35 minutes.

6   Stir in cherries.

7   Pour boiling mixture into sterilized half-pint or pint jars, leaving ¼ inch headspace; wipe rims and put on clean lids and rings.

8   Process using the boiling water bath method for 15 minutes.

Chokecherry Jelly

Total time: 30 minutes　　　　　　　　　Yields about 8 half-pints

Chokecherries (*Prunus virginiana*) are lovely little red, translucent berries that grow on a shrub or small tree. Chokecherries are a close relative of the black cherry (*Prunus serotina*). The berries are mouth-puckeringly astringent, but make food worthy of Heaven and were used in pemmican by the northern Native American tribes. When I was 7, we lived in Montana. We'd gather wild chokecherries, which my mother used to make chokecherry syrup for our pancakes. That syrup was sweet, a bit tart, and 100 percent delicious. Later, we moved to Wilson, Wyoming. Mildred Kelly, my step-grandmother, lived in nearby Jackson Hole. She shared this recipe with my mother. Many years later, my mother gave me the same index card she'd received from Mildred. (I suspect my mother's own recipe, like most of her recipes, was entirely in her head.) To get the chokecherry juice, use the instructions from the *Ball Complete Book of Home Canning* cited on page 238. Here's a summary of those instructions; they work for pretty much any kind of berry: Carefully de-stem, wash, and drain the berries. Combine berries with ½ cup water for every 4 cups berries. Bring to a boil over medium-high heat, stirring often. Reduce heat, cover, and boil gently, stirring often and crushing berries occasionally, until berries are just softened (5 to 10 minutes). (Remember! Berries are tender!) Carefully transfer berry mixture to a dampened jelly bag or a strainer lined with three or four layers of dampened cheesecloth. Set or suspend the cloth or strainer over a deep bowl to catch the juice. Let drip for two hours or overnight.

3½ cups chokecherry juice　　　4½ cups granulated sugar
1 package (1.75 ounces) regular　　¼ cup lemon juice
　　powdered fruit pectin

1　Bring chokecherry juice to a boil in a medium stockpot.
2　Add pectin and bring to a boil again.
3　Add sugar and lemon juice and boil hard for 2 minutes.
4　Remove from heat and skim off any foam.
5　Ladle into sterilized half-pint jars, leaving ¼ inch head room.
6　Wipe rims and put on lids and rings.
7　Process using the boiling water bath method for 10 minutes.

Cranberry-Orange Relish

Total time: 1 hour 15 minutes   Yields 6 cups

This recipe can also be called a chutney. Serve it with your next turkey dinner for a change of pace from straight cranberry sauce. I don't remember where I got this recipe—it could have been from my brother Peter in the 1980s. You can process this recipe in a boiling water bath, or refrigerate for up to a week.

1 pound cranberries
2 large oranges
zest of two oranges
1 cup orange juice
1 tablespoon lemon zest
1¾ cups granulated sugar

¾ cup seedless raisins
1 apple, peeled and diced
1 teaspoon minced crystallized ginger
¾ cup toasted, slivered almonds

1   Clean cranberries.
2   Finely grate oranges and reserve zest.
3   Remove white pith and seeds from oranges, then coarsely chop the oranges.
4   Put cranberries, oranges, orange zest, orange juice, lemon zest, sugar, raisins, apple, and ginger into a pot.
5   Bring to a simmer. Simmer, uncovered, for about 45 minutes, stirring now and then.
6   When mixture is done cooking, add almonds. (It's easy to forget this step.)
7   Ladle boiling hot into sterilized half-pint or pint jars, leaving ½-inch headspace.
8   Wipe rims, add lids and rings, and process using the boiling water bath method for 10 minutes.

Curried Apricot Chutney

Total time: 1 hour 15 minutes   Yields 4 pints

Adapted from a recipe in the sixth edition of Irma Rombauer and Marion Rombauer Becker's *The Joy of Cooking* (Bobbs-Merrill Company, Inc, 1975), this recipe produces a spicy chutney perfect as an accompaniment for lamb curry. Stay on the light side with the curry powder. You can vary the amount of cayenne from nothing to ¾ teaspoon or more depending on your preferences. Someday, look up the story of *The Joy of Cooking*—how Irma had a running battle with the original publisher, and how she surprised Julia Child by saying that she didn't test all her recipes. Oh, and how Irma's half-brother, Max Starkloff, introduced social distancing during the 1918 flu pandemic. Casually share these facts with your guests as you hand around this lovely chutney.

4 cups dried apricots, chopped
1 quart water
1½ cups chopped onions
¾ cup packed brown sugar
3 cups apple cider vinegar
2 teaspoons ground ginger

1 teaspoon curry powder
½ teaspoon cayenne
2 three-inch sticks cinnamon
½ teaspoon salt
4 cups raisins (regular or
    golden) or currants

1 Combine apricots with water, onions, and sugar. Simmer 30 minutes. (Since water is such a major ingredient, I recommend using distilled, purified, or filtered water.)
2 In a separate pan, combine vinegar, ginger, curry powder, cayenne, cinnamon sticks, and salt. Bring to a simmer. Simmer 5 minutes.
3 When done cooking, remove cinnamon sticks. If you want to put them in the jars, break each stick into two pieces.
4 Combine apricot and vinegar mixes.
5 Add raisins and ladle chutney into sterilized pint jars. Leave ½ inch headspace. Remove as much trapped air as you can by poking a clean chopstick or similar tool (must be wooden, not metal!) into chutney.
6 If you saved the cinnamon sticks, poke one half of a cinnamon stick into each jar.
7 Process using the boiling water bath method for 10 minutes.

Gingered Pear Conserves

Total time: 2 hours   Yields about 30 half pints

A former sister-in-law shared this recipe in the 1980s. The bite of ginger and tanginess of lemon help offset the sweetness of these conserves. You can halve the recipe if 30 half pints is too many.

8 ounces fresh ginger   **10** pounds cooking pears
2 lemons, zested and juiced   **5** cups granulated sugar

1 Grate ginger. You can also mince the ginger if you don't mind tiny bites of ginger in the conserves. But grating, though tedious, is best.
2 Wash, quarter, and core pears. (According to the original recipe, you can also mince the pears. I prefer them quartered so you have nice chunks of pear in the conserves. Otherwise, the conserves become more like pear sauce.)
3 Place lemon zest, lemon juice, ginger, and pears in a large pot.
4 Bring to a boil over medium high heat.
5 Gently stir in sugar. (Gently so you don't crush the pears.)
6 Reduce heat to medium low and cook until conserves are amber or until they are as thick as desired (about 1½ hours).
7 Ladle not conserves into sterilized half-pint jars, leaving ¼ inch headspace. Process using the boiling water bath method for 10 minutes.

Kimchi

Total time: Yields

Kimchi, a treasured Korean food, is cabbage mixed with gochugaru (a Korean chile pepper), and other ingredients, then fermented. It's a wonderful source of probiotics and deliciousness. If you aren't familiar with kimchi, think of it as a spicy sauerkraut and you'll be close. Kimchi comes in many varieties. A Korean neighbor who shared her recipe said every household in Korea has its own recipes. (This isn't her recipe, though. It's from the Nourished Essentials website. For peace of mind, I recommend their Easy Fermenter lids.) You can eat kimchi as a snack, mix it into various foods (cottage cheese, for example), or use it in "Tofu and Kimchi Stew" (page 58). Once you open a jar, refrigerate it a few days to a week.

1 medium head (2 pounds) Napa cabbage
¼ cup sea salt or kosher salt filtered or distilled water
6 garlic cloves, coarsely chopped
1 one-inch length fresh ginger, diced (no need to peel)
3 tablespoons fish sauce or water

3 tablespoons gochugaru or cayenne pepper
8 ounces daikon, sliced into thick circles, then each circle cut into matchstick-sized pieces
4 scallions, cut into 1-inch lengths
2 to 4 quart-sized canning jars with lids

1 Cut cabbage into quarters lengthwise. Remove cores and cut each quarter crosswise into 2-inch strips.
2 Place cabbage strips into a large mixing bowl.
3 Add salt and mix together thoroughly. Add water to cover cabbage. Place a plate on top of cabbage. Weigh down plate with something heavy to keep the cabbage submerged. (I use the water jug.)
4 Let stand for 1 hour.
5 After standing, rinse cabbage. Drain and set aside in a large bowl.
6 In a small bowl, combine garlic, ginger, fish sauce, and gochugaru. Stir until it forms a uniform paste.
7 Add radish, scallions, and paste to cabbage. Put on food prep gloves. Using your hands, mix until everything is coated with paste.
8 Pack cabbage tightly into leaving 1-inch headspace.
9 If you have fermentation weights (not required), place one on cabbage in each jar.
10 Put a lid on each jar. Store at room temperature (60 to 70°) in a dark place for 1 day to 2 weeks.

Marinated Mushrooms

Total time: 30 minutes plus 2 weeks   Yields 9 half pints

Marinating can give almost anything an interesting dimension. This delicious recipe from the USDA *Complete Guide to Home Canning* (cited on page 238) can be an easy yet impressive addition to your repertoire. You can process the mushrooms or store them in the refrigerator. **Important**! You can only use the water bath process on *marinated* mushrooms. If you want to can *plain* mushrooms, you must use a pressure canner and follow the USDA instructions. You're using bottled lemon juice because it has a standardized acidity.

2 pounds small, fresh whole unopened button mushrooms with caps less than 1¼ inch in diameter
½ cup bottled lemon juice
2 cups olive oil
2½ cups apple cider vinegar (5% acidity)
1 tablespoon dried oregano

1 tablespoon dried basil
1 teaspoon dried thyme
1 tablespoon pickling salt
½ cup diced onions
¼ cup drained and diced pimentos
2 garlic cloves, quartered
25 whole black peppercorns

1 Clean mushrooms and cut stems off, leaving a short stub (about ¼ inch) attached to cap. Soak in cold water to remove embedded dirt, then rinse in clean, cold water.
2 Place mushrooms in a large non-reactive pot, add lemon juice, and cover with water.
3 Bring to a boil, then simmer 5 minutes.
4 Remove from heat and drain.
5 Combine olive oil, vinegar, oregano, basil, thyme, and salt in a saucepan.
6 Stir onions and pimento into oil and vinegar mix. Bring to a boil.
7 Place ¼ garlic clove and 2 to 3 peppercorns each in hot, sterilized half-pint jars.
8 Fill jars with mushrooms and the hot, well-mixed oil/vinegar solution, leaving ½-inch headspace. Wipe rims, put lids on, and finger-tighten rings.
9 Process using the boiling water bath method for 20 minutes.
10 Try to wait two weeks at least before eating so the flavors can permeate the mushrooms.
11 Drain before serving.

Plum Chutney

Total time: 2 hours   Yields about 4 cups

Along with the Apricot-Currant Chutney on page 241, this is one of my favorite chutney recipes. Scientists think plums were one of the first fruits domesticated by humans. In his Santa Rosa home, American botanist Luther Burbank (1849 to 1926) developed a Japanese plum into the Santa Rosa plum (*Prunus salicina* "Santa Rosa") and introduced it in 1906. The Santa Rosa plum is a large, plump plum with deep red to purple skin, a lovely red-orange flesh, and a sweetly tangy taste. The only drawback is that it's a clingstone, not a freestone, so getting the fruit off the stone is messy. But you're making chutney, so it doesn't matter if the chunks of fruit are bedraggled. In the late 1980s, I rented a home in Santa Cruz that had an abundantly productive Santa Rosa plum tree. I'd make this chutney when the plums were coming ripe (July through August).

2 pounds plums, unpeeled (Santa Rosa plums are great)
¾ cup packed brown sugar
¼ cup apple cider vinegar
¼ cup golden raisins

1 garlic clove, minced
1 tablespoon dried smoked red chile pepper flakes
2 tablespoons minced fresh ginger

1 Pit plums and chop coarsely to finely depending on the size of chunks you want in final product. Reserve about three coarsely chopped plums.
2 Put plums (except reserved pieces), sugar, vinegar, raisins, garlic, chile pepper, ginger, and cayenne into a non-reactive saucepan. Bring to a boil.
3 Reduce heat and simmer for one hour, stirring occasionally. Be careful not to burn it! Because liquid will be boiling off, you may need to gradually reduce heat to maintain a simmer without scorching the chutney.
4 Stir in reserved plums.
5 Place in sterilized jars, leaving ½ inch headspace, and store in refrigerator for up to a week, or process using the boiling water bath method for 15 minutes.

Refrigerator Pickled Beets

Total time: 1 hour   Yields 4 pints

I love beets in almost any form, especially steamed, pickled, and juiced. This recipe from the USDA *Complete Guide to Home Canning* book makes an excellent pickled beet that you can store in your refrigerator or process for longer-term storage. Don't discard the fresh beet greens when you trim the beets. Use them in salad or steam them—they're delicious.

3½ pounds small fresh beets (2 to 2½ inches diameter)

2 to 3 onions, 2 to 2½ inches in diameter each (optional)

2 cups apple cider vinegar (5% acidity)

¾ teaspoon canning or pickling salt

1 cup sugar

1 cup water

1 three-inch stick cinnamon

6 whole cloves

1   Trim off beet tops, leaving 1 inch of stem and roots to prevent color bleeding.

2   Wash beets thoroughly. Boil or steam until tender (about 25 to 30 minutes). **Caution**: If you boiled the beets, drain and discard the boiling liquid.

3   Cool beets. Trim off the rest of the stems and roots and slip off skins. Slice into ¼-inch slices.

4   Peel and thinly slice onions.

5   Combine vinegar, salt, sugar, and 1 cup water.

6   Put cinnamon and cloves into a cheesecloth bag and add to vinegar mixture.

7   Bring vinegar mixture to a boil.

8   Add beets and onions to vinegar mix. Simmer 5 minutes.

9   Remove spice bag.

10 Fill hot, sterilized jars with beets and onions, leaving ½ inch headspace.

11 Add hot vinegar solution, again leaving ½ inch headspace.

12 At this point, if you want to refrigerate the beets, wipe the rims, adjust lids, and refrigerate for up to a week.

13 To can the beets, remove air bubbles and adjust headspace if needed. Wipe rims, adjust lids, and process using the boiling water bath method for 30 minutes.

Refrigerator Dill Pickles

Total time: 12½ hours   Yields 2 to 3 pints

Refrigerator pickles (also called fresh dill pickles) are so easy to make, you may never buy pickles again. If you want a sweet pickle recipe, you can find a safe one in one of the sources I cited on page 238. Note that it's super important to use vinegar of a known acidity and to follow the instructions exactly. Small cucumbers are best and stay crisper.

- **2** pounds of 3- to 5-inch pickling cucumbers
- **½** gallon water
- **⅓** cup canning or pickling salt (divided)
- **1½** cups vinegar (5% acidity)
- **3** teaspoons sugar
- **2** cups water
- **½** tablespoon whole mixed pickling spices

- **1** tablespoon mustard seed (1 teaspoon per pint jar)
- **3** to 5 sprigs fresh dill (1½ sprigs per pint jar)
- **2** to 3 tablespoons dill seed (1½ teaspoons per pint jar); dill seed gives the pickles their distinctive dill flavor

1 Wash cucumbers. Thinly slice off the blossom end and discard, but leave ¼ inch of stem attached.
2 Optional if making refrigerator dills: Dissolve 8 teaspoons salt in ½ gallon water. Pour over cucumbers and let stand 12 hours. After 12 hours, drain cucumbers.
3 Combine vinegar, the remaining salt, sugar, and 2 cups water.
4 Add mixed pickling spices tied in a clean white cloth. Heat to boiling.
5 As desired, slice cucumbers into spears or disks, or leave whole. You'll be able to pack more sliced cucumbers into each jar.
6 Fill hot, sterilized jars with cucumbers. Add 1 teaspoon mustard seed, 1½ heads fresh dill, and 1½ teaspoons per pint.
7 Cover cucumbers with boiling pickling solution, leaving ½ inch headspace.
8 If keeping in refrigerator: Put lids on and refrigerate.
9 If canning: Temove air bubbles and adjust headspace if needed. Wipe rims of jars, adjust lids, and process using the boiling water bath method for 10 minutes (if using pints) or 15 minutes (if using quarts). You can also use the low-temperature pasteurization method described in the USDA *Complete Guide to Home Canning*.

Tomato Chutney

Total time: 2 hours 30 minutes   Yields 4 cups

Quite spicy and quite gingery. I don't remember who shared this recipe with me—it might have been the same former sister-in-law who shared the recipe for Gingered Pear Conserves (page 247). This chutney is excellent with savory foods, such as chicken, or served on a charcuterie board (page 2).

7 fresh Anaheim chile peppers
3 fresh jalapeño peppers
1 fresh cayenne pepper
4½ cups packed brown sugar
1 quart apple cider vinegar (5% acidity)

½ pound fresh garlic, coarsely chopped
1½ pounds fresh ginger, minced
6 pounds tomatoes, washed, skinned, and chopped
2 cups seedless golden raisins

1 Roast fresh chile peppers in a hot oven (400° to 450°) or under broiler for 6 to 8 minutes.
2 Put rubber gloves on! Remove skins, stems, and seeds from chile peppers using one of the following methods:

  • Wrap chiles in a wet towel after removing from oven. Let stand 15 minutes, then skin them.
  • Place chiles in plastic bags. Freeze several hours, then skin them.

3 Bring sugar and vinegar to a boil over medium heat. Stir and scrape sides of pot to push down any sugar crystals. Continue to boil until sugar is dissolved and a thin syrup forms.
4 Stir in garlic and ginger and return to a boil.
5 Add tomatoes, raisins, and chiles.
6 Keep boiling (or bring to a boil again), stirring, then reduce heat to low.
7 Simmer until mixture thickens and solids soften.
8 Remove from heat.
9 Pour into hot, sterilized jars, leaving a ½ inch headspace, and process using the boiling water bath method for 20 minutes.

Wine Jelly

Total time: 30 minutes   Yields 4 cups

This recipe came from the December 1988 *Sunset* magazine. A set of small jars of these, made from different wines, makes a great holiday gift. The wine you choose determines the taste and appearance of the jelly, so it's great to use a good wine of known vintage than generic table wine. Sugar softens the tannins in a red wine; that means even young reds make a delicious jelly. Try, for example, a Pinot Noir or a Syrah for the red, and a Pinot Grigio or a Gewürztraminer for the white. If making several batches, don't multiply the recipe. Prepare everything you need for each batch (jars, lids, and so on), then cook one batch at a time. Note that for safety, I've updated my old recipe using the Red Wine Jelly recipe from the *Ball Complete Book of Home Preserving* (book cited on page 238).

3¼ cups good wine
½ cup bottled lemon juice

1 package (1¾ ounces) regular powdered fruit pectin
4½ cups granulated sugar

1. Wash four half-pint canning jars, lids, and rings with hot, soapy water. Drain; no need to dry.
2. In a 5- to 6-quart non-reactive pot, combine wine with lemon juice, then mix in pectin until dissolved.
3. Bring to a boil over high heat, stirring frequently.
4. Add sugar all at once and return to a full rolling boil, stirring constantly. The mixture will foam quite high.
5. Boil hard for 2 minutes, stirring constantly.
6. Remove from heat and skim off foam.
7. Ladle into prepared jars, leaving ¼-inch headspace. Wipe rims clean. Put lids and bands on jars, then

- If jellies are to be stored in refrigerator: Let jars cool, then refrigerate 6 months to a year. Use within one month of opening.
- If jellies are to be stored at room temperature: Process using the boiling water bath method for 10 minutes. Store in a cool dark place for 1 to 2 years.

Ingredients for Three Batches

5 pounds granulated sugar
1½ cups lemon juice
3 packages (5¼ ounces) regular powdered fruit pectin

3 bottles of 3 different wines (only 2 bottles of wine if you are using the same wine for all)
12 half-pint jars with lids

Salads & Salad Dressings

Many of the spectacular salad recipes in this chapter are healthful. Yet they're tasty and quite easy to make, rewarding you with a salad delectable beyond what you'd expect for the effort involved. Most recipes are vegan or vegetarian, or can be made so by leaving out some of the optional ingredients. Experiment with different uses for the dressings, such as using them as dips or in wraps.

Basic Mixed Green Salad

Total time: 15 minutes   Yields 4 servings

This recipe is a good start for a great mixed green salad as it is, and you can make it even better by customizing it to your tastes. Experiment freely with different ingredients; for example, try ½ cup chopped walnuts and ¼ cup dried cranberries, or, if you like sprouts, try sunflower or mung bean sprouts. This recipe is particularly delicious with a simple blend of balsamic vinegar and olive oil, or with the Basil Salad Dressing on page 257. I was taught long ago that when you tear greens, they tear naturally along cell borders, whereas when you cut them, you're cutting through the cells, making the leaves brown more quickly. Tearing along the cell borders is said to reduce browning and makes for an aesthetic presentation. That makes sense to me, but what I was taught might not be true; there's a lively debate on the topic on Stack Exchange. In my experience, for salads you're making casually to eat right away, it doesn't matter whether you cut or tear the greens.

2 cups mixed salad greens (such as arugula, baby beet greens, baby spinach, kale, radicchio, rhubarb chard, and young mustard greens), torn into bite-sized pieces
1 cup romaine or other lettuce, torn into bite-sized pieces
¼ cup fresh basil leaves, torn into small pieces
¼ cup roasted sunflower seeds
1 bell pepper, chopped
2 tomatoes, chopped
2 avocados, chopped
½ cup feta cheese, crumbled

1 Combine salad greens, romaine, basil, sunflower seeds, bell pepper, tomatoes, avocados, and feta.
2 Toss with your favorite dressing, or serve with a selection of dressings on the side.

Basil Salad Dressing

Total time: 5 minutes   Yields about 2¼ cups

My brother Peter experimented with raw foods in the 1990s. During that time, he shared this healthful and incredibly delicious recipe with me. Intended as a salad dressing, it also tastes great in wraps, over baked potatoes, on eggs, and with other savory items. I learned through experimentation that you *must* remove the basil stems; if you leave the stems on, the dressing will never become smooth no matter how long you blend it, and it won't result in the lovely rich deep green this dressing, should have. Lesson learned: There's only so far you can strip a recipe to its core elements before you have to stop. On the plus side, your kitchen will smell amazing as you pluck the tender basil leaves from the stems. (Remember to compost those stems!) Bragg's liquid amino acids are naturally gluten-free, though they aren't certified gluten-free, so use your judgment on this. The original recipe called for flaxseed oil, but I'm not fond of the taste, so I use the milder avocado oil instead. Also, although flaxseed was once thought to be a good source of omega-3 oils, researchers now say it's only useful as a backup for the omega-3s in fish oil. If you want to find out more, look up the October 2006 *Harvard Health Letter*, "Why not flaxseed oil?" Serve immediately or store in the refrigerator for 2 to 3 days. This dressing doesn't keep longer than that, though if you love it as much as we do, using it up will be a pleasure.

½ cup avocado oil or olive oil
¼ cup Bragg's liquid amino
  acids

½ cup lemon juice
2 cups fresh basil leaves, stems
  removed

1 Combine oil, Bragg's amino acids, lemon juice, and basil leaves in a blender.
2 Blend at high speed until thick and smooth. The dressing should thick, creamy, and bright green.

Bean and Tuna Salad

Total time: 30 minutes   Yields 6 servings

Complex flavors of tart and tangy ingredients meld with the beans and tuna in this healthful salad. It's hearty enough to be a main dish. I don't remember who shared this recipe with me; I started making it in the late 1990s. The recipe originally called for albacore, but according to the May 2020 *Harvard Health Letter*, light tuna has less mercury than albacore. You can use any kind of onion instead of the shallots. To make this vegetarian/vegan, leave out the tuna.

1 can (15 ounces) cannellini or Roman beans, drained and rinsed
2 cans (6½ ounces each) light tuna, drained
1 large tomato, diced
¼ cup chopped shallots

1 tablespoon lemon juice
2 teaspoons Dijon mustard
¼ cup olive oil
¼ cup fresh basil, chopped, plus a few leaves for garnish
black pepper to taste

1 Combine beans, tuna, tomato, and shallots in a large bowl.
2 Combine lemon juice and mustard in a small bowl.
3 Gradually whisk oil into lemon juice mixture.
4 Pour lemon juice mixture over bean/tuna mixture. Toss with chopped basil.
5 Add pepper to taste. Serve garnished with fresh basil leaves.

Caesar Salad

Total time: 5 hours   Yields 4 servings

Caesar salad is a classic American salad with foggy origins. Some say Caesar Cardini invented the recipe; some say it was his brother Alex. Others claim they invented it and that Caesar Cardini only made it famous. Since all the principals are long gone, we may never know. Aside from the infighting over who came up with the recipe, everyone agrees the salad is a classic. In 1953, three years before Caesar Cardini's death, the International Society of Epicures in Paris said Caesar salad was "the greatest recipe to originate from the Americas in 50 years." (Stephanie Curtis, "And Tossed Tales," *Washington Post*, July 25, 1984.) Caesar first served the recipe in his restaurant in Tijuana, Mexico; hence "the Americas" rather than "America," meaning the US. When researching this recipe's history, I was surprised to find that Alex Cardini said the original recipe used limes, not lemons. If you're not a fan of eggs or anchovies, you can leave out those two ingredients. But then some would argue you're omitting the essence that makes it a Caesar salad. For gluten free, use the Lea & Perrins Original Worcestershire sauce sold in the US; versions sold in other countries aren't gluten free.

1 clove garlic, minced	**3** tablespoons lemon juice
1/3 cup olive oil	**1** teaspoon Lea & Perrins Original Worcestershire sauce
1 head young romaine, washed, patted dry, and chilled	
1/2 teaspoon salt	**2** anchovy fillets, drained and minced
1/4 teaspoon freshly grated black pepper	**1/4** cup grated Parmesan cheese
1 large egg in unbroken shell	

1 Mix garlic and olive oil. Set aside at room temperature several hours. Just before assembling remaining ingredients, strain garlic pieces out of oil and discard or use in another recipe. Keep the oil.
2 Trim root end of romaine. You can cut it into bite-sized pieces if you like, but the original recipe calls for whole leaves, with the intention of guests lifting each leaf by hand to eat it.
3 Toss romaine with garlic/oil mixture, salt, and pepper.
4 Boil egg for exactly one minute, then rinse under cold water to stop cooking.
5 Break egg over lettuce. Cover egg with lemon juice, Worcestershire sauce, and anchovy fillets; toss to mix.
6 Arrange romaine in a circle on a large serving platter or in a large salad bowl, cut ends to the outside. Sprinkle with cheese. Serve immediately.

Fusion Dressing

Total time: 5 minutes   Yields a scant ½ cup

This recipe represents the kind of results you can get when you throw together several disparate ingredients and it works. I concocted this one night for fun—a bit of this, a dash of that—and my daughter liked the results so well she ate an entire otherwise plain romaine salad based on the tastiness of the dressing alone. And she's not a fan of salads. Use on salad or as a marinade for chicken. Store in refrigerator for up to a week.

3 tablespoons olive oil
1 tablespoon sesame oil
2 tablespoons rice wine
   vinegar

1 tablespoon balsamic vinegar
½ teaspoon Italian seasonings
   (page 300)

1 Combine olive oil, sesame oil, rice wine vinegar, balsamic vinegar, and Italian seasonings in a small jar with a lid.
2 Put lid on and shake very well. By some magic, the dressing becomes thick and opaque.

Carrot and Raisin Salad

Total time: 30 minutes   Yields 8 servings

Worldwide, everyone has their favorite version of carrot salad. Some cultures make it with cooked carrots, though most make it with raw. Sometimes the salad is pickled. I'm sure they're all delicious, and someday it would be fun to experiment with making all the different types of carrot salad recipes from around the world. This is my favorite version, which my mother would sometimes make. Serve immediately, or chill and serve later.

3 cups grated carrots
1 tablespoon lemon juice
1½ cups raisins
1 cup mayonnaise
1 cup walnuts, chopped

1 can (6 to 8 ounces) crushed pineapple
1 apple, peeled, cored, and shredded
2 tablespoons honey (adjust to taste)

1   Combine carrots, lemon juice, raisins, mayonnaise, walnuts, pineapple, apple, and honey.

Cranberry Fluff

Total time: 30 minutes plus overnight
chilling time

Yields 12 servings

This simple and delicious recipe leans toward the dessert side. It's perfect for winter holiday meals, either during or after the meal, depending on whether you think of it as a dessert or a side dish. If you have the foresight to freeze packages of fresh cranberries when they are available in the winter, you can use them in the summer to make a cool and refreshing summer salad. The original recipe was shared with me in the late 1990s. That recipe called for imitation whipped cream, which is made with about fifteen ingredients, including hydrogenated oils and high-fructose corny syrup. I immediately replaced that with the much simpler and more healthful homemade whipped cream made with only two ingredients—cream and sugar. (Making your own whipped cream is also less expensive than buying the imitation stuff.) It's best to make this recipe one day ahead, though you can make it at the last minute with good results.

5 cups fresh uncooked cranberries
1 can (6 ounces) crushed pineapple
½ cup granulated sugar
½ cup flaked or shredded unsweetened coconut
5 ounces miniature marshmallows
½ cup heavy cream
½ cup powdered sugar

1 Chop cranberries coarsely in a blender or food processor.
2 In a large bowl, combine cranberries with pineapple, granulated sugar, coconut, and marshmallows.
3 Cover and refrigerate 8 hours or overnight.
4 The next day, whip cream with powdered sugar until it is quite stiff. Just before serving, fold whipped cream into salad.

Curried Lentil Salad

Total time: 30 minutes   Yields 6 servings

Easier and faster than it looks, this recipe came from Natalie LaGuardia, a co-worker in the early 2010s. Like most of the recipes in this chapter, this salad is vegan (unless you add feta). These instructions tell how to make this salad from scratch, including cooking your own lentils, but you can purchase steamed lentils from Trader Joe's and skip the lentil cooking step. (If you buy the lentils from Trader Joe's, use one package.) This is such a huge favorite in my home that I always have on hand a large batch of the spice mixture for the vinaigrette. For the spice mixture in the vinaigrette (starting with black pepper and ending with cinnamon), you can substitute three tablespoons Sweet Curry Powder (page 314).

Lentils

3 cups cooked brown lentils or 1 cup uncooked brown lentils

Water for cooking uncooked lentils

Vinaigrette

⅓ cup avocado oil or olive oil
¼ cup apple cider vinegar
2 tablespoons maple syrup
2 tablespoons stone ground mustard
1 teaspoon sea salt
2 teaspoons ground black pepper
1 teaspoon ground cumin
1 teaspoon ground turmeric

½ teaspoon ground coriander
½ teaspoon ground cardamom
½ teaspoon cayenne
¼ teaspoon ground cloves
¼ teaspoon ground nutmeg
1 teaspoon ground cinnamon,
2 tablespoons Madras-style curry powder (page 303)

Optional Ingredients

1 medium red onion, diced
1 cup chopped walnuts
1 cup dried currants or raisins
½ cup feta

1 cup kale, deribbed and thinly sliced
3 sprigs fresh cilantro, finely chopped

1   **If using uncooked lentils**: Rinse lentils well. Place in a medium saucepan and cover with about 3 to 4 inches of water.
2   Bring to a boil, then reduce heat and simmer.
3   Cook lentils 15 to 20 minutes or until they're tender but still have a bit of tooth. Don't cook until completely soft—the recipe won't work well with softer lentils.

4 Remove lentils from heat and drain. Rinse with cold water to stop the cooking process. Before adding the vinaigrette, make sure the lentils are cool.

5 **While lentils are cooking, make the vinaigrette**. Combine oil, vinegar, maple syrup, mustard, black pepper, cumin, turmeric, coriander, cardamom, cayenne, cloves, nutmeg, cinnamon, and curry powder in a jar with a lid and shake well.

6 Once lentils have cooled, add onion, walnuts, and currants to lentils and mix well.

7 Pour vinaigrette over lentil mixture and mix well.

8 If serving right away, add any additional or optional ingredients you want to use. Otherwise, refrigerate lentil salad until you serve the salad, then stir in additional or optional ingredients right before serving.

Deluxe Tuna Salad

Total time: 30 minutes   Yields 6 servings

With its blend of ingredients, this tuna salad keeps your taste buds intrigued and delighted. A co-worker shared their tuna salad recipe long ago and I riffed on it to come up with my own version. You can skip the mayonnaise and use this mixture as a salsa. To serve, spread on bread as a sandwich, or use in recipes that call for plain tuna, or stuff into hollowed large tomatoes, or double all the vegetable ingredients and serve on lettuce as a salad or main course.

Core Ingredients

2 large cans light tuna
1 can (4 ounces) marinated artichoke hearts, well drained and cut up
1 medium tomato, diced
1 large dill pickle, diced
¾ cup sliced kalamata olives
½ red onion, minced

2 stalks celery, minced
½ cup chopped fresh cilantro
½ teaspoon fresh oregano
3 tablespoons lemon juice
2 tablespoons spicy mustard or 2 teaspoons dry mustard
¼ cup mayonnaise or to taste

Optional Ingredients

¼ cup grated carrots
½ teaspoon fresh dill weed, minced
4 large leaves fresh basil, chopped

2 tablespoons capers
1 teaspoon za'atar spice
¼ teaspoon cayenne
¼ teaspoon freshly ground pepper

1   Drain tuna. Give juice to your cats.
2   Put tuna in a large mixing bowl.
3   Add artichoke hearts, tomato, pickle, olives, onion, celery, cilantro, oregano, lemon juice, mustard, and mayonnaise. Mix well.
4   Add any optional ingredients you want to experience.

Easy Romaine Salad

Total time: 5 minutes   Yields 4 servings

lthough the ingredients are simple, this combination is delicious. Try it with the Basil Salad Dressing (page 257) or the Fusion Dressing (page 260).

2 heads romaine lettuce, chopped	**1** cup cherry tomatoes, whole or sliced in half
1 cup walnut pieces	**2** stalks celery, coarsely diced

1   Toss together romaine, walnuts, tomatoes, and celery.
2   Top with your favorite salad dressing.

Eggless "Egg" Salad

Total time: 45 minutes   Yields 4 servings

This delicious tofu-based sandwich spread is perfect for strict vegans, though non-vegetarians enjoy it too. If you aren't a vegan, you can use regular mayonnaise, though Sir Kensington's Vegan Mayo is excellent.

- **1** package silken tofu (firm)
- **3** tablespoons vegan (eggless) mayonnaise
- **¼** teaspoon honey
- **¼** teaspoon ground turmeric
- **⅛** teaspoon salt
- **⅛** teaspoon ground black pepper
- **⅛** teaspoon dry mustard
- **2** teaspoons dill pickle relish
- **1** teaspoon capers or minced cornichons
- **2** tablespoons minced green onions (green and white parts)
- **2** tablespoons minced celery

1. Drain tofu and pat dry.
2. Grate tofu into a medium bowl.
3. In another bowl, combine mayonnaise, honey, turmeric, salt, and pepper.
4. Add tofu to mayonnaise mixture.
5. Mix in mustard, relish, capers, green onions, and celery.
6. Refrigerate 30 minutes before serving.

Green Goddess Dressing

Total time: 15 minutes   Yields about 2 cups

The story of the original Green Goddess dressing is that it was invented in San Francisco in 1923 by the Palace Hotel's chef to honor actor George Arliss and his then-popular play, *The Green Goddess*. This variation of the recipe is flexible, tangy, and delicious. Try making it for a holiday dinner. If you don't have watercress, substitute parsley or cilantro or other, similar fresh green herbs. Serve immediately as a salad dressing or dip, or refrigerate for up to a three days.

½ cup mayonnaise
½ cup plain yogurt or sour
   cream
1 cup (packed) watercress
3 anchovy fillets or 2
   teaspoons anchovy paste
2 tablespoons fresh dill weed,
   chopped

2 tablespoons fresh basil or
   tarragon, chopped
1 teaspoon fresh mint,
   chopped
1 tablespoon green onions,
   chopped
1 garlic clove
½ teaspoon salt

1   Combine mayonnaise, yogurt, watercress, anchovies, dill, basil, mint, green onions, garlic, and salt. Purée until smooth.
2   Pour into a jar with a tightly sealing lid.

Kale and Lemon Salad

Total time: 15 minutes   Yields 6 servings

I got a version of this recipe from a nutrition class I took in 2012. I stripped the original recipe of many unnecessary ingredients, refining it to a fast, simple, easy, tasty, and healthful salad. Asiago is a delicious hard cow's-milk cheese that originated in Northern Italy. It has a subtle but distinct flavor. You can substitute Parmesan for the Asiago if you prefer Parmesan's stronger flavor. Serve immediately. Refrigerated, this salad keeps well for about a day.

4 cups kale
2 tablespoons olive oil
2 tablespoons lemon juice

¼ cup finely grated Asiago cheese (or another hard cheese of your choice)
¼ cup sunflower seeds (raw or roasted)

1   Remove ribs from kale. Tear or chop kale into bite-sized pieces.
2   Combine oil and lemon juice and toss with kale.
3   Add cheese and sunflower seeds and toss again.

Layered Green Salad

Total time: 1 hour plus 1 day   Yields 10 servings

The first time I heard about this salad (in the 1980s), it sounded weird. But my friend Johnette brought it to a company potluck, and then I was sold. This is her recipe. For a vegan version, leave out the bacon, eggs, and cheese, and use egg-less mayonnaise. Some versions of this salad combine the mayonnaise with ½ cup sour cream and put that on top as a dressing. Other versions stick with a strict seven ingredients and are called seven-layer salad. To serve, dig your serving spoon in to get something from all layers in each serving.

Layers

- 1 medium head iceberg lettuce, shredded
- 1 cup thinly sliced celery
- 3 large hard-boiled eggs, coarsely chopped
- 1 can (8 ounces) sliced water chestnuts
- 1 package (10 ounces) frozen peas, broken apart
- 1½ cups mayonnaise
- ½ cup grated Parmesan cheese
- ¼ teaspoon garlic powder

Toppings

- ¾ pound bacon, cooked, cooled, and crumbled
- ½ cup chopped green onions
- 2 medium tomatoes, cut in wedges

1 Layer ingredients in a large, deep serving bowl in this order: lettuce, celery, eggs, water chestnuts, peas, mayonnaise, Parmesan cheese, and garlic powder.
2 Cover and chill 24 hours.
3 Just before serving, sprinkle top with bacon and green onions. Arrange tomato wedges on top.

Mom's Coleslaw

Total time: 15 minutes   Yields 8 servings

To get the ingredients and instructions, I had to watch my mother assemble her tangy, sweet coleslaw. This salad gets juicier upon standing. Most cabbages work fine; my mother used green or red cabbages, but any cabbage will do. I make it with the non-traditional Napa cabbage, and I leave out the bell pepper. Serve immediately.

Salad

1 medium cabbage
1 medium carrot, grated

1/2 green bell pepper, diced or sliced

Dressing

6 heaping tablespoons mayonnaise
1 can (20 ounces) pineapple chunks, drained
2 tablespoons balsamic vinegar

1 1/2 teaspoons honey or granulated sugar
1/4 teaspoon salt
1/4 teaspoon pepper

1   Shred or chop cabbage as coarsely or finely as you like. My mother shredded her cabbage finely.
2   Add carrot and bell pepper. Mix well.
3   In a separate, non-reactive bowl, mix mayonnaise, pineapple chunks, vinegar, honey, salt, and pepper. Add more salt and pepper if you want.
4   Add cabbage to dressing and toss until cabbage is well coated with the dressing.

Mom's Potato Salad

Total time: 1 hour 30 minutes   Yields 16 servings

This is another genuine "Mom" recipe; when I asked her for it, she said, "take some potatoes, some vinegar, some onions...." As always, I had to watch her make it to get the exact ingredients and instructions. My mother used russets or red potatoes, and that's how I've always made it, but I bet it would be tasty made with Yukon Golds. My mother told me vinegar is the key to this recipe.

4 pounds potatoes
1 cup apple cider vinegar
2 medium onions, chopped
6 hard-boiled large eggs, coarsely chopped
6 large dill pickles, coarsely chopped
¼ cup fresh parsley or cilantro, coarsely chopped (optional)
¼ cup fresh basil, finely chopped (optional)

4 stalks celery, chopped (optional)
1 teaspoon dill weed, fresh or dry (optional)
mayonnaise to taste
1 tablespoon dry mustard or 1 teaspoon prepared mustard
salt and pepper to taste
¼ cup sour cream (optional)

1 Boil potatoes in their skins. To speed up the cooking, cut potatoes into bite-sized chunks before cooking. When potatoes are cooked but still firm, pour off water and let potatoes sit until cool enough to handle (though still warm).
2 If you didn't cut up the potatoes before cooking, chop them now into bite-sized pieces. You can peel them first if you like, but peeling isn't necessary.
3 Pour vinegar over potatoes. Let potatoes cool. The potatoes will absorb a lot of vinegar. The more vinegar, the tangier the end product. Add more as desired or needed.
4 When potatoes are cool, drain any excess vinegar.
5 Add onions, hard-boiled eggs, and dill pickles; the more egg and pickle, the better, my mother used to say. These ingredients are essential.
6 If desired, add one or more optional ingredients: parsley, basil, celery, and dill weed.
7 Mix potato mixture with mayonnaise and mustard.
8 Add salt and pepper to taste.
9 Add sour cream if you like. Serve immediately or chill if desired.

Pasta Salad

Total time: 30 minutes

Yields 6 servings

I came up with this recipe while experimenting with pasta salads. The cheeses I use work very well together; the Mahón and Parmesan are flavorful drier cheeses, the Blarney is tasty but not overbearing, and the Gouda's touch of smokiness adds that final perfect flavor. I use Tinkyada brand gluten-free brown rice noodles.

12 ounces dry, gluten-free rotini pasta
½ cup mayonnaise
1 tablespoon apple cider vinegar
2 cloves fresh garlic, diced, or 2 teaspoons garlic granules

2 cups grated cheese, either one kind or a mixture (I like to use Parmesan, Spanish Mahón, Irish Blarney, and smoked Gouda)

1 Cook pasta and rinse in cool water until cool. Drain well.
2 While pasta is cooking, combine mayonnaise, vinegar, and garlic and let stand.
3 When pasta is cool, stir in mayonnaise mixture, then stir in cheese.

Smoked Salmon Salad

Total time: 10 minutes   Yields 4 servings

Fabulously delicious when you use a tasty smoked salmon, and very fast. Serve on a bed of leaves or in sandwiches. I threw these ingredients together when I had some delicious smoked salmon and wanted to make it last as long as I could. The salmon should be on the dry side, but not hard. This salad is great on romaine or on freshly baked bread as a sandwich. You could also added one large beaten egg and 1½ cups bread crumbs, and bake this as a smoked salmon loaf.

1 pound smoked salmon
¼ cup mayonnaise
1 teaspoon dill weed, fresh or
    dried

¼ teaspoon freshly ground
    black pepper
3 stalks celery, diced
2 hard-boiled large eggs, diced

1   Crumble salmon until it is in fine flakes.
2   Mix in mayonnaise until salmon is of the desired moistness. Add more mayonnaise if needed.
3   Add dill weed, pepper, celery, and eggs. Mix thoroughly.

Sunomono

Total time: 15 minutes

Yields about 2 cups

Sunomono is a vinegar-based Japanese vegetable salad served in tiny amounts as an appetizer or as small accompaniment to a meal. Typically, sunomono is made with cucumbers, but I encourage you to experiment with similar vegetables or even fruits, such as apples. Japanese, English, Persian, or Vietnamese cucumbers are best because they have thin skins and virtually no seeds. You can use American cucumbers if you need to, or lemon cucumbers for an interesting variation. Serve sunomono as a side dish with any meal from any cuisine. It's great with any savory Japanese dish, such as the fantastically tasty Chicken Karaage on page 180.

3 cucumbers
¼ teaspoon salt
3 tablespoons rice wine
 vinegar or mirin
½ teaspoon minced fresh
 ginger

1 tablespoon granulated sugar
1 teaspoon toasted sesame oil
¼ teaspoon tamari
1 teaspoon sesame seeds

1 **This step is only if you're using American cucumbers**. Skip to the next step if using Japanese, English, Persian, or Vietnamese cucumbers. Peel cucumbers, then cut in half lengthwise. Scrape out and discard seeds.
2 Slice cucumbers into the thinnest slices possible.
3 Sprinkle slices with salt, mix until coated, and set aside for 5 minutes. The salt is to pull water out of the cucumber slices, making them crunchy. Resist the temptation to use more salt—you won't be rinsing the cucumber slices, so most of the salt will remain in the salad, even after draining.
4 Combine vinegar, ginger, sugar, and oil in a small bowl. Stir until sugar dissolves.
5 Gently squeeze water out of cucumber slices. Discard water. Do not rinse.
6 Stir vinegar mix into cucumber slices, making sure each slice is coated.
7 Chill 1 hour.
8 Sprinkle with sesame seeds and serve.

Syrian Fattoush

Total time: 30 minutes   Yields 6 servings as a side dish

A *fattoush* is a Middle Eastern salad that combines flat bread, vegetables, and spices. I first tasted this recipe in the same nutrition class where I learned the Kale and Lemon Salad (page 269). Fortunately, the instructor shared her recipes with no restrictions, though of course I've rewritten it in my own words and changed ingredients to suit my taste. Although ingredient quality, freshness, and flavor are important to all recipes, they're especially important to the success of this salad. To serve, divide salad into six bowls. Because of the pita pieces, this salad doesn't keep.

Pita Chips

2 whole rounds pita bread

Vinaigrette

2 large garlic cloves, minced
1/4 cup fresh lemon juice
1 tablespoon rice wine vinegar
3/4 teaspoon ground cumin

1 cup olive oil
Salt and freshly ground black
   pepper to taste

Salad

3/4 cup cherry tomatoes, halved
3/4 cup cucumber, peeled,
   seeded, and diced in 1/4 inch
   cubes
1/4 cup thinly sliced red onion
   (about 1/2 of a small onion;
   don't overdo this ingredient)
1/4 cup fresh cilantro, finely
   chopped

1/4 cup finely chopped fresh
   mint
6 cups hearts of romaine
   (about three hearts), roughly
   torn
2/3 cup crumbled feta
1/4 cup pitted Kalamata olives
   (about 12 olives)

1   Split each pita into halves, then cut each half into 6 triangles. Arrange on a baking sheet.
2   Toast in oven at 350° for about 12 minutes or until chips are crisp and golden brown. Remove from oven and set aside to cool.
3   When chips are cool, break into large pieces.
4   Prepare vinaigrette while pita chips are toasting. In a medium bowl, combine garlic, lemon juice, rice wine vinegar, cumin, and olive oil. Add salt and pepper and set aside.
5   In a large bowl, combine tomatoes, cucumber, onion, cilantro, mint, romaine, feta, and olives.
6   Toss salad and vinaigrette together in a large bowl, coating salad ingredients well with vinaigrette. Stir in pita pieces.

Tabouli

Total time: 1 hour 15 minutes   Yields 8 servings

Tabouli (also spelled tabbouleh) is a traditional Middle Eastern salad made with bulgur, tomatoes, mint, and lemon juice. Like most common recipe, tabouli has many variations. This easy, delicious version tastes great freshly made or after refrigeration. If you don't like cilantro, you can leave it out, but the parsley and mint are essential. Bulgur is wheat that is parboiled, dried, and cracked, with much of the bran still present; it's considered a whole grain. It's similar to cracked wheat, except for the parboiling. You can cook bulgur as a breakfast cereal or use it in many other recipes. Serve immediately (while warm), or refrigerate for one hour or up to a day.

$1\frac{3}{4}$ cups medium or coarse bulgur

$1\frac{3}{4}$ cups water

$\frac{1}{2}$ cup olive oil

$\frac{1}{3}$ cup lemon juice

$\frac{1}{2}$ teaspoon salt

1 teaspoon ground allspice or nutmeg

2 stalks celery, diced

1 cup chopped green onions (white and green parts)

$\frac{1}{4}$ cup fresh cilantro, finely chopped

1 cup fresh parsley, finely chopped

2 medium tomatoes, diced

5 fresh basil leaves, finely chopped

5 fresh mint leaves, finely chopped

1   Combine bulgur and water in a medium saucepan. Bring to a boil. Reduce heat and simmer until water is barely absorbed (about 5 minutes). Remove from heat.

2   While bulgur is still hot, combine bulgur with olive oil, lemon juice, salt, and allspice. Set aside to cool slightly (about 10 minutes).

3   Once cooled, mix in celery, green onions, cilantro, parsley, tomatoes, basil, and mint.

Savory Sauces & Spices

Spices are exceptionally useful. They add delicious flavors to your food so you can get away with using less (or no) salt. They can make the same main ingredients (meats, vegetables) taste appetizingly different.

In this chapter, you'll find our family favorite everyday spice blends, such as Italian seasonings and curry powder. You'll also find a few rare spice blends I dug up here and there. In the first pages of this chapter, I include information on how long to keep spices, how to distinguish among spices by their names, some excellent, give a list of fair-trade online sources for spices, and so on.

Roughly half the recipes in this chapter are spice blends: my versions of classics, created after diligent and delicious experimentation. If you're content buying your favorite spice blends, there's no reason to use the spice blend recipes in this chapter. However, making your own spice blends can be quite satisfying. You can use your choice of ingredients; in my case, organic, fair trade herbs and spices (my favorite source is MountainRoseHerbs.com). You can experiment with these recipes until you come up with something you can call your very own. You will have the freshest and tastiest spice blends possible.

In this chapter, in addition to the spice blends, you'll find recipes for our favorite savory sauces; for example, my mother's unmatchable salsa, a friend's complexly flavored barbecue sauce, another friend's perfect ponzu sauce (ponzu is a citrusy liquid used in Japanese cooking), the deceptively simple curried sour cream, and the best tartar sauce I've ever tasted.

Why "savory" in the chapter title? I still remember my long-ago delight in finding out that in cooking terms, "savory" refers to salty or spicy foods, as opposed to sweet foods. The origin of the term has its roots in the Latin word *sa-*

pere, meaning "to taste; to savor." Although you could say (and if you do, I won't disagree) that we savor desserts, in modern terms savory sauces and spices aren't sweet, and we serve them with main or side dishes. For desserts, you'd use sweet sauces and spices; you'll find a few sweet spice blends in this chapter.

Should You Use Fresh or Dried Herbs?

You can almost always use either fresh or dried herbs in a recipe, whichever you have on hand. Fresh herbs smell wonderful, and are excellent for cooking with. And most dried herbs taste as good as (or sometimes even better than) their fresh versions. For example, you can use either fresh or fried dill weed and the results, flavor-wise, will be fine. Fresh rosemary is lovely and imparts more flavor than dried, but dried rosemary is also excellent.

But sometimes, either the fresh or dried versions of some herbs and spices are better. For example, dried bay leaves pack more flavor than their fresh equivalents, but you can use either and still get good flavor.

And some dried herbs are just not worth buying. For example, I love fresh cilantro, so I once bought a large bag of dried cilantro, thinking it would be handy when I don't have fresh cilantro on hand. Alas, dried cilantro has all the flavor of straw. (I can thank my rural childhood for knowing what straw tastes like.) That bag sat in my pantry for a year. I deeply dislike waste, and kept thinking I'd find a use for it. I never did, and eventually composted it.

Most cooks develop a sense for which herbs are best fresh or dried and stock their pantry accordingly. In this cookbook, if a recipe specifies a version (fresh or dried), it's because that form works best in the recipe.

How Long Should You Keep Spices?

In *The Tenth Kingdom* (a favorite fairy tale miniseries), when preparing a grandmother for cooking, the character Wolf looks around the kitchen and asks in dripping disdain, "What do we have here? Three-year-old dried spices?" It's a funny scene and not nearly as macabre as you might think. The point is that herbs, spices, and seasonings lose their flavor over time, and need to be used up or replaced before they become tasteless.

Whole herbs and spices keep longer than ground versions, which is why many cooks prefer to mainly keep whole herbs and spices on hand, then prepare or grind their seasonings as needed. And that's what I do.

How can you tell when it's time to replace your spices? Sniff the spice and check its appearance. If it's faded or has lost its taste or smell, that's a good indication that it's time to replace it. The more organized among us might even date their spices; some spice companies also add dates to their packaging.

How you store your herbs and spices affects how long they last. Exposure to light, heat, and moisture will cause them to lose their potency much more quickly, so store them in airtight, inert containers (such as glass) in a cool, dry, dark place. You can refrigerate cayenne, chili powder, and paprika to help retain their scent and color; don't refrigerate anything else, and don't freeze any herbs or spices except whole ginger root and curry leaves.

The following table shows when to replace your dried herbs, roots, rhizomes, extracts, spices, and seasonings. The dates are approximations and your mileage may vary. When in doubt, throw it out and replace it with new.

How long will that herb or spice keep?

Type of Spice	Replace After
Dehydrated vegetables (such as chives, garlic, onion)	1 year
Extracts (except pure vanilla extract, which lasts indefinitely)	4 years
Ground roots and rhizomes (such as ginger, turmeric, wasabi)	2 years
Ground barks, leafy herbs, and seeds (such as cinnamon, basil, sage, cumin)	6 to 8 months
Hot pepper flakes	2 years
Seasoning blends (such as curry powder or chili powder)	2 years
Dried whole leafy or flowery herbs (such as basil, lavender, thyme)	2 years
Dried whole roots, rhizomes, barks, and seeds (such as ginger root, cinnamon sticks, cumin seed)	3 to 4 years

Making Your Own Spice Blends

The recipes in this chapter give step-by-step instructions for creating the herb and spice blends.

At a high level, for an herb blend, you just combine the required amounts of whole, dried herbs. Sometimes the recipe calls for grinding the herbs into a fine powder; for that, I love using my Waring WSG30, a sturdy workhorse of a spice grinder. If buying a different brand, look for one that can grind small to large quantities, and that has a stainless steel, not plastic, grinding cup.

For spice blend, such as curry powder, a recipe may call for dry toasting some of the spices before combining them with other spices (and then grinding them into a fine powder). After toasting the spices, you cool them, then grind them with other spices. (Using a sturdy grinder.)

Dry toasting drives out moisture, brings out complex flavors (though some disagree), and makes the spices easier to grind. Not all spices are suitable for dry-toasting; my recipes indicate which to toast and which not to. And even the recipes that call for dry toasting still give a perfectly fine product if you skip the dry toasting phase.

Tempering Spices When Cooking

Another way you can bring out a spice's best flavors is to temper your spices when cooking a recipe. Tempering means briefly heating spices in oil or ghee, if you have it. (Don't use olive oil—the flavor isn't right for this process.) You temper the spices right before adding them to a dish.

To temper spices, heat 1 or 2 tablespoons mild cooking oil or ghee over high heat until the oil is hot. Reduce heat to medium and toss in the spices (whole or ground, doesn't matter, but if you're using both, start with the whole seeds, then add the ground spices). Cook for just a few seconds. The tempering process is finished when the seeds change color or crackle; cumin and mustard seeds might pop. You'll also smell the spices's fragrance. If you burn the spices, throw them out and start over; that burned flavor will transfer to your food.

After tempering the spices, you can either start adding other ingredients to the oil (for example, if the recipe calls for sautéing onions next), or you can drain off the oil and add the tempered spices to whatever food you're preparing. Save the oil for later cooking, because you now have a spice-infused oil!

Which Herbs and Spices to Get First

I call for such a large variety of spices in this chapter, you may be wondering how you can make some of the recipes. I see two barriers to making the herb-and-spice-rich recipes:

1   Having the herbs and spices on hand, and
2   finding good sources for those herbs and spices.

The rest of this section can help you overcome both barriers.

Starting Your Herb and Spice Collection

Unless your budget allows you to go on a buying spree and buy every herb and spice used in this chapter, I recommend choosing one or two recipes and buying just the herbs and spices you need for those recipes. Then add more to your pantry as you make more recipes.

In case you *do* have the budget, here's a list of my favorites that I always have on hand. I also stock a variety of specialty spices (fenugreek, lavender buds, long pepper, nigella, and white pepper, for example), but you could make almost every recipe in this cookbook if you have the herbs and spices in the following list. I mostly only have the whole versions and grind what I need when I need it. If you don't have a good spice grinder, the ground versions of most of these spices will do just fine. Start small, think big, as an instructor in a management class once said.

- allspice (whole berries)
- basil (fresh and dried)
- bay leaves (dried)
- black pepper (whole)
- cardamom, both green and black, both whole pods and hulled cardamom
- cayenne (and ancho and bird's eye chile powders)
- celery seed (whole)
- true sweet cinnamon (sticks and ground cinnamon)
- coriander seed (whole)
- cumin (whole white cumin seed)
- dill weed (fresh and dried) and dill seed
- five-pepper blend (a blend of five types of whole peppercorns from Mountain Rose Herbs)
- garlic (fresh cloves and granulated garlic)
- ginger (fresh and ground)
- mace blades (whole dried blades; a little mace goes a long way)
- marjoram (dried)
- mustard (dry powder and both brown and yellow seed)
- nutmeg (whole)
- oregano (dried)
- rosemary (fresh from my garden and dried)
- sage (dried)
- thyme (dried)

You'd need a few more (for example, fenugreek) to make the curry powders in this chapter.

Finding Herbs and Spices Online

As for where to buy herbs and spices, fortunately, you have many excellent sources for spices available. For example, you can find almost all the (dried) herbs and spices called for in this cookbook from MountainRoseHerbs.com, my favorite source. They sell organic, fair-trade spices at fair prices. Mountain Rose Herbs doesn't carry everything, though, so you can order from any of the many ethically sourced specialty spice shops online.

In her article, "Where You Buy Your Spices is Just As Important As How You Use Them" (*Bon Appetit*, May 22, 2020), Mackenzie Fegan lists most of the following companies as carrying ethically sourced, short-supply-chain spices. (I've added more to the list.)

I buy from several of these sources (which I've commented on in the list) and am always pleased with the quality.

I've included the home country in this list. Many of these companies work directly with their sources; for example, DiasporaCo.com buys directly from spice farmers in India. Some of these companies ship internationally.

- BurlapAndBarrel.com (United States)
- CurioSpice.com (United States)
- DiasporaCo.com (United States)
- Frontiercoop.com; focus is on organic; consistently good quality (United States)
- MountainRoseHerbs.com (United States)
- OaktownSpiceShop.com; consistently good quality (United States)
- Penzeys.com; large chain, consistently good quality (United States)
- RumiSpice.com (United States)
- SavorySpiceShop.com (United States)
- TheSpiceHouse.com; consistently good quality; I love their flat packs, which are a great way to try a spice (United States)
- SpiceTrekkers.com (Canada)
- SpiceWallaBrand.com (United States)

When ordering, keep in mind that herbs and spices are often quite light; one ounce of basil will be a much larger amount than you anticipate. Order smaller quantities more often; perhaps as much as you think you'll need in a year. Because of shipping costs, it's more economical to buy everything you need from one source rather than buying from many sources.

Same Common Name, Different Spice?

Sometimes spices share a common name with other spices. How do you know which one is meant? For example, are cumin and black cumin the same? (No.) The best way to know what you have is using the scientific names. Unfortunately, most recipes don't provide the scientific names; only the common names. To make the puzzle a bit harder, some recipes use the wrong name for a spice, leaving it up to you to figure out which one is meant. This section provides information on some spices and herbs that share common names, or that are commonly confused with other spices and herbs, and gives the scientific names to help you distinguish among them.

Several Kinds of Bay Leaves

Several leaves are called bay or laurel, though only two can be substituted for each other. The one that is usually used in cooking is the bay laurel, sometimes also called sweet bay, whose scientific name is *Laurus nobilis*. When you buy bay leaves from the store, this is what you get.

For *Laurus nobilis*, some people substitute leaves of the California bay laurel (also called California bay). California bay only grows in the western coastal regions of the US. I've often walked through redwood forests, relishing the sharp, unforgettable fragrance of the California bays growing among the redwoods.

The scientific name for the California bay is *Umbellularia californica*. Despite the different scientific name, it's still within the *Lauraceae* (laurel) family. (Though it's the only species in the genus *Umbellularia*.) In Oregon, *Umbellularia californica* is called the myrtle or Oregon myrtle. The tree also has a variety of other common names, including pepperwood, spicebush, headache tree (because lengthily inhaling the smell from crushed fresh leaves can bring on a headache), mountain laurel, and balm of heaven.

A slow-growing tree, *Umbellularia californica* produces a lovely golden wood with a deep grain; the older the tree, the more lovely the wood. Because making objects of the wood for tourists is a big industry in Oregon, it's increasingly hard to find old myrtle trees. If you've seen myrtlewood furniture, you'll understand the attraction.

One way to tell between *Laurus nobilis* and *Umbellularia californica* is that the leaves of the *Laurus nobilis* are wider, with finely crinkled edges, while the leaves of *Umbellularia californica* are narrower and smooth-edged. Another difference is the *Umbellularia californica* leaves are more pungent than those of *Laurus nobilis*.

Whether *Umbellularia californica* is toxic is still a matter of scientific disagreement. My two small *Umbellularia californica* trees have often contributed to my cuisine, but you must decide for yourself. For legal reasons, I must recommend you use *Laurus nobilis*. Some people put California bay leaves in their cornmeal, flour, rice, and other dry goods to repel insects. I do this too, but I don't know whether it works.

While the Indian bay leaf, *Cinnamomum tejpata* (*malabathrum*), like all cinnamons, is in the laurel family, it is not a substitute for *Laurus nobilis*. Instead, it tastes mildly of cinnamon.

The scientific name of the Indonesian bay leaf (also known as the Indonesian laurel or salam leaf) is *Syzygium polyanthum*. This herb is also not a substitute for *Laurus nobilis*.

Two Kinds of Black Cumin and One Kind of White

The name "cumin" is applied to several spices. Two are called black cumin. The cumin you may be most used to using is called white cumin (*Cuminum cyminum*).

Both black "cumins" are commonly used in East Indian and Middle Eastern cooking. The scientific names for the two spices are *Nigella sativa* and *Elwendia persica* (also known as *Bunium persicum*).

Nigella sativa, commonly called nigella and kalonji, and also called black caraway, black cumin, black seed, fennel flower, and Roman coriander, is the intriguingly shaped three-sided seed of an annual plant in the ranunculus family. Imagine a tiny, compact American football with a velvety black surface and three curved sides and three sharp edges. That's what nigella seed looks like. Despite its common names, nigella is neither caraway, coriander, cumin, nor fennel; it's not in the cumin family; and taste-wise, it's not a good substitute for cumin.

To further confuse matters, some people also refer to the other kind of seed that is called black cumin, *E. persica,* which *is* in the cumin family, as black caraway or black seed. *E. persica* looks like white cumin, but is darker, a bit longer, narrower, more curved, and pointier at the ends. In cooking, this black cumin, and white cumin, though not identical in flavor, are similar enough to interchange.

Three Kinds of Cardamom

With the three common varieties of cardamom, their flavors vary but they are definitely sisters. Botanically, they all belong to the ginger family, *Zingiberaceae.* The scientific names for the three cardamoms are *Elettaria cardamomum, Amomum subulatum,* and *Lanxangia tsaoko* (formerly *Amomum tsao-ko*).

Elettaria cardamomum is more commonly known as green cardamom. In its whole form, it is a pale grey-green, fibrous pod about a half inch long filled with small, hard, dark brown or black seeds. It has a sharp flavor; a little goes a long way. It's one of my favorite spices, and is a key flavor in masala chai, a spiced milk tea. (For my admittedly over-the-top masala chai recipe, see page 73.) Green cardamom is lovely in both sweet and savory dishes. Unless I specify otherwise, all cardamom called for in my recipes is green cardamom.

The second kind of cardamom is *Amomum subulatum,* also known as black cardamom or Nepal cardamom. The majority of black cardamom comes from Nepal, and it gets its distinctive smoky smell and flavor from being smoked over open flames. Think of that. When you use black cardamom, you are connected across the world to someone who grew it, harvested it, smoked it over what may have been a fragrant open fire, and sent it on to you.

Whole black cardamom has a dark brown, fibrous, hairy pod a little larger than green cardamom. Like green cardamom, black cardamom pods are also filled with small, hard, dark brown or black seeds. It is often used whole in East Indian cookery, almost always in savory dishes. (To add flavor; you don't eat the pod unless you're brave.) Black cardamom is also sometimes used sparingly in masala chai.

Both green and black cardamom are used extensively in India and in some Pakistani cuisines. When you buy decorticated (hulled) cardamom, you're buying the seeds that have been removed from the pod. Hulled cardamom is more expensive, but saves much time; removing the seeds from the pods is time-consuming.

The third type of cardamom I mentioned, also called black cardamom or Chinese black cardamom, has a larger pod than *A. subulatum* and is used in Sichuan (China) and Vietnamese cuisines. One common name for it is *cao guo*. Grown wild and also cultivated, the plant is only known to grow in three small regions: at high altitudes in the Yunnan region in southern China, one province in northern Lao PDR, and one province in northern Vietnam. It's on the International Union for Conservation of Nature's near threatened list.

Four Kinds of Cinnamon

Cinnamon can be one of the following:

- The mild, delicately flavored true cinnamon (commonly called Ceylon cinnamon, scientific name *Cinnamomum verum*, formerly known as *Cinnamomum zeylanicum*). This is my favorite; I buy mine from Mountain Rose Herbs.
- Indonesian or Korintje cassia cinnamon (*Cinnamomum burmannii*). Korintje is the most commonly sold cinnamon in the US. Its color is richer and darker than *C. verum*, and its flavor may be the most familiar to you.
- Vietnamese or Saigon cassia cinnamon (*Cinnamomum loureiroi*). Many people love Saigon cinnamon, which is much easier to find in the US than it used to be.
- Chinese cinnamon (*Cinnamomum cassia, Cinnamomum aromaticum*), rare in the US and usually used for medicinal purposes. (According to Wikipedia, it's one of the 50 fundamental herbs in traditional Chinese medicine.)

All cinnamons are in the *Lauraceae* (laurel) family.

Cassia cinnamons pose a health hazard when consumed in large quantities because of the much greater quantities of coumarin than in *C. verum*. Coumarin is a blood thinner that can cause liver damage if consumed in large amounts.

Parsley and Cilantro

Parsley and coriander leaf (cilantro in the US) are two similar-looking but different-tasting leafy herbs. Parsley, Herb of the Year in 2021, has a curly-leafed version and a flat-leafed version; the flat-leafed version is sometimes called Italian parsley.

Flat leaf parsley looks enough like cilantro that sometimes recipes confusingly call for parsley when in fact cilantro is meant (or vice versa). Part of the confusion is in the appearance. Flat-leaf parsley and cilantro look almost identical; only an experienced cook can tell the difference. (Parsley leaves are a little thicker and darker than cilantro; cilantro leaves are softer and more delicate.) Even then, a cook can make a mistake. You have to smell and taste it to be sure.

Parsley's scientific names are *Petroselinum crispum* for the curly-leafed variety, and *Petroselinum neapolitanum* for the flat-leafed variety. The inoffensive parsley tastes grassy and mild.

Every part of the coriander plant (*Coriandrum sativum*) is edible and is used in cooking worldwide: the leaves, the fruit (coriander seed is technically a fruit), and the roots.

In the US, the leaves are commonly called cilantro, Chinese parsley, or coriander leaf, and the seeds are called coriander. (We seldom use the root in the US.)

In the rest of the world, the leaves, seeds, and roots are all called coriander, and are used in a wide variety of cuisines—Greek, East Indian, Mexican, Middle Eastern, Spanish, and Thai, to name a few. For clarity, in my recipes I use the term coriander seed for the whole seeds, and cilantro for the leaves.

Like parsley, cilantro is best when used fresh; but unlike parsley, cilantro has an unfortunate taste to some people. Those people have a gene that makes cilantro taste soapy; to the rest of us, cilantro has a sharp, rich, clean flavor that's hard to describe but easy to love. If you don't know whether your guests enjoy cilantro, serve it on the side so they can decide whether to use it.

Coriander is one of the oldest documented spices; coriander seeds were found in Israel associated with a culture called Pre-Pottery Neolithic B, which ended about 8,000 years ago. Manna was compared to coriander seed in Exodus 16:31: *"Thus the House of Israel called it 'Man' [Manna], and it was like a seed of coriander, white; and the taste of it was like cakes and honey."* (Ferrar Fenton Bible, 1903; note that manna wasn't coriander; it's just that manna was similar in color to coriander seed.) Coriander was found in Tutankhamun's tomb; it doesn't grow wild in Egypt, so it had to have been either imported, or cultivated from imported seeds. And the Romans also used coriander extensively. Coriander has been popular throughout history down to our modern times.

Keeping Parsley, Cilantro, and Basil Fresh

One way to have both fresh parsley and cilantro last longer in the refrigerator is to trim about ½ inch from the stem ends and place the bundle in a jar with a few inches of water, just as you would a bouquet of flowers. Remove what you need as you need it, and change the water daily. Compost it all when it's wilted or yellowing and buy yourself a fresh bunch. Some people mince their parsley and cilantro and store it in an airtight container in the refrigerator. They swear it lasts longer.

You can also keep fresh basil by trimming the stems and putting in a jar of water, but keep the jar on the counter, not in the refrigerator.

AJ's Barbecue Sauce

Total time: 30 minutes   Yields 3 cups

Y ou can store this tangy homemade barbecue sauce in the refrigerator for up to two weeks. My friend AJ invented this recipe on the spot one day in my kitchen. This recipe is gluten-free if you use the US version of Lea & Perrins Original Worcestershire sauce.

1 small yellow onion, chopped
1 tablespoon oil (olive or other)
6 garlic cloves, diced, or 3 teaspoons garlic powder
1 tablespoon grated fresh ginger
2 teaspoons ground ginger
1 tablespoon mustard powder
1 teaspoon ground cumin
1/2 teaspoon black pepper

1 tablespoon light molasses
1/2 teaspoon ground coriander
1/2 teaspoon paprika
1 cup ketchup
1 tablespoon Lea & Perrins Original Worcestershire sauce
4 tablespoons A.1. Steak Sauce
1 tablespoon apple cider vinegar

1 Sauté onion in hot oil a few minutes or until slightly translucent.
2 Add garlic and grated ginger and cook a few minutes more.
3 Add powdered ginger, mustard powder, cumin, pepper, molasses, coriander, paprika, ketchup, Worcestershire sauce, A.1. sauce, and vinegar. Stir well.
4 Cook a few more minutes, then store in a sterilized container.

Baking Powder

Total time: 10 minutes   Yields 4 teaspoons

Sometimes you need baking powder and you're out of it, or the baking powder you have has expired. (It loses its oomph after about six months to a year.) Just as baking soda is a leavening, so is baking powder. They aren't interchangeable. But if you're stuck with no baking powder, you can make your own with baking powder and cream of tartar.

This recipe makes a small batch of single-acting baking powder. If you are allergic to cornstarch, use very dry rice flour or wheat starch (dried in an oven at very low heat) in place of the cornstarch, or just leave it out. If you don't add the cornstarch, use the mixture immediately; the cornstarch prevents the cream of tartar and baking soda from reacting with each other, and therefore helps it last longer.

If you want to make a larger batch, use the same proportions of 2:1 (two units of cream of tartar to one unit of baking soda). Note that, like baking powder, cream of tartar also looses its potency over time, so if your cream of tartar is a bit long in the tooth, you may need to buy more. Cream of tartar (tartaric acid) is also a leavening agent. It's an acidic byproduct of making wine. My favorite brand of commercial cream of tartar is Frontier's..

To use this baking powder, substitute the same amount of this mix for any single-acting baking powder called for in your recipe. However, most recipes mean double-acting when they call for baking powder, so unless a recipe specifically calls for single-acting baking powder, use 1 teaspoon of this mix in place of every ¾ teaspoon of (double-acting) baking powder that the recipe calls for.

To test whether baking powder (homemade or commercial) is still good, combine ½ teaspoon baking powder with ½ cup hot water. If it bubbles rapidly, it's still good. To test your cream of tartar, put ½ teaspoon and a pinch of baking soda in ½ cup hot water. If it bubbles, it's good.

2 teaspoons cream of tartar   1 teaspoon cornstarch
1 teaspoon baking soda

1 Combine cream of tartar, baking soda, and cornstarch. Stir well.
2 Store in an airtight container away from light and moisture.

Best-Ever Tartar Sauce

Total time: 15 minutes   Yields about 1½ cups

You can prepare this classic accompaniment to batter-fried fish up to two days in advance. It's the absolute best tartar sauce I've ever tasted. I adapted this recipe from NatashasKitchen.com. It's fantastic made with fresh dill pickles. (For a pickle recipe, see Refrigerator Dill Pickles on page 252.) If you prefer your tartar sauce sweet, you can use a half cup of sweet pickle relish instead of the dill pickles. You can make this vegan by using vegan mayonnaise. Once made, store in the refrigerator for up to five days.

1 cup mayonnaise
1 cup diced dill pickles
1 teaspoon lemon juice

2 tablespoons finely chopped fresh dill weed
1½ teaspoons dill seed

1 Combine mayonnaise, pickles, lemon juice, dill weed, and dill seed. Stir well.
2 Store in an airtight container in the refrigerator.

Cajun Seasoning

Total time: 5 minutes   Yields 2½ cups

T his recipe makes a good amount of seasoning to have on hand for use in Cajun or Creole recipes. (For a succinct description of the differences between Cajun and Creole cooking, see NewOrleans.com.) There isn't one definitive Cajun season- ing mix, though paprika, salt, pepper, garlic, and oregano are key ingredients. And although filé powder is a definitive Cajun spice (and absolutely essential to gumbo), filé is an unusual ingredient in a Cajun seasoning blend. I like it, but if you can't find filé, you can leave it out. Filé is the dried and powdered leaves of the sassafras tree (*Sas- safras albidum*), though most commercial filé powders include additives like oregano or thyme. (For pure filé, try Penzeys or Zatarain brands.) When I searched the internet for how to make your own filé powder, I was deeply amused that the first step is to "find some sassafras trees." Onion powder cakes after a while, so store this spice mix in an airtight, well-sealed container. It should last up to a year, but keep an eye on it and shake well before using. Once you've made this mix, try it on fish (it's a delight with catfish or salmon), shrimp (of course!), turkey, chicken, or beef; or sprinkle over steamed vegetables like zucchini (or any other summer squash), popcorn, or, if you're in the mood for it, cottage cheese.

½ cup paprika
6 tablespoons sea salt
¼ cup coarsely ground black
  pepper
3 tablespoons dried basil
3 tablespoons filé powder
2 tablespoons garlic powder
2 tablespoons cayenne

2 tablespoons dry mustard
2 tablespoons onion powder
2 tablespoons dried oregano
2 tablespoons paprika
2 tablespoons ground white
  pepper
2 tablespoons dried thyme
½ teaspoon celery seed

1 Combine paprika, sea salt, pepper, basil, filé powder, garlic powder, cayenne, mustard, onion powder, oregano, paprika, white pepper, thyme, and celery seed.

2 Mix well. I like the charming texture of this mix as it is, though you can whir it up in a spice grinder if you wish.

Curried Sour Cream

Total time: 10 minutes   Yields 1¼ cups

T his super easy and deceptively simple sauce is excellent with thick, firm, broiled fish fillets, such as cod. You can serve it immediately, but it tastes better after standing one hour.

1 tablespoon unsalted butter
1 tablespoon finely grated
   onion

2 teaspoons curry powder
1 cup sour cream or yogurt

1   Melt butter in a frying pan.
2   Add onion and curry powder, stir to combine well, and warm for 2 to 3 minutes.
3   Remove from heat and stir butter/curry into sour cream.
4   Let rest 1 hour (to develop flavors) before serving.

Garam Masala (Ground)

Total time: 20 minutes   Yields about ½ cup

G aram masala (literally, hot spices) is a popular spice blend that originated in India. Many say it's delicate and therefore should only be added at the end of cooking. Others say it's very strong and you should use it sparingly. I've had excellent results adding it at the start of cooking, and I do use it sparingly. In whatever way you choose to use it, garam masala makes an excellent and unusual addition to a number of recipes. I came up with this blend after experimenting with a number of different spice combinations and proportions.

Toasting Spices

1 teaspoon cumin seed
½ teaspoon coriander seed
1 tablespoon hulled green cardamom (*Elettaria cardamomum*)
½ teaspoon black peppercorns
4 teaspoons stick cinnamon, broken into pieces

½ teaspoon whole cloves
1 teaspoon whole nigella (*Nigella sativa*)
½ teaspoon hulled black cardamom (*Amomum subulatum*)

Non-Toasting Spices

¼ ground nutmeg
1 bay leaf
½ teaspoon mace blades

1 star anise
¼ teaspoon ground cinnamon
½ teaspoon saffron

1   Combine cumin, coriander, green cardamom, peppercorns, cinnamon, cloves, nigella, and black cardamom. Place in a dry skillet (cast iron is best) on medium low heat. Toast for 1 to 2 minutes, stirring constantly. **Be careful not to burn the spices.**
2   Remove from heat and transfer to a small, cool bowl to stop the cooking immediately.
3   Let toasted spices cool completely.
4   Combine nutmeg, bay leaf, mace, anise, cinnamon, and saffron with toasted spices.
5   Grind and sift, then store in an airtight container.

Garam Masala (Whole)

Total time: 5 minutes   Yields enough for one use

This version of garam masala is meant to be used immediately in one recipe. It has a stronger, more pronounced presence than ground garam masala recipe on the previous page. If you don't have Indian bay leaves, you can use bay laurel leaves, though the taste won't be quite the same.

2 Indian bay leaves
   (*Cinnamomum tejpata*)
1 whole clove

1 half-inch stick cinnamon
¼ teaspoon black cumin seed
   (*Elwendia persica*)

1 Combine bay leaves, clove, cinnamon, and cumin.
2 Use immediately.

Ginger–Garlic Paste

Total time: 5 minutes   Yields ½ cup

Ginger-garlic paste is a staple in Southern and Southeast Asian cookery. Normally, you make enough ginger-garlic paste to use immediately, though you can make more than needed and store it in an airtight container in the refrigerator for a few days. You can also freeze it in ice cube trays, then store the cubes of frozen paste in an airtight container in the freezer. If you freeze it, use the paste within two months. (You can also freeze pesto the same way.) If you want to make less paste, the proportions are equal quantities of ginger and garlic. However, if you want to make this is larger amounts, for food safety, use water instead of oil. You can use other oils aside from sunflower, but I like the mildness of sunflower oil.

¼ cup garlic cloves, peeled   ½ teaspoon salt
¼ cup chopped fresh ginger   1 teaspoon sunflower oil

1   Put garlic, ginger, salt, and oil in a blender. Blend into a fine paste. If needed, you can add a bit more oil.
2   Keep blending until it's a lovely rough texture (like horseradish).

Herb Butter

Total time: 10 minutes

Yields about 2 cups butter and 1 cup buttermilk

I f you have a good stand mixer, you can make your own butter in just a few minutes. If you have your own milk cow, you'll especially appreciate this process. The recipe doesn't work with ultra-pasteurized heavy cream, though I've discovered through experimentation that it can work with older heavy cream that's still sweet, but has separated. I adapted this recipe from ALittleInsanity.com, with additional information about butter from LandOLakes.com. You can use this recipe to make plain butter—just leave out the herbs. Once you get the feeling for making herb butter, experiment with other flavorings. Consider lime or lemon zest, for example, or chili seasoning or other dry spice blends. Store herb butter in an airtight container in the refrigerator and use within a week. You can store plain butter in an airtight container in the refrigerator for up to four weeks, or freeze for up to four months.

1 quart heavy cream, *not* ultra-pasteurized
2 quarts ice water
1 teaspoon salt (optional)

4 tablespoons fresh minced herbs (garlic, parsley, rosemary, thyme, or whatever you like), optional

1   Pour cream into an absolutely clean, dry stand mixer bowl.

2   Attach wire whisk and whip cream. Start at the lowest speed and ramp up over a few minutes as you mix.

3   In 3 to 5 minutes, the cream starts to separate into butter and buttermilk.

4   Once butter is sticking to the whisk and looks nicely butter-like, stop mixer. Pour off as much buttermilk as you can. Save buttermilk for drinking or baking. It may well be the most delicious buttermilk you've ever tasted.

5   Pour about 2 cups ice water over butter in mixer bowl. Whisk on medium speed to blow out remaining buttermilk. Drain and discard rinse water.

6   Repeat step 5 two or three times, or until water runs clear.

7   **For food safety**, you must remove as much fluid as you can, so don't stint on this phase. Remove whisk and pry butter off the whisk, putting butter back into the bowl. Press butter against sides of mixing bowl to expel water. Drain and repeat until you've gotten as much water as you can out of the butter. If you want, wrap butter in a clean cotton towel and squeeze it (gently) to remove fluid.

8   Mix in salt and/or herbs.

Herbes de Provence

Total time: 5 minutes   Yields about ¾ cup

The Provence region in France is known for its lovely and fragrant lavender fields. Herbes de Provence means basically, "herbs like those used in Provence": Mediterranean seasonings. The exact herbs in an herbes de Provence recipe vary, but typically include basil, oregano, rosemary, savory, and thyme. Other herbs can include bay leaf, chervil, fennel, mint, marjoram, oregano, and tarragon. The herbes de Provence blend doesn't classically include lavender buds; that's a controversial American addition. (Controversial, because some people dislike the lack of authenticity, and others dislike the taste of lavender in their food. I'm not a big fan of lavender in food either, but a small amount is fine.) This is my own recipe for herbes de Provence, American-style. When I had a mix of scented thymes in my garden, I dried the leaves and flowers and used them in this mix. You will need this recipe, or a commercial version, to make the Seasoned Flour (page 312). Store in an airtight container.

3 tablespoons dried marjoram
3 tablespoons dried savory (summer or winter)
3 tablespoons dried thyme
3 tablespoons dried oregano
1 teaspoon dried rosemary
1 teaspoon dried lavender flowers

1 Combine marjoram, savory, thyme, oregano, rosemary, and lavender.
2 Mix well and store.

Honey Barbecue Sauce

Total time: 15 minutes   Yields about 2½ cups

Made in a blender, this sauce is thick and tasty. Since it is on the sweet side, it's a great base for pulled pork or barbecued chicken. For some interesting taste variations, experiment with different types of honey. This recipe is gluten-free if you use the US version of Lea & Perrins Original Worcestershire sauce. Other brands usually contain gluten. Store in a clean container in refrigerator for up to a week.

1 cup honey
¼ cup molasses
1 cup ketchup
⅛ teaspoon ground cinnamon
½ teaspoon smoked paprika
⅛ teaspoon grated fresh ginger
⅛ teaspoon freshly ground
    black pepper
¼ teaspoon salt
⅛ teaspoon dried oregano

1 clove garlic, coarsely
    chopped
2 tablespoons Lea & Perrins
    Original Worcestershire
    sauce
1 tablespoon mustard seed,
    ground (prepared mustard
    is also okay)
¾ cup brown sugar (not
    packed)

1   Combine honey, molasses, ketchup, cinnamon, paprika, ginger, pepper, salt, oregano, garlic, Worcestershire sauce, mustard, and sugar.
2   Blend on medium speed until it is a uniform texture and color. It should be quite thick and a dark honey brown.

Italian Seasonings

Total time: 5 minutes   Yields about 1 cup

This is a staple in my kitchen, so I make it in large quantities. A gallon jar of this blend lasts perhaps eight months in my household. For this recipe, I reduced my normal quantities and retained the proportions. Store in an airtight container.

2 tablespoons dried basil
2 tablespoons dried marjoram
2 tablespoons dried oregano
2 tablespoons dried thyme

2 tablespoons dried summer savory
1 tablespoon dried sage
1 tablespoon dried rosemary

1   Combine basil, marjoram, oregano, thyme, summer savory, sage, and rosemary. Mix well.

Jamaican Curry Powder

Total time: 30 minutes   Yields about 1 cup

Jamaican curry powder has its roots in East Indian curry powder, but is distinctively its own flavor. Jamaican curry powders usually include allspice and thyme. This version is excellent with chicken or lamb. Or goat, if you happen to have some. (The spices in this blend are strong enough to stand up to stronger flavors.) You can also use it with roasted root vegetables such as carrots and beets. As with my Madras-style curry powder (page 303), this version is tamer than is traditional because I lost my hot spice *wu* when I was nursing my daughter. If you want to heat up this recipe, add 1 teaspoon to 1 tablespoon cayenne to the spice mix, or go whole-hog and use the ferociously intense Scotch bonnet chiles in whatever dish you're cooking. Or add Scotch bonnet chile powder to the blend. (Scotch bonnets are kissing cousins with habanera peppers.) Store this blend in an airtight container out of the light.

2 tablespoons anise seed or 2 star anise pods
¼ cup coriander seed
2 tablespoons cumin seed
2 teaspoons mustard seed (brown or yellow)

1 tablespoon whole fenugreek
1 tablespoon whole allspice
1 whole clove
1 teaspoon dried thyme
5 tablespoons ground turmeric

1 Toast coriander, cumin, mustard, anise, and fenugreek in an dry skillet over low heat until seeds are fragrant and darkened slightly—five to eight minutes. Watch closely so spices don't burn. Remove from heat and remove from skillet immediately so spices don't keep toasting.

2 Cool spices thoroughly (at least 20 minutes). If you try to grind them while still warm, it might harm your spice grinder.

3 Once spices are cool, add allspice, clove, and thyme. Grind until finely ground.

4 Stir in turmeric and mix well.

Lemon and Herb Marinade

Total time: 5 minutes   Yields 3 tablespoons

Use this excellent sauce to marinate fish or chicken before baking, or simply sprinkle it over cooked fish right after you pull it from the oven. It's also tasty on vegetables, such as steamed broccoli. Use this marinade immediately or refrigerate for up to a week. Just a reminder: For food safety's sake, throw out the marinade after it's touched raw fish.

2 tablespoons olive oil   ¼ teaspoon dried oregano
3 tablespoons lemon juice   ¼ teaspoon dry mustard

1   Combine olive oil, lemon juice, oregano, and mustard.
2   Mix well.

Madras-Style Curry Powder

Total time: 25 minutes   Yields about 1 cup

In India, there isn't just *one* curry powder blend; there are many. Generically, these spice blends are called *masala*, meaning spice blend (for example, garam masala). According to Spiceography.com (a fascinating site—I recommend visiting it), curry may go as far back as 4,000 years ago, and the word curry comes from a Tamil word, *kari*, meaning "a thin sauce containing spices." Curries come in both savory and sweet versions. In the United States, we've come to call all curry blends by the one term, curry powder, though many US cooks understand the distinctions among the many kinds. Madras-style curry powder is named after the Indian city Madras (now Chennai). Despite its name, Madras-style curry powder isn't used in India. Although Madras-style curry powder is typically hot—not volcanic, but getting there—my own Madras-style curry powder is mild. You can make it hotter by adding more cayenne. It's immodest of me to say this, but I'm saying it anyway: I would put my curry powder up against anyone else's—it's that good. And it gets better over time.

Toasting Spices

10 tablespoons cumin seed
2 tablespoons coriander seed
2 teaspoons yellow mustard seed

1 teaspoon whole allspice
1 teaspoon fennel seed
1/4 teaspoon hulled green cardamom

Non-Toasting Spices

4 tablespoons whole fenugreek
1½ teaspoons black peppercorns
1 tablespoon whole dried turmeric root or 1 tablespoon ground turmeric

2 teaspoons dried ginger pieces
½ small dried cayenne pepper or ½ teaspoon ground cayenne pepper

1 Combine cumin, coriander, mustard, allspice, fennel, and cardamom. Spread in a single layer in a dry skillet over medium-low heat. (I like to use a cast iron skillet.)
2 Toast 1 to 2 minutes, stirring constantly. Be super careful not to burn the spices. You may need to toast it in batches.
3 Remove from heat and immediately transfer to a small bowl to stop the cooking. Let spices cool completely.
4 Combine fenugreek, peppercorns, turmeric, ginger, and cayenne with the toasted spices.
5 Grind until fine, then sift and store in an airtight container.

Mom's Salsa

Total time: 15 minutes   Yields about 5 cups

The savory food category includes salsa, which in Spanish simply means "sauce," but which in North America has come to mean a specific kind of mix (often scooped up with tortilla chips) made with fresh tomatoes, onions, chile peppers, cilantro, and potentially a variety of other ingredients. The ginger, oranges, and limes in my mother's salsa add an unmatchable, delicious tang. As with all other recipes from my mother, I was only able to get a list of ingredients from her ("you take some tomatoes..."), and not specific quantities. I wrote down the quantities after she made it one day while everything was fresh in my memory. Serve immediately, or chill and serve later. You can refrigerate this salsa for up to a week.

8 firm medium tomatoes, diced

1 bunch scallions, diced

1 large fresh Anaheim chile, finely chopped

2 teaspoons grated fresh ginger

2 ripe but still firm avocados, diced

1 teaspoon garlic powder

salt to taste

several drops hot pepper sauce

juice of 4 limes

1 cup fresh cilantro, finely chopped

1 large navel or Valencia orange, peeled and chopped

1   Combine tomatoes, scallions, Anaheim chile, ginger, avocados, garlic, salt, hot pepper sauce, lime juice, cilantro, and chopped orange.

2   Mix gently but quite well.

Moroccan Spice Blend

Total time: 10 minutes   Yields ½ cup

The original version of this recipe was in an issue of *Better Homes and Gardens.*, though I didn't write down which. I've adapted their recipe to use whole spices. Unlike many other spice blends that use whole spices, you don't need to toast anything. You can use ground spices if you don't have the whole spices. This blend is savory but not hot; add more cayenne if you want some kick. Use with roasted vegetables or fruits, or on chicken, beef, and pork. Store in an airtight container.

2 teaspoons whole allspice
1 teaspoon smoked black peppercorns
1 teaspoon hulled green cardamom
1 teaspoon coriander seed
1 teaspoon cumin seed

1 teaspoon cayenne pepper
2 tablespoons paprika
1 tablespoon ground turmeric
1½ teaspoons ground Ceylon cinnamon
2 teaspoons ground ginger

1   Combine allspice, peppercorns, cardamom, coriander, and cumin.
2   Grind to a fine powder, then pour into a medium mixing bowl.
3   Stir in cayenne, paprika, turmeric, cinnamon, and ginger.
4   Mix well.

Ponzu Sauce

Total time: 10 minutes   Yields about 2½ cups

Ponzu sauce is a classic thin, lightly citrusy Japanese sauce sprinkled on just about anything savory. I love ponzu sauce, but the commercial varieties don't agree with me. I was delighted when our friends Daniel and Mary Ironwood gave us a bottle of their homemade ponzu sauce one Christmas. Turns out their recipe, which they gladly shared, doesn't affect me like the commercial varieties. (Daniel and Mary asked me to also credit their friend Kazuko Okamura, the Japanese friend who taught them the recipe.) The one change I made to their recipe was to swap in tamari for the soy sauce their recipe called for. Tamari is typically gluten-free, but if you're gluten sensitive, double-check the ingredients on the tamari bottle to make sure you're getting a gluten-free version. If you're lucky enough to have yuzus (*Citrus junos*, an indescribably fragrant East Asian citrus), you can use yuzu juice instead of or in addition to the lemon and lime juices (keeping the proportions the same). Try this ponzu sauce sprinkled over chicken, rice, or in my Stir-Fried Vegetables and Beef (page 232). Refrigerated, this ponzu sauce keeps for up to a month.

2 tablespoons finely chopped fresh ginger	**6** garlic cloves, minced
1 scant cup rice wine vinegar	**1** lemon, juiced
1 scant cup tamari	**1** lime, juiced
	1 lime, cut into quarters

1   Combine ginger, rice wine vinegar, tamari, garlic, lemon juice, and lime juice.
2   Put lime quarters into sterilized jar with a lid.
3   Pour sauce over lime quarters. Put lid on.
4   Refrigerate a few days to a week before using.

Pork Roast Rub

Total time: 5 minutes   Yields ½ cup

When I roast beef or pork, I like to slice up a lot of fresh garlic. I then use a paring knife to poke many holes into the roast, especially into the fat (fat holds and spreads flavor), and insert the garlic slivers into those holes. As the meat roasts, the garlic permeates everything. It's time consuming, but gives the roast a fantastic flavor. If you love garlic, that is. Which I do. One night, I wanted to cook a pork roast. I was tired and it was late and I wanted to speed up the prep process. But plain roast pork just wasn't an option. So I put together this rub as an experiment. It gave the roast a wonderfully crispy outer crust, and the meat absorbed the flavors. This rub is now my favorite way to roast pork. Za'atar is both a savory Middle Eastern spice blend with ancient roots, and an herb. For the spice blend, although za'atar recipes vary, the defining ingredients are oregano, salt, sesame seeds, sumac, and thyme. (Not poison sumac, but the sumac whose dried fruits are used as a tangy, common Middle Eastern seasoning.) Za'atar is an Arabic word referring to an herb or family of herbs. The single herb is *Origanum syriacum*, Syrian oregano. (For the fascinating history of za'atar the herb, za'atar the spice blend, and Biblical connections, see the Wikipedia entry for za'atar.) I buy my za'atar spice blend from TheSpiceHouse.com (one of my favorite sources for ethically sourced spices). If you don't have za'atar, you can substitute ½ teaspoon each whole oregano and whole thyme. To make this recipe, I used a heavy granite mortar and pestle that works beautifully for crushing spices. You can use a spice grinder instead, but be careful not to over blend. When using as a rub, pat liberally on all sides of the pork roast before roasting.

2 bay leaves	½ teaspoon cumin seed
¼ teaspoon hulled green cardamom	¼ cup garlic granules
	1 teaspoon za'atar
¼ cup whole dried sage	2 tablespoons Himalayan salt

1 Crumble bay leaves with your fingers and put into a mortar.
2 Add cardamom, sage, cumin, and za'atar. Crush everything well with pestle about 2 minutes or until spices are a coarse powder.
3 Add salt and mix well.

Poultry Seasoning

Total time: 10 minutes   Yields a scant ½ cup

I love Bell's Seasoning, a savory blend of finely powdered rosemary, oregano, sage, ginger, marjoram, thyme, and black pepper used when cooking poultry. Once I started making my own spice blends, of course I had to try making my own version of Bell's Seasoning using organic spices. In the mid-1990s, I found a copycat recipe (apologies to whomever's it was—I didn't record the source), then kept adding spices and modifying quantities until it was perfect. This recipe is a close approximation to Bell's Seasoning, though I've added a bay leaf to the mix, and Bell's doesn't contain bay.

1 tablespoon whole dried rosemary
4 teaspoons whole dried oregano
2 tablespoons whole dried sage
1 tablespoon whole dried marjoram

1 tablespoon whole dried thyme
1 teaspoon black peppercorns
½ teaspoon white peppercorns
1 bay leaf
1 teaspoon ground ginger

1 Combine rosemary, oregano, sage, marjoram, thyme, black and white peppercorns, and bay leaf.
2 Grind to a fine powder.
3 Add the ground ginger and mix thoroughly.
4 Store in an airtight container.

Pumpkin Pie Spice

Total time: 5 minutes   Yields ¼ cup

When you need a pumpkin pie spice blend, you have three options: you can buy a commercial blend, you can put together the necessary spices every time you need it, or you can make your own. I usually put everything together when I need it, but it's convenient to have a blend on hand, whether store-bought or homemade. Most pumpkin pie spice blends comprise cinnamon, cloves, ginger, and nutmeg. Some blends use allspice instead of cloves. I like to use both. I also add mace, resulting in a more subtly complex mix. Avanelle Day and Lillie Stuckey's excellent *The Spice Cookbook* (David White Company, 1964; long out of print but readily available used) calls for the classic four, with the surprising addition of black pepper, which I found to be a revelation. I immediately made the milder white pepper a part of my own blend. When I make my blend, I start with cinnamon sticks, whole cloves, whole white pepper, and whole mace blades, all of which I grind myself. For your convenience, I've presented my recipe using ground spices.

4 teaspoons ground cinnamon
4 teaspoons ground ginger
1½ teaspoons ground nutmeg
1 teaspoon ground cloves

1 teaspoon ground allspice
⅓ teaspoon ground mace
⅓ teaspoon ground white pepper

1 Combine cinnamon, ginger, nutmeg, cloves, allspice, mace, and white pepper.
2 Place spice blend in a small airtight glass jar with a lid. Shake well.
3 Store in a cook dark place.

Quatre Épices

Total time: 20 minutes   Yields a scant ⅓ cup

Pronounced KAH-tray-PEES, the French name of this spice blend means "four spices," usually, cloves, ginger, nutmeg, and pepper. Despite the name, many recipes for this common French blend contain five or more spices, and the proportions can vary wildly from recipe to recipe. This is my version. It's surprisingly excellent in bean or meat dishes. Or try it with roasted fruits, like pears or apples. Compare this with the pumpkin pie spice blend (page 309) to see of how the same (or nearly same) ingredients blended in different proportions can result in something completely different.

10 whole cloves
1 tablespoon white peppercorns

1 tablespoon stick cinnamon, broken into pieces
1 small nutmeg, grated
1 teaspoon ground ginger

1   Combine cloves, peppercorns, and cinnamon. Toast in a dry cast iron skillet over medium-low heat for 1 to 2 minutes, stirring constantly. Be careful not to burn the spices.
2   Remove from heat and pour toasted spices into a small, cool glass bowl to stop the cooking.
3   Cool completely.
4   Grind cool, toasted spices (cloves, peppercorns, and cinnamon bark) to a fine powder.
5   Add nutmeg and ginger. Mix well.
6   Store in an airtight container in a cool, dark, dry place.

Red Enchilada Sauce

Total time: 20 minutes   Yields about 4 cups

Y ou can store this rich, full-flavored red enchilada sauce in the refrigerator for up to a week. As this sauce sits, its flavors marry, making it even better, so make it a day ahead if you want. One of the key ingredients, masa harina, is a staple in Mexican and Central American cooking that gives many foods from those regions their distinctive flavor. Masa harina is ancient. Long ago, the inhabitants of Central America discovered a process called nixtamalization. (From the Aztec Nahuatl language, *nixtamalli* or *nextamalli*.) The process starts with soaking whole maize (corn) in an alkaline solution at a near boil for many hours, then soaking for a while longer, after which it's rinsed thoroughly. At this stage the maize is called nixtamal (in the Southern US, this is called whole hominy). The nixtamal is then ground and used fresh as a dough (to make corn tortillas, for example), or ground and dried, resulting in masa harina. Nixtamalization is a brilliant process; it not only removes most mycotoxins from mold-contaminated maize, it improves maize's nutritional value by making bioavailable calcium and freeing the niacin bound in the maize. Beans and masa together make a complete protein, thereby preventing the nutritional problems people would otherwise have had with non-treated maize. No one knows how ancient the nixtamalization process is, though archaeologists have found nixtamalization equipment dating back to over 3,000 years ago on Guatamala's southern coast. (Sources: various Wikipedia articles, and *Cereal Grains for the Food and Beverage Industries*, by Elke Arendt and Emanuele Zannini, Woodhead Publishing, 2013.) You can substitute all-purpose flour for the masa harina in this recipe, but masa harina is better for flavor and texture.

1 tablespoon unsalted butter
2 tablespoons masa harina
4 cups plain tomato sauce
1 tablespoon garlic powder

2 tablespoons Ancho chile powder
1 tablespoon ground cumin

1   Melt butter in a medium saucepan.
2   One ingredient at a time, add masa harina, tomato sauce, garlic, Ancho chile powder, and cumin, blending well after each addition. The sauce should be smooth, without lumps.
3   Heat gently and simmer 10 minutes.

Seasoned Flour

Total time: 10 minutes   Yields 6 cups

This is my own recipe. Use it to bread chicken pieces, beef stew meat, pork chops, or lamb stew meat, either to fry or to cook in a stew. If using a commercial version of Herbes de Provence, make sure it includes lavender flowers, as that is a defining ingredient. When using this seasoned flour, scoop out only as much as you need, and, for food safety, discard any remaining used flour. Yes, this recipe calls for catnip. Don't let your cats find out. Za'atar is also a nice addition. If not storing in the refrigerator, leave out the Parmesan. To make this recipe gluten free, substitute brown rice flour for the all-purpose flour. It works just as well.

6 cups all-purpose flour
6 tablespoons Herbes de Provence (page 298)
2 teaspoons catnip
1 teaspoon cayenne
2 tablespoons garlic powder
2 teaspoons garlic powder

½ teaspoon salt
1 tablespoon Italian seasonings (page 300)
1 tablespoon grated Parmesan cheese
½ teaspoon paprika
½ teaspoon long pepper

1   Combine flour, Herbes de Provence, catnip, cayenne, garlic powder, salt, Italian seasonings, Parmesan, paprika, and long pepper. Mix well.

2   Store in an airtight container in the refrigerator (because of the Parmesan cheese).

Spice Blend à la Carême

Total time: 10 minutes   Yields a scant ½ cup

Marie Antonin Carême, an early nineteenth-century French chef (1784–1833), can justifiably be said to have laid the foundations of much of our modern cookery. Referred to as "the king of chefs and the chef of kings," Carême cooked for such luminaries as Napoleon Bonaparte and the politically slippery food-lover and French diplomat, Charles Maurice de Talleyrand-Périgord. Talleyrand once challenged Carême to produce an entire year's worth of menus, without repetition, using only local and seasonal produce, a challenge that Carême met.

This spice blend is from page 140 of Carême's cookbook, *The Royal Parisian Pastry-cook and Confectioner, from the original of M.A. Carême, of Paris* (edited by John Porter (F.J. Mason, 1834). Carême said of this blend, "In order to season dishes well, and *au haut goût*, adopt the following mixture of spices, every one of which should be of the very best quality." (*Au haut goût* means "of high taste.") I agree with Carême that everything you cook with should be of good quality. Carême also suggests creating your own seasoning salt by taking a pound of salt and adding to it an ounce of this spice blend. Carême calls for the seasoned salt throughout the part of his book that begins with this spice blend recipe. The original amounts in Carême's recipe are given in drams, which I converted to ounces, then to teaspoons. Use this blend to impart an interesting, faintly exotic flavor to just about anything you cook, both savory and sweet. This blend is also especially good with savory stews. Every time I use this, I like the thought that I'm using a spice blend unchanged from when it was first used almost 200 years ago. **Note**: Although I give instructions using ground spices, this blend is most potent if you grind your own whole spices. Store in a cool, dark place.

1½ teaspoons ground nutmeg
1½ teaspoons ground cloves
1½ teaspoons ground white pepper
¾ teaspoon ground allspice

¾ teaspoon ground mace
¾ teaspoon ground bay leaves
¾ teaspoon ground basil
¾ teaspoon ground thyme

1 Combine nutmeg, cloves, white pepper, allspice, mace, bay leaves, basil, and thyme. Stir until well mixed.
2 Place in an airtight container.

Sweet Curry Powder

Total time: 10 minutes   Yields about ¾ cup

This curry isn't sweet in the sense of having sugar, but instead because the spices used are predominantly considered sweet in the spice sense. It lends itself well to being used in sweeter curries, such as the Curried Lentil Salad (page 263). Store this curry blend in an airtight container in a cool, dark place.

6 tablespoons ground black pepper

4 teaspoons ground cumin

4 teaspoons ground turmeric

5 teaspoons ground coriander

5 teaspoons ground green cardamom

1 tablespoon cayenne

2½ teaspoons ground cloves

2½ teaspoons ground nutmeg

5 teaspoons ground cinnamon

1 Combine pepper, cumin, turmeric, coriander, cardamom, cayenne, cloves, nutmeg, and cinnamon. Mix well.

Vanilla Extract

Total time: 10 minutes plus 6+ months   Yields 4 cups double-fold extract

Vanilla extract, made using the beans of the vanilla orchid, is indispensable to baking. Yet prices can rise steeply. According to a 2018 *Business Insider* video by Alyssa Pagano and Gina Echevarria, high vanilla prices are due to "vanilla bean theft, complex pollination, extreme weather, and the rise of the 'all natural' food movement." To offset the cost, you can make your own vanilla extract. It's still going to be expensive, but not as expensive as commercial extracts, which often contain water, sugar, and other unnecessary ingredients. Vanilla orchids are chiefly grown in Indonesia, Central and South America, Madagascar, Papua New Guinea, Tahiti, and Uganda. Of the many vanilla species, the following three are grown for the vanilla trade: *Vanilla planifolia*, *V. pompona*, and *V. tahitensis*. Each variety has its characteristic flavors; they're all wonderful. You can use either grade A (culinary grade) or B (extract grade) beans in this recipe. Use inexpensive, decent vodka. When buying vanilla extract, you may have noticed the terms "single fold" and "double fold." Fold means the amount of beans by weight you use per volume of alcohol. Single fold is the standard weight (1 ounce beans per cup of alcohol); double fold is twice as much (2 ounces per cup). See http://danieltalsky.com/vanilla/ for a calculator for determining how much alcohol and beans you need. This recipe makes a double-fold extract; you can reduce the beans to 2 ounces if you want single fold. When using double-fold vanilla, reduce the vanilla recipes call for to one-third; for example, if a recipe calls for 1 tablespoon vanilla extract, use 1 teaspoon of this extract. When you remove the beans (see recipe), dry them thoroughly, then put the beans in your granulated sugar to give your sugar a hint of vanilla scent. (An old tip from my mother.)

4 ounces vanilla beans
2 cups vodka or other 80-proof alcohol (brandy, bourbon, or rum)

2 one-cup (8-ounce capacity) sterile bottles with secure lids

1 Slice vanilla beans down their length with a sharp knife. You're not cutting them in half; just opening them to expose the seeds inside.
2 Evenly divide beans and alcohol between bottles. Make sure alcohol completely covers beans. If you need to, cut beans into smaller pieces to fit. Put lids on.
3 Store bottles in a cool, dark place for 6 to 12 months. The longer it sits, the better the flavor. Gently shake bottles each month.
4 Gently shake bottle before using. When you've used enough extract that beans are poking up above extract, remove beans.

Appendix A: Recipe Guidelines

As is true for any cooking adventure, it's a good idea to read each recipe all the way through to make sure you know what you need and what's involved. The first time I make a recipe, I like to make it exactly according to the instructions. After that, I freely experiment and revise.

In this cookbook, I list the ingredients within each recipe in the order in which you'll use them. And each step in a recipe's instructions is one action. For example, if you are to combine two ingredients, that's one step..

This commonsense approach makes it easier for you to stay on track with the recipe. If you find that the instructions call for an ingredient that's listed after an ingredient you don't recall using, double-check the previous steps of the recipe to see if you missed a step. A helpful cooking practice is to set all ingredients out on the counter in the order in which the recipe calls for them.

In recipes where an ingredient is used for two or more parts of a recipe, I list the ingredient once but give the individual measurements. For example, a recipe might call for 1 cup plus 1 tablespoon cocoa. The cup is used in one part of the recipe, and the tablespoon in another. That way, you know up front how much you need.

For the best results and flavors, use the best ingredients you can afford, and use organic ingredients and eggs from pasture-raised chickens when possible.

Special Dietary Requirements

My daughter is healthier when eating **gluten-free foods**, so over the years I've worked at either converting favorite recipes to gluten-free versions, or finding good gluten-free recipes. Most of my experiments have been with America's Test Kitchen's (ATK) gluten-free flour mix. Because I don't want to ask you to make your own ATK gluten-free flour (it's a bit fussy and requires purchasing a number of ingredients you're not likely to have on hand), I haven't included any gluten-free recipes that use ATK's flour blend. ATK's *The How Can It Be Gluten Free Cookbook* (America's Test Kitchen, 2014) has many excellent recipes, all of which work. I highly recommend it.

However, this cookbook includes many naturally gluten-free recipes, all of which you can find listed under "gluten-free recipes" in the index. By "naturally," I mean recipes whose ingredients are naturally gluten-free, not recipes that use gluten-free substitutes. For example, many beverages and vegetable dishes don't require gluten-containing ingredients. You can also adapt some recipes by swapping in brown rice flour for the all-purpose flour called for. I've made notes in some recipes where that works.

If you're **avoiding salt**, you'll find that most recipes call for no salt and instead use spices to add savor.

Many recipes are **vegetarian** (mostly for lacto-ovo vegetarians, though many are also more strictly vegetarian) or **vegan**; again, check the index for recipes that suit these diets. Many recipes that seem to not be vegan or vegetarian can often be easily adapted to conform to your dietary choices.

About Using Butter

In recipes that call for butter, that's US grade AA unsalted butter (unless otherwise specified). If you only have salted butter, slightly reduce any salt the recipe calls for. (And see the note about American and European butters on the next page.) Also, fats absorb flavors more readily than other ingredients, so for many of my recipes, I add flavorings to the butter first.

Since the 1990s, we've been told to avoid trans fats (found in partially hydrogenated oils such as shortening and margarine). I was raised on butter and butter-based recipes, so over the years, I've adapted my recipes as needed to remove trans fats. For example, if someone shared a recipe that called for margarine or shortening, I tested it with butter and, if butter worked, I kept the recipe. If the recipe didn't work with butter, I discarded the recipe.

However, some people are concerned about butter's cholesterol and saturated fats. If you're one of those folks, you can substitute equal amounts of margarine or shortening for the butter in most of these recipes, though the results won't always be the same.

About Flour, and Sifting It
● ●

Unless otherwise specified, all recipes that call for flour are for unbleached, all-purpose flour. At the risk of horrifying some people, decades ago I stopped sifting flour, even for breads and desserts. Not sifting is one less step and speeds the baking that much more. My recipes always come out fine. Sift if you like, but these recipes don't need it.

Be aware that, aside from a few exceptions, ingredients for baked desserts must be well mixed to come together for baking magic. Likewise, when baking, you should always measure flour (and all ingredients!) carefully and spoon it into the measuring cup (rather than scooping), but even that's not essential.

Understanding Prep/Cook Times
● ●

Each recipe includes a *Prep/cook time*. This time represents how much time you can expect to spend on a recipe from start to finish. Prep/cook time includes all preparation tasks (grating, chopping, measuring, and so on), as well as all mixing, cooking, cooling, and setting-up times.

The prep/cook times are as accurate as I can make them based on my own experiences. However, take them as approximations. Many things can make a difference in the amount of preparation and cooking time required.

Cooking Outside the US
● ●

All these recipes work in any country, though you may need to adjust a bit.

- **American measuring cups and spoons** are smaller than cups and spoons used in Australia, Canada, and the UK. See Ingredient Weights and Measures on page 324 for tables of equivalent capacities and metric weights and volumes.
- **Temperatures** in these recipes are in Fahrenheit. For a table of temperature equivalents in Celsius or gas marks, see Oven Temperatures and Formulas on page 325.
- **American butter** and European-style butter differ. European-style butter has a higher butterfat content, less water, and is a tiny bit sour (because it's cultured). American butter has a lower percentage of butterfat, more water, and a more neutral flavor. The water in American butter helps leaven baked goods. If you substitute European style butter for American style in baked goods, the results will be greasier and drier. To counteract that, use ¾ of the amount of butter called for, and add a splash of water. For example, if a recipe calls for 1 cup butter, use ¾ cup European style butter with a teaspoon of water.
- **Egg sizes** can differ, as well as type of eggs (goose, for example, or duck). The eggs used in this cookbook are large, US Grade AA or A chicken eggs. For more information, see Egg Sizes and Substitutions on page 322.

Appendix B: Weights and Measures

I n 1896, Fannie Farmer introduced the idea of standardized measurements with the publication of her popular (and still in print) *The Boston Cooking-School Cook Book* (Little, Brown & Company, 1896). And historically, American recipes have called for ingredients by standardized measurements by volume (tablespoons and cups), not weight (grams or ounces).

More than a century later, cooks all over the world are sharing their recipes, recipes whose ingredients are specified either in the same-sounding volume (cups, for example), but whose volumes aren't the same (a measuring cup in America holds less than a measuring cup in the UK), or are specified in metric units (grams, milliliters). Recipes can go wrong, sometimes disastrously wrong, if you use the wrong volume or weight.

Paired with this American practice of specifying ingredients by volume has been the practice of specifying ingredients by package or unit (one package cream cheese, one stick butter, for example). This practice makes sense—a package is, after all, a type of volume. But packages have changed in America, so a package of cream cheese is no longer always eight ounces—it could be five ounces, or three. And sticks of butter vary in volume as well. Likewise, baking chocolate is now sold in a variety of shapes and sizes. One popular baking chocolate bar, which was once sold in packages of one-ounce squares, is now sold in half-ounce squares. If you didn't know that, and you were following a recipe that called for three squares of baking chocolate, your recipe wouldn't have enough chocolate, and that's just tragic. To address the issue of changing package sizes, I've updated and standardized all recipes so that they call for the volumes or weight of ingredients.

In these recipes, I've kept the American volumes (cups, teaspoons, and so on). But for cooks who prefer to cook by weight, or who are in another country, this appendix has tables of weight and volume equivalents (including metric) for many common ingredients, rounded to the nearest whole number in most cases. Precision isn't essential in most recipes.

The tables in this appendix are not exhaustive. To convert other quantities than in the tables in this chapter, I recommend the following resources:

- For almost every possible conversion, I relied heavily on the following website to create the list of equivalent weights: convert-me.com/en/convert/cooking/. (That site has been on the internet since 1995!).
- For lists of ingredients in US measurements and their UK equivalents, see allrecipes.co.uk/how-to/44/cooking-conversions.aspx.
- For different types of converters for specific cooking ingredients, see traditionaloven.com/tutorials/conversion.html.

Egg Sizes and Substitutions

Unless otherwise specified, eggs in these recipes are large, US Grade AA or A chicken eggs. You can substitute small, medium, extra large, or jumbo chicken eggs, but you may need to adjust how many eggs you use. Goose eggs, which are much larger than chicken eggs, are often used in European baking, so I've included the equivalents for goose eggs. If you need to divide a goose egg, beat the egg first.

Egg size substitutions table

If the recipe calls for this many chicken eggs	Use this many chicken eggs				Or this many goose eggs
Large eggs	Jumbo	Extra large	Medium	Small	(144 grams per egg)
1	1	1	1	1	½
2	2	2	2	3	1
3	2	3	3	4	1½
4	3	4	5	5	2
5	4	4	6	7	2½
6	5	5	7	8	3

In addition to goose eggs, you can also use duck, ostrich, or quail, though be aware the flavors will vary. Here are the average weights for those eggs, plus a few notes.

- **Duck eggs each** weigh about 70 grams, about the same as a jumbo chicken egg in the US. Use the "Jumbo" column in the egg size substitutions table for how many duck eggs to use. Duck egg shells are thicker than chicken eggs (so they're harder to crack) and, depending on what the duck eats, the flavor can be stronger.
- **Ostrich eggs** weigh 3.5 to 5 pounds (1,600 to 2,300 grams), and are about the equivalent of 28 to 41 large US chicken eggs. With eggs that big, it doesn't make sense to talk about substituting numbers of eggs. Instead, beat the ostrich egg and weigh out how much you need. For example, if you're replacing 2 large chicken eggs, you'll need 144 grams of ostrich egg.
- **Quail eggs** weigh about 9 grams. You need about six quail eggs to substitute for one large chicken egg in the US.

The following table shows the standard chicken egg size names and weights in grams for Australia (AU), Canada (CA), the Europe Union (EU), New Zealand (NZ), and the US. The data were taken from the websites of each country's equivalent of the United States Department of Agriculture (USDA).

Standard chicken egg weights in grams in different countries

Chicken egg size	AU	CA	EU	NZ	US
King size (AU)	73 g				
Mega, XXXL (Western AU)	72 g				
Jumbo	68 g	70 g		68 g	70.9 g
Extra large (XL)	60 g	63 g	73 g	62 g	63.8 g
Large (L; NZ: standard)	52 g	56 g	63 g	53 g	56.7 g
Medium (M)	43 g	49 g	53 g	44 g	49.6 g
Small (S)		42 g	>53 g		42.5 g
Peewee (NZ: pullet)		>42 g		35 g	35.4 g

Freezing Eggs

What do you do when you have leftover egg whites or yolks, or just have an abundance of eggs?

You can freeze raw egg yolks, egg whites, and whole eggs (but never in the shell). Freeze eggs in labeled, freezer-safe containers.

Use the guidelines in this section to freeze eggs, which can keep in the freezer for up to a year.

To freeze eggs,

- For **whole eggs,** beat lightly, then package, label, and freeze.
- For yolks, mix with ⅛ teaspoon salt (or 1½ teaspoons sugar) per ¼ cup (about four) yolks. Then package, label, and freeze. The salt or sugar help slow down the yolk becoming gelatinous. You'd use the salted yolks for savory dishes, and the sugared yolks for sweet dishes.
- For **whites**, don't beat. Just package, label, and freeze.

When labeling, include the number of eggs (or yolks or whites), whether you used salt or sugar, and the date. To use frozen yolks or whole eggs, thaw overnight in the refrigerator, then use immediately. If using thawed whites, bring to room temperature, then use immediately.

Eggnog lovers, you can freeze commercial eggnog (but not homemade—never freeze that) for up to six months.

For more on eggs, including nutrition, safe handling, and what you can and can't freeze, see the USDA's "Shell Eggs from Farm to Table" (fsis.usda.gov/wps/portal/fsis/topics/food-safety-education/get-answers/food-safety-fact-sheets/egg-products-preparation/shell-eggs-from-farm-to-table/#17).

Ingredient Weights and Measures

Imagine that you have one cup of feathers and one cup of rocks. They are both one cup in *volume*, but the rocks *weigh* much more. Likewise, the same *volume* of different food ingredients can *weigh* differently. For example, one cup of powdered sugar weighs less than one cup of granulated sugar. Because many cooks use weights rather than volumes, and many US recipes specify volume (including this book), it's useful to know how much something weighs.

In addition, measuring cups and spoons vary from country to country. For example, measuring cups and spoons in the UK are slightly larger than in the US; 1 UK cup holds a bit more than 1 US cup. And fluid ounces are also different between the US and the UK (because the ounces are from different systems).

With ingredients you use in smaller quantities, the volume difference isn't important: 1 teaspoon of vanilla extract (which is called vanilla essence in the UK and Australia) is going to be fine whether it's a US teaspoon or a UK teaspoon. (The exception is salt—small variations in salt are quite noticeable.) But with the ingredients you use in larger quantities, the difference can be important.

For the common ingredients used in this book where weight or volume can make a difference (butter, sugar, flour, and so on), the following table lists those ingredients with their weights and volumes in US, UK, and metric units. (I've rounded most UK and metric units.)

You'll need to do a little math to figure out the units not listed in this table. For example, if a recipe calls for ½ cup sugar, divide the US 1 cup weight and volume for sugar in half. For other volumes or weights, see the conversion websites listed on page 321.

If you live in the UK and you don't want to fuss with conversions, you can buy US measuring cups and spoons online in the UK.

Weights and volumes for specific ingredients

Ingredient	US (Imperial) Units	UK Units	Metric Units
Butter	2 cups (16 ounces)	2 cups	454 grams
Butter	1 cup (8 ounces)	1 cup	227 grams
Butter	½ cup (4 ounces)	½ cup	114 grams
Buttermilk, sour cream, yogurt	½ cup (4 fluid ounces)	.46 cup (4.2 fluid ounces)	118 ml
Buttermilk, sour cream, yogurt	⅓ cup (2.6 fluid ounces)	.32 cup (2.7 fluid ounces)	78.8 ml
Chocolate chips	1 cup (6 ounces)	.95 cup	170 grams
Cocoa powder	1 cup (3.5 ounces)	.9 cup	100 grams
Cream, heavy (double cream)	1 cup (8 fluid ounces)	.98 cup (8.3 fluid ounces)	237 ml
Flour, all purpose, unsifted (plain flour)	1 cup (4.25 ounces)	.96 cup	120 grams
Flour, almond (almond meal)	1 cup (3.4 ounces)	1 cup	96 grams
Milk, whole	1 cup (8 fluid ounces)	.98 cup (8.3 fluid ounces)	237 ml
Sugar, brown	1 cup (7 ounces)	.9 cup	198 grams
Sugar, granulated	1 cup (7.1 ounces)	.9 cup	200 grams
Sugar, powdered (icing sugar)	1 cup (4.4 ounces)	.9 cup	125 grams
Sugar, superfine (castor sugar)	1 cup (7.9 ounces)	.9 cup	225 grams

Remember, the fluid ounce systems in the US and UK are different. And these equivalents are all as close as I could get, but volumes and weights can vary.

Oven Temperatures and Formulas

Different countries use different temperature systems. In this cookbook, all temperatures are in degrees Fahrenheit (°F) in a conventional electric oven. Your oven may cook hotter or cooler than mine. If you have a convection (fan) oven, you'll need to reduce cooking times.

Also, I almost never preheat the oven. (The United States Department of Agriculture says it's not necessary in most cases.) When preheating is important, I say so in the recipe. If you don't preheat, and the instructions call for preheating, you may need to bake the item a little longer. If you do preheat and the instructions don't call for that, shorten your baking times.

A fast, approximate oven temperature conversion is to halve the Fahrenheit degrees to get the Celsius equivalent, or double the Celsius degrees for the Fahrenheit equivalent. For example, 350°F is approximately 175°C. With most recipes, a precise temperature isn't vital.

If you're used to cooking in Celsius or with a gas mark oven, you can use the following table to see the temperatures/marks to use. Note that the Celsius temperatures are the conventional equivalents, not the precise conversions.

Oven temperature equivalents

Fahrenheit (°F)	Celsius (°C)	Gas Mark	Descriptive Term
150 to 194	66 to 90	NA	Drying
200 to 230	93 to 110	1/4	Very slow/very low
248 to 266	120 to 130	1/2 or .5	Very slow/very low
275	140	1	Slow/low
300	150	2	Slow/low
325	160	3	Moderately slow/warm
350	180	4	Moderate/medium
375	190	5	Moderate/moderately hot
400	200	6	Moderately hot
425	210	7	Hot
450	220	8	Hot/very hot
475	240	9	Very hot
500	260	10	Extremely hot

If you want a precise equivalent, you'll need to do a tiny bit of math: to convert from Fahrenheit to Celsius, take the temperature in degrees Fahrenheit (°F), subtract 32, then multiply the result by $\frac{5}{9}$ (which is .5555). The final number is the temperature in degrees Celsius (°C). Here's the formula:

```
((Temperature in °F) - 32) × .5555 = temperature in °C
```

So, for example, to convert 350°F to its precise Celsius equivalent,

```
(350°F - 32) x .5555 = 176.6649°C or 177°C, rounded
```

The formula to from degrees Celsius to degrees Fahrenheit is as follows:

```
(Temperature in °C x 1.8) + 32 = temperature in °F
```

Sugar Terms
· ·

The following table pairs the US term for different types of sugar with the UK terms.

Sugar types and terms

US Term	UK Term
Brown sugar, light	Demerara sugar
Brown sugar, dark	Dark soft sugar
Granulated sugar, white sugar, sugar	Baking sugar, sugar
Molasses	Black treacle
Powdered sugar, confectioner's sugar	Frosting sugar, icing sugar
Superfine sugar, baker's sugar	Castor (or caster) sugar

Index

Made in the USA
Middletown, DE
30 December 2021

57338003R00205